THE BEAST
IN THE
GARDEN

THE BEAST IN THE GARDEN

*A Modern
Parable of Man
and Nature*

DAVID BARON

W. W. NORTON & COMPANY   NEW YORK   LONDON

Copyright © 2004 by David Baron

Title page image © Daniel J. Cox / Getty Images
Part I opener, Union Pacific Rail Road poster circa 1891, courtesy of Archives,
University of Colorado at Boulder Libraries.
Part II opener, lion print at the corner of Ninth Street and Arapahoe Avenue, Boulder,
January 1989, courtesy of Michael Sanders.
Part III opener, Animal Control Officer Clay Leeper and Boulder police with tranquilized
lion on University Hill, August 24, 1990. Photo by Charlie Johnson, courtesy of *Colorado Daily*.

Visit the companion Web site at www.beastinthegarden.com.

For information about permission to reproduce selections from this book, write to Permis-
sions, W. W. Norton & Company, Inc., 500 Fifth Avenue, New York, NY 10110

Manufacturing by the Courier Companies, Inc.
Book design by BTDnyc
Maps on pages 2 and 3 by Paul J. Pugliese. All other maps by John McAusland.
Production manager: Amanda Morrison

Library of Congress Cataloging-in-Publication Data

Baron, David, 1964–
The beast in the garden : a modern parable of man and nature /
David Baron.—1st ed.
p. cm.
Includes bibliographical references (p.   ).
ISBN 0-393-05807-7 (hardcover)
1. Puma—Colorado—Boulder Region. 2. Human-animal
relationships—Colorado—Boulder Region. I. Title.
QL737.C23B26524 2003
599.75'24'0978863—dc22
2003016111

W. W. Norton & Company, Inc.
500 Fifth Avenue, New York, N.Y. 10110
www.wwnorton.com

W. W. Norton & Company Ltd.
Castle House, 75/76 Wells Street, London W1T 3QT

1 2 3 4 5 6 7 8 9 0

For Paul

"And to every beast of the earth, and to every bird of the air, and to everything that creeps on the earth, everything that has the breath of life, I have given every green plant for food."
And it was so.
—Genesis 1:30

CONTENTS

Part Three

PLAGUE

THE BEAST
IN THE
GARDEN

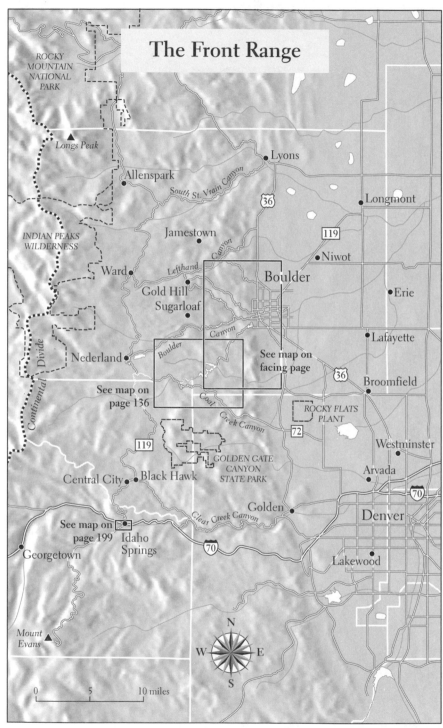

The Front Range: A north-south trending massif of the Colorado Rocky Mountains, historical habitat of *Puma concolor*, the mountain lion.

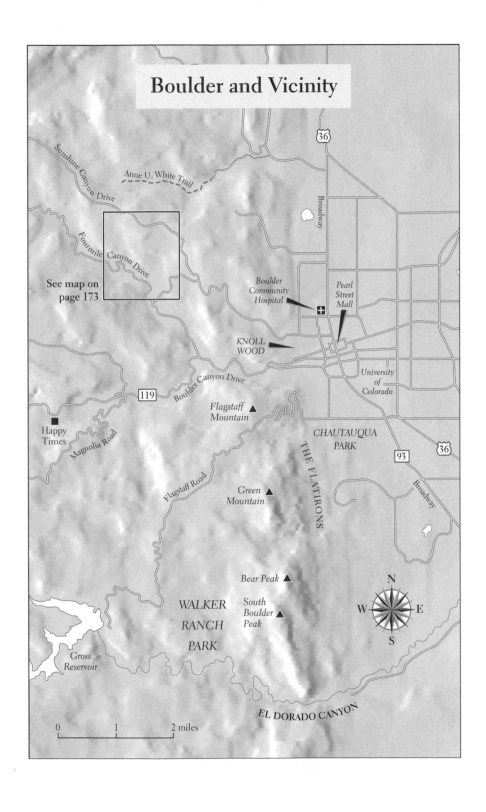

Boulder and Vicinity

Anne U. White Trail

Sunshine Canyon Drive

Fourmile Canyon Drive

See map on
page 173

Broadway

Boulder
Community
Hospital

Pearl
Street
Mall

KNOLL
WOOD

Boulder Canyon Drive

University
of
Colorado

119

Flagstaff
Mountain

CHAUTAUQUA
PARK

Happy
Times

Magnolia Road

93

36

Flagstaff Road

Green
Mountain

THE FLATIRONS

Broadway

Bear Peak

South
Boulder
Peak

N
W E
S

WALKER
RANCH
PARK

Gross
Reservoir

EL DORADO CANYON

0   1   2 miles

Prologue

DEATH IN THE ECOTONE

JANUARY 16, 1991

The Colorado sun burned through a mantle of winter gloom, dappling the rocks, the trees, the snow with a warm glow, giving an air of spring to the January hillside. Ponderosa pines, their needles carpeting the ground, shimmered in the silvery light beside a town that owed its existence to gold. The forest lay open, trees interspersed with grasses and shrubs that could tolerate the heat and low moisture of the south-facing slope, vegetation that provided excellent cover for a creature in hiding.

The sounds of civilization—trucks on the interstate, dogs in backyards, students at the high school—carried up the hill, where half a dozen men had gathered. Wearing boots, gaiters, and wool hats, the men assembled in a line along a ridge and trudged eastward in unison. Heads pivoted and necks craned as the search party scanned the terrain for clues: a piece of clothing, a candy wrapper, a footprint, anything that might help explain how a healthy, young athlete had vanished in the middle of an average Monday on the edge of a small Rocky Mountain city. The men looked behind trees, under bushes, beside rocks and fallen logs, but they found nothing.

Two days had passed since the disappearance. So many sheriff's deputies, search dogs, and townsfolk had scoured the hillside that no one expected this piece of earth to yield anything dramatic, yet Steve Shelafo intended to be thorough. The twenty-eight-year-old emergency medical technician, who wore a small mustache and an air of gravity of purpose, had been assigned to lead the final search of this area. With the first pass complete, Steve shifted his men south onto an adjacent swath of hillside and started the line moving back upslope. The team climbed a sunny ridge beneath high-tension power lines and gained a view that stretched from the old cemetery to downtown. The men lowered their gaze and inspected around their feet. Pine cones lay in melting snow. Prickly pear cacti poked through soil of decomposing granite. Deer droppings littered the ground like piles of Milk Duds.

It was then that one of the searchers pointed beneath a juniper. "We found him," the young man said. Steve Shelafo approached through crunching snow, and as he neared, his eyes widened in disbelief. "None of us were prepared [for what we found]," he said later. "Not in the remotest sense."

During his years in wilderness rescue, Steve had seen plenty of corpses—dismembered in plane crashes, bloated from drowning, crumpled after falling from cliffs. But this sight was more than gruesome; it was both haunting and indescribably weird. The body, clothed in athletic gear, wasn't sloppily mangled; it was carefully carved, hollowed out like a pumpkin. Someone had cut a circle from the front of the sweatshirt and the turquoise T-shirt beneath, sliced through the skin and bones, exposed the chest cavity, and plucked out the organs. After conducting this ghoulish backwoods surgery, the killer had removed his victim's face and then sprinkled moss and twigs on the lower torso as if to signify something profound, as if performing a macabre ritual. *Is the murderer still on the mountain?* Steve wondered. Then, urgently and cryptically, one of the other searchers said, "Hey. Right behind you." Steve turned, fearing a madman with a shotgun. Instead he saw a wild animal.

The creature was large, its body muscular, its visage unmistakably feline. It sat sphinxlike in a copse of trees just five yards away and watched the men intently. The head seemed small for such a massive beast, but its face was mesmerizing: rounded ears that stood erect, whiskers fanning outward, sloping forehead, cherubic cheeks, and determined eyes. Linnaeus had dubbed the species *Felis concolor*,* "cat of one color," a description not quite accurate, for the animal's back was the hue of sand, its belly eggnog, with patches of white around its mouth and black on the sides of its muzzle and the tip of its tail. In common parlance, the creature was known as cougar, puma, panther, or mountain lion. ("Mountain lion" was also something of a misnomer. Although often found in rugged, rocky terrain, cougars were once the most widely distributed land mammal in the Americas, occupying not merely mountains but swamps, grasslands, deserts, and forests from sea level to fourteen thousand feet, California to Maine, British Columbia to Patagonia.)

The mountain lion is by far the largest wild cat in the United States, excepting the occasional jaguar that slinks across the border from Mexico. A full-grown female weighs as much as a German shepherd. An adult male may be more massive than a Great Dane and even heftier than Theodore Roosevelt, who, on a Colorado hunting trip while vice president–elect in the winter of 1901, killed a cougar that tipped the scales at 227 pounds.

The lion that faced Steve Shelafo was not exceptionally large. A young adult male, weighing one hundred pounds, it was normal in most every respect but one. As authorities soon discovered, after a frantic chase violently ended by a bullet in the cougar's chest, the cat's stomach contained fragments of a human heart.

The grisly scene that Steve Shelafo and his group from Alpine Rescue Team encountered was not the result of a homicide; it was something more bizarre. They had located the remains of the first adult known to be killed and consumed by a mountain lion in more than a century. In the following days, newspaper headlines told the disturbing story: "Lion suspected in jogger death," "Human remains found in cougar," "Fatal attack believed unprecedented in North America." *USA Today* labeled its report simply "Cougar Mystery."

The death was especially troubling because, according to experts, it should not have occurred. Until that time, mountain lions were considered timid creatures of the night that avoided humans and human habitation. Although nineteenth-century American lore told of bloodthirsty cougars ambushing unsuspecting victims, scientists discounted such tales as the product of active imaginations and dime-store novels. Authenticated

*Taxonomists have since reclassified and renamed the species *Puma concolor*.

accounts of cougar attacks on people were so rare that Theodore Roosevelt, a great student of the outdoors, once wrote, "There is no more need of being frightened when sleeping in, or wandering after nightfall through, a forest infested by cougars than if they were so many tom-cats." And yet in Colorado, in 1991, at midday, a mountain lion slew a young man in sight of an interstate highway and a high school. Forensic tests would prove that the lion had been the killer.

But no autopsy or bite-mark analysis or examination of the bloody attack site could solve the deeper mystery. What prompted a cougar to make such an exceptional and discomfiting choice of prey? The answer was to be found not in the cat's bullet-pierced body, or in the remains of its human victim, but in the landscape.

This book tells the story of a death that was not supposed to happen and the forces that made it inevitable. It is a tale of politics and history, and ecology gone awry, all come to life in feline form. It is the chronicle of a town that loved its own version of nature with such passion that its embrace ultimately altered the natural world. The comparison may seem far-fetched, but much as the Aztecs hauled prisoners up high pyramids and cut out their beating hearts as an offering to the sun, the human mauled five centuries later on a frozen hill in 1991 was, in effect, a sacrifice, killed by a community embracing a myth: the idea that wilderness, *true* wilderness, could exist in modern America.

Wilderness—from the Old English *wilddēornes,* "the place of wild beasts"—responds not only to Darwinian but also to market forces. The scarcer the supply, the greater the value of the remaining commodity.

When the New World was new and America seemingly boundless, colonists and pioneers viewed the abundant wilderness as an enemy to be conquered, a monster to be tamed. Carving a civilization out of the forest required hard labor: felling trees, planting crops, extirpating undesirable animals along with America's native people. Throughout the first four centuries after European discovery of the Americas, the continents' wilderness appeared menacing and evil, and, to all but a handful of inspired thinkers—such as Henry David Thoreau, who famously wrote, "In Wildness is the preservation of the World"—it was worthless. "In Europe people talk a great deal of the wilds of America," wrote Alexis de Tocqueville, perhaps the most renowned chronicler of nineteenth-century American culture, "but the

Americans themselves never think about them; they are insensible to the wonders of inanimate nature and they may be said not to perceive the mighty forests that surround them till they fall beneath the hatchet."

Some 170 years after his famous journey, Tocqueville would no longer recognize the untrammeled territory he once described. Manifest Destiny, industrialization, and a twentyfold growth in population since 1830 have converted the United States into a land of megalopolises and superhighways, a nation in which "sprawl" figures in political debates, a country where, outside of Alaska, it is impossible to place oneself more than twenty miles from a road. (The most remote spot in the lower forty-eight states, by the distance-from-a-road standard, is in the southeastern part of Yellowstone National Park.) And civilization's tendrils continue to spread. Phoenix's urban edge creeps outward at the rate of half a mile per year, consuming another acre of desert each hour. Atlanta's swelling metropolitan region is expected to add almost two million residents in the next quarter century. Even urban areas with stagnant populations are expanding. Suburban Americans are consuming more land per capita. We are spreading out.

In this increasingly paved and sanitized environment, wilderness has acquired a different hue. Americans have come to treasure what little remains of a world that is uncontrolled, natural, wild. When asked in a recent poll, "How important is it to you personally that wilderness and open spaces are preserved?" most American adults answered, "Extremely important," and almost all of the rest said, "Somewhat important." Protecting nature, at least in theory, has become a core American value.

This shift in attitude is forcing a change in the nation's landscape, as undeveloped parcels of land, large and small, are protected. Between 1998 and 2002, voters across the United States passed ballot measures authorizing more than $20 billion in public spending to preserve open space. At the same time, private organizations dedicated to that same goal have prospered. The Nature Conservancy, an extraordinarily wealthy and successful conservation group, has protected land nationwide equal in area to Vermont and New Hampshire combined. More than twelve hundred local and regional land trusts have preserved an additional New Jersey's worth of open space, including vacant lots (now community gardens) in downtown Philadelphia, a eucalyptus grove that serves as a roost for monarch butterflies near Santa Barbara, a 73-acre farm on Maryland's Eastern Shore, and a 12,000-acre ranch outside Yellowstone National Park.

Natural areas are not only being preserved; they're being restored. The federal government and the state of Florida have launched a bold, $7.8-billion project to resuscitate the parched and ailing Everglades. Military bases and atomic weapons facilities, among the world's most polluted landscapes, are being cleaned and converted to wildlife refuges. Other habitats that were once highly modified are recovering thanks to neglect. New England's forests, once heavily logged for firewood and farms, have reclaimed millions of acres left fallow since the early twentieth century. The Great Plains are depopulating, and there is serious discussion of giving the range back to the bison.

Americans have also changed their minds about wildlife, no longer seeing animals merely as an exploitable resource. According to the U.S. Fish and Wildlife Service, which tracks such things, the number of hunters in America declined 8 percent in the past decade while the nation's population rose 13 percent. Since 1990, voters in California, Colorado, Arizona, Oregon, Alaska, Massachusetts, Michigan, and Washington have passed ballot measures that restrict the hunting and trapping of bears, beavers, bobcats, wolves, wolverines, foxes, lynx, and cougars. No surprise, then, that wildlife is rebounding.

Although many species (the Stephens' kangaroo rat, the California condor, the black-footed ferret) face serious threats to their survival, others (white-tailed deer, raccoons, an assortment of large carnivores) are thriving and reclaiming old territory. In the Northeast, black bears have encroached on Boston's inner suburbs for the first time in almost two centuries, and New Jersey's ursine population has grown by a factor of twenty in the past thirty years. In the upper Midwest, the once endangered and now regionally prospering tribe of *Canis lupus*, the gray wolf, is "rapidly adapting to human presence," according to a recent study that found the animals frequently cross major highways as they roam across Wisconsin and Minnesota. (Wolves have been tracked to within nineteen miles of downtown St. Paul, and in 1999 one that had apparently *not* learned to cross roads safely was killed by an eighteen-wheeler inside Minnesota's fifth-largest city, Rochester.) In Florida, alligators—hunted toward extinction in the 1960s, then protected by the Endangered Species Act—have become so abundant that if each consumed just sixteen humans, the reptiles would thoroughly depopulate the Sunshine State. Coyotes, previously confined to a swath of land from the western plains to the desert Southwest, have spread across the entire nation and now reside even in major cities: Boston (a coyote recently turned up on a South End doorstep), New York (a coyote captured in Central Park in 1999 now resides at the Queens Zoo), Seattle (in 1997, a coyote running from crows triggered the automatic door of the Henry M. Jackson Federal Building, sped through the lobby, and entered a waiting elevator). And across the American West, mountain lions have become so numerous that, some biologists believe, the cats may be as abundant today as when Lewis and Clark paddled through the region two centuries ago.

These countervailing forces—humans moving out and wildlife moving in, lands being developed and neighboring lands being restored—present both an unprecedented paradox and a surprising phenomenon: the return of the American frontier, which historian Frederick Jackson Turner defined as "the meeting point between savagery and civilization," more than a century after it was officially declared closed. This modern frontier is not a line of human progress marching resolutely westward, but rather a convoluted boundary ringing cities and suburbs. It cuts behind new subdivisions in Wallingford, Connecticut, where yards abut forests that harbor deer. It runs along the edge of Auburn, California, where the city meets a 35,000-acre state recreation area, home to a healthy population of mountain lions. Today's American frontier is an increasingly fractal edge that, like a craggy coastline, enhances the area of contact between two habitats, in one case land and water, in the other the urban and the wild.

Ecologists call the zone of transition between habitats (for instance, forest and prairie) an ecotone. America is becoming one vast ecotone where civilization and nature intermingle. To some, this suggests a utopian state of affairs. Peregrine falcons nest regally atop skyscrapers. Foxes den in vacant lots. Deer stroll suburban streets. Indeed, ecotones can be areas of great biological richness.

These new transition zones, however, create dynamics that cannot be completely predicted or controlled. In ecotones, species mix that otherwise remain separate. The dynamics of predator and prey change. Such changes, termed "edge effects," can propagate and alter the functioning of ecosystems some distance from the boundary. In the continental United States in the twenty-first century, these urban-wild edge effects are increasingly unavoidable. The presence of almost three hundred million people inevitably transforms, alters, and distorts the natural world in myriad ways.

Yet this is what our nation is becoming: a country where people build new homes on undeveloped land, pay to preserve the open space beside it, attract animals into their yards, and—by embracing wilderness and wildlife—alter the very nature of what they presume Nature to be. In this way, and on a much larger scale, the future of America looks a lot like a place in Colorado where, on a mild winter's day in 1991, a large cat killed a young man and ate his heart.

Part One

THE PEACEABLE
KINGDOM

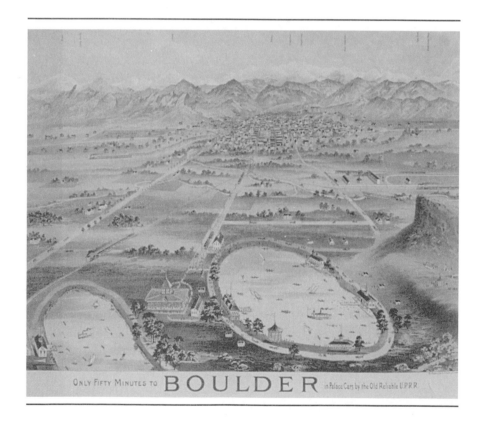

ONLY FIFTY MINUTES TO BOULDER in Palace Cars by the Old Reliable U.P.R.R.

1

A LAND WITHOUT CARNIVORY

DECEMBER 20, 1987

Snow dusted the mountains like confectioner's sugar. In the distance, glacier-carved peaks cut a jagged line of white against the sky, while the rolling foothills in the foreground looked placid, the sea of evergreens transformed into a forest of a million sparkling Christmas trees. Below, in a slight depression where the Great Plains met the Rockies, a small city was in motion.

Parka-clad shoppers crowded downtown stores, emerging with last-minute gifts and stopping for croissants at *Pour la France!*, a popular bakery and café. At St. John's Episcopal Church on the corner of Fourteenth and Pine, the Boulder Messiah Chorale and Orchestra was preparing for its fifth annual sing-along of Handel's famous oratorio. Up on University Hill, a student-filled neighborhood of fraternities and group homes, undergraduates grabbed duffels of dirty laundry and packed cars to head home for winter break. At the Humane Society, the obligatory Santa posed for photographs with domesticated dogs and cats. It was the weekend before Christmas, and Boulder, Colorado—like the rest of America—was consumed by activity in pursuit of peaceful holidays.

Boulder, however, was not the typical American town, not the sort of place depicted in Frank Capra movies; the signs of Christmas's approach were slightly askew here. A band of protesters picketed stores that sold war toys—guns, tanks, and science fiction items—that "glorify destruction of the Earth and domination of the universe." A local New Age group was organizing an event called the World Instant of Cooperation, a global simultaneous meditation for peace scheduled for New Year's Eve day and intended to create a "mind link" among participants. In advance of the holidays, someone had snuck up Flagstaff Mountain, where a string of holiday lights shined over the city in the shape of a star, and transformed the star into a peace sign.

Long known for its freethinking nonconformity, Boulder was, in 1987, an island of liberalism in the era of Reagan conservatism. The city's inhabitants, 82,000 in number, were whiter, wealthier, and more progressive than the nation as a whole. Boasting a youthful image, Boulder was a college town—home to the University of Colorado (CU) and its 23,325 students—filled with cafés and art galleries, health food stores and acupuncturists (the yellow pages listed fourteen practitioners), a thriving live music scene and the aroma of marijuana on downtown streets. Boulderites embraced the bumper-sticker slogan "Think Globally, Act Locally"; in a single-handed attempt to defuse Cold War hostilities, the community had established sister-city ties with a Soviet municipality—Dushanbe, the capital of Tajikistan—prompting an exchange of delegations, pen-pal letters, and gifts between the United States and the USSR. During a visit by Soviet officials, the president of the Boulder-based herbal tea company Celestial Seasonings had jokingly offered another swap: "Send us two missiles and we'll give you a box of tea."

Boulder enjoyed a "stuck in the sixties" reputation, with T-shirts, torn jeans, and sandals a common wardrobe. The *Denver Post* called the city "the little town nestled between the mountains and reality." To the *Colorado Daily*, Boulder was "the Peaceable Kingdom, where the lion lies down with the lamb and everybody eats. (Remember: Vegetarian entrees are *always* available.)" *Newsweek* dubbed Boulder "laid-back city," and the populace— an amalgamation of students, professors, athletes, artists, scientists, massage therapists, and aging hippies—did appear friendly and laid-back to outsiders, but Boulderites harbored an understated arrogance about their city. They believed their hometown to be better than others, its residents more enlightened, its landscape more sublime.

The city sat on the plains beneath an especially handsome stretch of the Rockies known as the Front Range, in a region bookended by two prominent, treeless crags—Longs Peak (14,259') to the north, with a flat, broad summit large enough to fit a football field, and Mount Evans (14,265') to the south, the top of which could be reached by the highest paved road in the United States. Between these two peaks, the land was corrugated into ridges separated by canyons named St. Vrain, Lefthand, Sunshine, Fourmile, Boulder, Eldorado, Coal Creek, and Clear Creek, which concealed small towns and unincorporated villages filled with ramshackle cabins and luxury homes. The nearby canyons were Boulder's bedroom communities, and the mountains were the city's playground, offering slopes to ski, peaks to climb, and cliffs to scale.

The boundary between the flatland and the mountains ran along the edge of downtown, on a north–south line roughly marked by Third and Fourth Streets. Immediately to the west, on the leading edge of the Rockies, enormous slabs of rusty sandstone and conglomerate emerged from the plains and soared taller than the Chrysler Building. These ancient sediments—compacted into rock, tilted upward at a fifty-degree angle by tectonic forces, and sculpted into colossal triangles by gravity and time—were the Flatirons, geological formations that lent their name to a local golf course, movie theater, automobile dealership.

Below the Flatirons, the city was lush, with jade lawns, spring tulips, and an urban forest of maples and oaks, elms and chestnuts, locusts and ashes, as well as apple, pear, and peach trees that provided food for abundant wildlife. Brick cottages and broad-porched bungalows occupied old sections of town, giving the neighborhoods the feel of a simpler, quainter America. Boulder Creek rambled among the houses, paralleled by a park with a jogging and bicycle path that became a busy thoroughfare on sunny days, of which the city had more than the usual allotment. Birders congregated with Canada geese, mallards, warblers, tanagers, orioles, and herons around shallow lakes, the still waters reflecting the mountains peakside down.

With its small-town charm, spectacular scenery, growing high-tech industry, and the benefits of a big city—Denver—just half an hour away, Boulder approximated the Beat poet and environmental activist Gary Snyder's idyllic vision of how humans should live—gently on the land, in harmony with nature, in small communities populated by "computer technicians who run the plant part of the year and walk along with the Elk in their migrations during the rest."

Indeed, elk picturesquely inhabited the nearby foothills and occasionally migrated down into people's yards; in 1986, a yearling wandered as far as the Pearl Street pedestrian mall, an area of bricked-over pavement in the heart of downtown, and was eventually captured by wildlife officers in an alley between Thirteenth and Fourteenth Streets. But far more common than elk were mule deer. Boulder boasted its own urban herd—estimated to number more than a thousand—that wandered backyards and city streets.

This harmonious relationship between civilization and nature encouraged people and wildlife to interact in intimate ways. In other times, this mingling would have been perceived as a worrisome sign, as in seventeenth-century England, where "the encroachment of wild creatures into the human domain was always alarming," historian Keith Thomas has noted. "In 1604 the House of Commons rejected a bill after the speech of its Puritan sponsor had been interrupted by the flight of a jackdaw through the Chamber—an indisputably bad omen." But Boulder had moved beyond such superstitious notions. The friendly merger of wildlife and humankind was not a liability; it was, rather, what attracted many residents in the first place—the chance to bask in nature's glory from one's very own back porch.

Comparisons to Eden were common in Boulder, and apt. With its lofty heights, fair skies, fruit trees, and flowing waters, the Colorado city bore a more than casual resemblance to theological representations of the prelapsarian world. (Eden was "higher than all the rest of the earth," wrote John of Damascus. "It was temperate in climate and bright with the softest and purest of air.") But a deeper similarity between Boulder and the biblical garden was less obvious and more profound.

Eden was a land without carnivory. According to the standard reading of Genesis, plants provided the only food in Paradise. (This presents a puzzle, admitted Gregory of Nyssa: "What fruit does the panther eat? What fruit makes the lion strong? But nevertheless these creatures, when submitting to the laws of nature, ate fruits.") In fact, until an unfortunate incident involving a snake and an apple, Adam and Eve got along swimmingly with all of their nonhuman neighbors; no one ate anyone else, and the animals were tame. (Alexander Pope on Eden: "Man walk'd with Beast, joint Tenant of the Shade; The same his Table, and the same his Bed.") The ferociousness of wild animals did not arise until after the Fall. Predation was born of original sin.

Boulder, too, lacked carnivores; not entirely, but the city and nearby foothills—like most of America—were devoid of the large, meat-eating mammals that had once dominated the land. Wolves, which in the 1800s had ruled Colorado's plains, "where large bands preyed upon the buffalo," according to an early report, had vanished from the state by the 1940s, the intended outcome of a brutal campaign of extermination. A similar war against bears had reduced the state's grizzly population to a handful by the early 1950s and probably zero by 1980. ("Probably" because on September 23, 1979, long after the species had been thought extinct in the state, a lone, honey-colored grizzly turned up in southern Colorado; the sow, quite possibly the last of her kind in the region, was promptly killed by a big-game outfitter who stabbed her with an arrow—in self-defense, he claimed.) Mountain lions had also suffered from a century of persecution and had seen their numbers dwindle; although not eliminated from Colorado, they had been pushed into remote refugia, far from human settlement.

With its large carnivores gone, Boulder's herbivores flourished. This burgeoning of wildlife at first seemed a good thing, but small problems soon became evident, and these annoyances prompted an editorial in Boulder's newspaper of record, the *Daily Camera* (so named because of the large number of pictures it printed in its early years), on the Sunday before Christmas in 1987. Given the hectic preholiday activity, it is likely that few Boulderites noticed the newspaper's opinion piece, and those who did probably thought little of it, but the words would prove prophetic:

CONTROL WILDLIFE AGGRESSION

We have nothing but the greatest sympathy for the people who have to figure out what to do with Boulder's various out-of-control wildlife populations.

Deer, geese, ducks and raccoons are all thriving here, and while that pleases most of us most of the time, it is a problem that cries out for some kind of environmentally sound solution.

At the root of the problem is that natural predators have been so reduced that wildlife populations grow out of control, far beyond the carrying capacity of the host neighborhoods. The deer problem, for instance, reached a new level of outrage recently when at least one deer began attacking a dog.

That stands as a warning of things to come, in our opinion.

Michael Sanders read the words closely. As one of the people charged with managing wildlife in this animal-loving town, he considered the *Camera* editorial further evidence that his new job would keep him fully occupied.

A naturalist by training and an extrovert by temperament, Michael exuded a mix of scientific studiousness and down-home southern charm. A vocal twang revealed his upbringing, on a family farm near Memphis in a town so small that a person could, in theory, launch a bottle rocket at one end of downtown and have it land clear at the other, a feat that he attempted one Halloween and likely would have achieved if the launch pad had not teetered, sending the projectile through the beauty-shop window. To Michael, who at age thirty-four retained a boyish face despite his tall frame and brown mustache, Boulder seemed a big, impersonal city. He was glad to have full-time work and a regular, albeit small, paycheck, but he would have preferred to remain in his previous job had federal budget cuts not eliminated the position, which involved studying grizzly bears in Yellowstone National Park. Although the distance between Michael and the closest wild grizzly was now greater than the gap between Boston and Baltimore, his experiences with large, fearsome predators would prove far more relevant to his new job than he could imagine.

Big mammals had always captivated him. "I remember my very first experience with bears," he recalls. "My dad had this old '60 Pontiac car. It was one of these red, four-door—*fins*, you know—and it was a beautiful automobile, *huge* automobile, like a boat. And I remember we were in the Smoky Mountains and we were having a picnic, and it was with my aunt and uncle and my mom and dad and myself, and we were sitting there at a picnic table and down through the woods came this bear. And I remember my mom and dad and aunt and uncle, they kind of got behind the car, and *I* jump *in* the car and lock all the doors. I was about seven or eight years old. And the bear comes down and gets face to face with me. There was just the glass between us. And I was just fascinated by it, just *totally* fascinated by it. My dad took pictures of it, of me inside the car and the bear looking at me inside the car." Twenty years later, as a graduate student at the University of Tennessee, Michael was back in the Great Smoky Mountains studying black bears under the tutelage of renowned biologist Michael Pelton.

Later on, at Yellowstone, Michael Sanders studied the interaction between people and wildlife—specifically, how humans behaved around grizzlies, and how grizzlies behaved in the presence of humans. He spent his days in a broad valley along Antelope Creek, north of Canyon Village and in the shadow of Mount Washburn. He arrived each morning in his National Park Service truck, stopped along the two-lane road, and deployed a pneumatic device to count passing vehicles. Then he took out a radio receiver and antenna for tracking bears.

Before his own fieldwork began, biologists had fitted about a dozen grizzlies in the area with radio collars—thick leather neckbands that held fist-sized transmitters. By tuning his receiver to different frequencies and swiveling a handheld antenna that looked like a TV aerial until he heard a telltale *bip-bip-bip*, Michael could identify which animals were nearby and their approximate direction. He would then sit in his truck, read books (Stephen Herrero's *Bear Attacks: Their Causes and Avoidance* was a favorite), eat pickles (he loved all sorts: dill, bread and butter, gherkins), glass the hillsides with binoculars, and wait for the action to begin. He kept a shotgun in the truck, "in case any of the bears ever decided to take a person down."

Soon, bears would emerge from the trees. The grizzlies lumbered across a meadow of wildflowers and knocked over anthills to lap up a high-protein meal of insects. Inevitably, tourists would emerge from their vehicles. Winnebagos halted in the middle of the road. Doors flung open. Husbands shouted, "Get the camera!" Traffic jams ensued.

Michael counted both vehicles and tourists. He noted how humans acted when they spotted the bears and how grizzlies reacted when they spotted the people. Many bears fled. One, known unpoetically as Bear 59, almost never did.

With humped shoulders, a concave face, and the approximate body shape of an NFL linebacker, Bear 59 was a medium-sized sow, her pelt a hue of dark chocolate tipped with silver. She had recently delivered her second litter, and tourists cooed and giggled as they watched her teach her cubs to browse berries and eat ants. "She was the best bear," Michael remembers. "She was not elusive at all. I mean, she spent a lot of time right up along in plain view of people. She'd give the park visitors what they wanted. They could go home and say they saw a bear. But she was always far enough away that she never caused any problems."

Until one early-autumn day.

On October 7, 1986, rangers discovered Bear 59 feeding blithely alone in a rolling meadow of grasses and sagebrush beside open stands of lodgepole pine. Initially unconcerned with the grizzly's eating habits, park officials were seeking a missing person who had apparently abandoned his car, a 1963 Chevrolet Impala, aqua in color, a short distance away. (The car appeared as if parked in haste and had sat in the lot of a small picnic area, three-tenths of a mile south of Otter Creek, for three days.) Observing Bear 59, the rangers soon realized they had found the person they sought, though not in his entirety. The sow huddled over the lower portion of a human body, from waist to sneakers still largely intact and clothed in blue denims secured by a leather belt. Rangers shot the bear and then investigated the scene. In the front left pocket of the jeans, they found a dime and nickel. In the front right were keys to the Impala. Tooled into the back of the belt was the name Bill.

A board of inquiry, which included Stephen Herrero, author of *Bear Attacks: Their Causes and Avoidance*, divided blame for the fatal mauling between the sow and the nature lover. Bill Tesinsky, an automobile mechanic and aspiring wildlife photographer from Great Falls, Montana, bore responsibility for his own death, the board concluded; he had foolishly approached Bear 59 to take a picture, as evidenced by the blood-and-dirt-smeared Pentax K-1000 camera found near his body, the zoom lens set at 120 mm. At this setting, the investigators determined, the bear would have appeared full-frame at around thirty to fifty feet.

More significantly, the board concluded that Bear 59 had become especially dangerous by years of exposure to camera-toting tourists, who had instilled in the grizzly an unnaturally blasé attitude toward humans. The board wrote in its final report,

> Animals normally flee when exposed to unusual, potentially threatening situations, such as people approaching. However, repeated exposure to such situations, if not followed by negative consequences, may result in an animal that does not flee

as readily. Behavioral scientists refer to this waning of response upon repeated exposure to potentially threatening situations as habituation. . . . We believe that bear #59's habituation allowed Mr. Tesinsky to approach, but that due to his desire to get good, albeit dangerous, photographs, he approached too closely and was attacked and killed.

In other words: animal behavior is malleable, and a community of people—whose actions may seem innocuous, and who as individuals may have minor impact—can exert a powerful, cumulative effect on wildlife; and when the wildlife species in question is a large carnivore, the results can be deadly.

Michael Sanders assumed that, with his change in jobs, such grave matters involving predatory mammals were no longer part of his life. Now in Boulder, having recently hauled all his belongings here in a four-by-eight trailer behind his Ford Bronco, Michael, as a new employee of the Boulder County Parks and Open Space Department, was responsible for reducing conflict between humans and far more benign wildlife.

Residents would routinely call and plead for help with raccoons nesting in their chimneys. "Build a fire," Michael would say. "Not a hot fire, just take some newspaper. The smoke will run them out." He received complaints about flickers—gaudy woodpeckers with polka dot chests and rouged cheeks—drilling holes in the cedar siding of homes. "Put up a plastic owl on the top of the house" to scare the birds away, he'd recommend. And he heard from dozens of desperate homeowners whose flowers and shrubs were being devoured by deer. "Lifebuoy soap," was his answer. "Take Lifebuoy soap and shave it with a cheese grater, put it in a bowl, and make a solution out of it. Make it just a very thick soap solution. Put it into a sprayer and spray it onto your geraniums or tulips and things like that. It first of all is a natural insecticide, and secondly, the deer hate it."

Deer, raccoons, woodpeckers, bats, prairie dogs, skunks, geese, mosquitoes. The focus of Michael's professional life had shifted a long way down the food chain. No grizzlies in Boulder and, as far as he knew, no cats the size of Saint Bernards.

2

RETURN OF THE NATIVE

As Boulderites trimmed trees and wrapped gifts on the weekend before Christmas in 1987, a pair of unseen eyes watched the city from above. The eyes glowed bright amber, but they saw the world in subdued and impoverished color. Through them, the rolling hills of ponderosa pine looked more buttermilk than olive, the sky more robin's egg than cerulean. The creature was red-green color-blind, its eyes designed for night vision. To the animal, the scene looked grainy and muted, like an antique photograph of the Rockies hand-tinted in pastel shades of blue and yellow.

The beast moved silently, stealthily, and alone along the southern flank of South Boulder Peak, on parkland owned by the city. It followed a narrow path beneath snow-covered branches, tracing a contour as it hugged the steep hillside. The forest was patchy, interspersed with shrub land and meadow. A knob of weather-worn granite emerged from the hillside above, the outcropping's surface splotched with fluorescent-orange lichen advertising the presence of abundant mammals. (The lichen, *Caloplaca*, thrives on nitrogen compounds found in urine.) Deer scat lay piled nearby.

Proceeding with precision and grace, the cougar left distinct tracks in soft snow: four toes, their imprints like teardrops, above a three-lobed heel shaped like a fat M. The cat planted its paws firmly and carefully in such

a way that its hind feet stepped in the prints of its forefeet, thereby mini-
mizing the risk of snapping a twig or crushing a dry leaf. ("[The cougar]
never makes any noise," Sioux author Charles Eastman once wrote, "for he
has the right sort of moccasins.") To the untrained eye, the pugmarks
might look like those of a dog, but the prints were too round to be canine
and showed no claws. The cougar possessed claws, sharp as ice picks and
long as threepenny nails, yet they hid within sheaths of skin and extended
only when necessary.

The lion angled upward and slightly north of due west. The serrated
spine of the Continental Divide rose above the foothills ahead, and the muffled roar of South Boulder Creek drifted up from below. In the seclusion of
Eldorado Canyon, a deep notch in the mountains at the edge of the plains,
the cougar could hear little evidence of humankind except the occasional
moaning of a train whistle or the rumble of a jet. Few houses occupied this
section of forest, but civilization was inescapable. Denver appeared through
the opening of the canyon, its distant skyscrapers a hazy apparition on the
horizon.

As the lion looked across the foothills, it likely felt a sense of ownership.
Cougars, like humans, are possessive of land; they divide the terrain into
home ranges—interlocking realms that they come to know as intimately
"as you and I know the floorplan of our house," biologist Harley Shaw has
written. These ranges can be of enormous proportion. An adult male may
preside over a territory the size of a minor European principality; a tom
could easily rule Liechtenstein, perhaps Andorra. A lion patrols his home
like a cop on the beat, walking circuits from one end of his range to the
other, learning where prey congregates and at what time of day, where to
hide in ambush, where to find water and shelter. Males mark their territories by dragging claws down tree trunks, rubbing their faces on rocks to
deposit scent, and scraping together mounds of soil, pine needles, twigs,
and leaves onto which they urinate or defecate as a signal to others that the
area is occupied.

For millennia, these mountains belonged to the lions. Males sparred
over territory and mates. Females nurtured cubs from blind infancy
through adolescence, teaching their offspring the art of the kill. Deer—the
lion's primary prey—learned vigilance; those that failed to watch the
bushes for a hint of movement ended up broken-necked, devoured in a flash
of fur and fang and claw.

But the cats' reign had ended, brutally and suddenly, when another species arrived in great herds, enticed by a substance the color of a lion's eyes.

Twenty miles southwest of where the lion stood, and almost 129 years earlier, a young Missourian named George Jackson set up camp beneath a large fir at the confluence of two streams, known today as Clear Creek and Chicago Creek, in a secluded valley where the small town of Idaho Springs now sits along Interstate 70. Jackson had been lured to the Rockies by reports of gold. The preceding summer, a prospecting party had found trivial quantities of the precious metal in streams at the foot of the mountains, and news of the discovery spread like a bad rumor, propelled and exaggerated ("THE NEW ELDORADO!!!" proclaimed the *Kansas City Journal of Commerce*) by those who stood to gain from embroidered reality. The reports of easy wealth came at a time of economic depression, prompting Jackson and more than a hundred thousand others to head for the Rockies in one of the great mass migrations in American history, known misleadingly as the Pikes Peak Gold Rush. (The prominent mountain named for explorer Zebulon Pike lay almost one hundred miles from the original auriferous deposits.) These gold-seeking "fifty-niners"—who outnumbered California's *forty*-niners by more than two to one—flooded across the plains in a great wash of humanity, traveling by foot, horse, ox-drawn wagon, even sailcraft, many foundering, some perishing, one forced to engage in familial cannibalism. (Illinoisan Daniel Blue, stranded and ill provisioned on the high plains in winter, survived on a diet of snow, boiled roots, grass, one dog, the occasional rabbit, and portions of his two dead brothers and another deceased traveling mate.) When the hordes arrived at the goldfields, they found gold lacking, and many denounced the whole episode as a hoax and turned toward home just as paying quantities of the precious metal were finally being unearthed.

Jackson was the first to strike significant pay dirt. At his winter campsite in the foothills west of Denver, while on a lone hunting and prospecting foray, he built a large fire that thawed frozen stream gravels. On January 7, 1859, Jackson dug into the sediment with his knife and uncovered a golden nugget, and by the following day he had amassed about half an ounce of gold. "Will quit and try and get back in the spring," he wrote in his diary. He did return, and the "Jackson Diggings" and other deposits nearby proved so rich that they spawned a mining industry that would extract more than $50 million worth of gold within two decades, turn Boulder and Denver into bustling supply towns, and lead to the creation of Colorado first as a territory and, in 1876, as the nation's thirty-eighth state. A plaque commemorating George Jackson's central role in Colorado history sat bolted to a granite boulder in front of Clear Creek High School in Idaho Springs. It read,

ON THIS SPOT
WAS MADE THE FIRST
DISCOVERY OF GOLD
IN THE
ROCKY MOUNTAINS
BY
GEORGE A. JACKSON
JANUARY
7TH
1859
PLACED 1909

Unacknowledged on the plaque, or in most history books, was the feud George Jackson started with the native wildlife during his prospecting trip. Jackson recorded the struggle in his diary: Jan. 1—"Killed a mountain lion to-day"; Jan. 2—"Mountain lion within 20 steps, pulled my gun from under the blankets. Shot too quick. Broke his shoulder, but followed up and killed him"; Jan. 4—"Mountain lion stole all my meat to-day in camp. No supper to night, damn him!"; Jan. 5—"Wounded mountain lion before sunrise."

Jackson's contempt for the local feline inhabitants was to be expected. Slaughtering cougars was part of a longstanding American tradition. His victims were only the latest casualties in a war of extermination that had been waged for centuries, a bloody conflict that left a lasting mark on Boulder, the Front Range, and the nation.

It is difficult to overstate the animosity Americans have exhibited toward large carnivores. We have poisoned wolves with strychnine, dynamited grizzlies, shot coyotes from helicopters, and lured mountain lions to steel-jawed traps with catnip oil. We have invented ingenious devices of death such as the "coyote getter," a contraption similar to a Roman candle that shoots cyanide crystals into the mouth of the animal that tugs at the bait. We have tortured predators—wired their mouths shut so that they starve; doused them with gasoline and set them on fire; sawed off their lower jaws and thrown them, crippled, to packs of dogs. We have gassed their dens and strangled their young. All of this an attempt by humans, the ultimate predators, to eliminate the competition.

The beastly slaughter began with the arrival of Europeans in the New World. Resentful at losing horses and cows and sheep to carnivores, settlers put a price on the murderous animals' heads. The earliest recorded bounty on cougars dates to the 1500s, when Jesuit priests in Baja California offered natives one bull for each lion killed. A century later, the British colonies were paying cash. The town of Springfield, Massachusetts, offered five shillings per cougar and required that those seeking the reward "bring the heads & taile of every one soe killed unto the Select men or Towne Treasurer." A Connecticut law of 1694 provided that "whosoeuer shall kill any panter in this Colony and make it so appeare he shall be payd out of the pub: treasury twenty shillings p head." Nineteen years later, still vexed by the cats, Connecticut doubled its bounty.

To accelerate the killing, colonists organized "ring hunts," a bloody sport that proved horrifically effective at cleansing large areas of predators. Historian and conservationist Henry W. Shoemaker described one such mass execution perpetrated around 1760 in central Pennsylvania:

> Panthers and wolves had been troubling the more timid of the settlers, and a grand drive towards the centre of a circle thirty miles in diameter was planned. A plot of ground was cleared into which the animals were driven. In the outer edge of the circle fires were started, guns fired, bells rung, all manner of noises made. The hunters, men and boys, to the number of two

hundred, gradually closed in on the centre. When they reached the point where the killing was to be made, they found it crowded with yelping, growling, bellowing animals. Then the slaughter began, not ending until the last animal had been slain.

Among the creatures dispatched: 109 wolves, 112 foxes, 17 black bears, and 41 cougars.

By the time the United States celebrated its centennial, the unrelenting massacre had proved highly successful; mountain lions had been extirpated from Massachusetts, Rhode Island, New Jersey, Indiana, and Kentucky, and many other states quickly joined the ranks of the cougar-free. (Exactly when the animal became extinct in any given area is subject to debate, but authoritative sources suggest the following years for the last confirmed kill in these states: Pennsylvania, 1871; Vermont, 1881; Virginia, 1882; North Carolina, 1886; New York, 1894.) As the twentieth century began, cougars had been almost entirely extinguished from the eastern half of the United States, with the lone exception of Florida, where a small population of the animals, known locally as Florida panthers, survived by hiding in the Everglades.

Having accomplished its aim in the East, the war then shifted west. In 1915, under heavy lobbying from western ranchers, Congress created a federal predator-control program with its own cadre of government-paid killers. The agency, called the Division of Predatory Animal and Rodent Control, today known euphemistically as Wildlife Services, employed hunters who shot, trapped, and poisoned "problem" animals on behalf of ranching associations and individual stockmen.

The campaign of killing invoked the imagery of the Wild West, replete with stories of valiant lawmen bringing outlaws to justice. "Slippery Sally," a Colorado cougar that the *Denver Post* called "a hunted criminal, with government men tracking her all over the county," met an ignominious end after two years of pursuit. (Sally's crime: preying on deer.) Stock-killing cats, such as California's notorious "Crooked Nose," New Mexico's "Old Five-toe Tom," and Colorado's "Old Bob"—blamed for the deaths of "hundreds of cattle and young colts"—provoked particular vengeance, and their demise elicited special celebration.

The men, and at least one woman, who hunted down these criminals were hailed as heroes, and the most proficient among them became legendary. When California's state lion hunter Jay Bruce came to town, schools discharged students so they could hear about his storied exploits. (In *Cougar Killer*, his aptly titled autobiography, Bruce boasted a lifelong catch of 669 lions.) Arizona's famous Lee Brothers, a septet of lion-hunting siblings (until a firearms accident reduced their number by one), claimed to have killed more than a thousand cougars in twenty years. The great "Uncle Jim" Owens, a Texan who slaughtered cats from Montana to Wyoming to Arizona, killed so many animals that, as one New York writer calculated, "Uncle Jim destroyed more than two hundred tons of cougar. He destroyed more than three miles of cougar, enough to form a parade from Washington Square to Central Park, plus."

Yet the "dean of lion hunters" was Ben Lilly. A southern mountain man famed for his skill and perseverance in tracking cougars, Lilly was an expert shot ("I never saw a lion that I did not kill or wound," he bragged) who tempered his homemade knives in panther oil and ate lion meat to acquire the cat's agility and endurance. In 1907, Theodore Roosevelt hunted with Lilly in Louisiana and wrote, "He is a religious fanatic, and is as hardy as a bear or elk." Once on a lion's trail, Lilly would follow for days without food or shelter, stopping only for the Sabbath. Lilly read the Bible regularly and believed he was doing God's work. According to big-game hunter and author Frank Hibben,

> It seemed that Ben Lilly regarded himself as a policeman of the wild. He was a self-appointed leavener of nature. Certain animals—bears and lions to be specific—were endowed by their very nature with a capacity to wreak evil. They couldn't help it, but evil they were and should be destroyed. Ben Lilly several times referred to panthers as the "Cains" of the animal world. They were slayers and should be killed in their turn.

Sportsmen shared this hatred of mountain lions because the cats ate deer and were therefore a "menace to other wholly attractive and more desirable members of our American fauna." In other words, cougars were taking game that human hunters would rather kill themselves. (And the lions enjoyed an unfair advantage, showing "no respect for hunting seasons, hunting hours, [or] bag limits," remarked a U.S. Forest Service employee.) For a while, even ardent conservationists were convinced by this line of reasoning.

Consider the case of William Temple Hornaday, first director of the New York Zoological Park and founder of the American Bison Society, a man who, according to his *New York Times* obituary, "spent practically a lifetime fighting against the extinction of the birds and beasts of the North American Continent." Hornaday lobbied tirelessly for the creation of animal preserves and against wanton hunting. "The only thing that will save the game is by stopping the killing of it!" he wrote in his conservation manifesto *Our Vanishing Wild Life*. But even though Hornaday fought vigorously to protect buffalo and fur seals and migratory birds, he had no sympathy for wolves or cougars, which he denounced in a 1914 speech at Yale University as a "curse" to deer and elk: "The eradication of the puma from certain districts that it now infests to a deplorable extent is a task of immediate urgency. . . . [W]e consider firearms, dogs, traps and strychnine thoroughly legitimate weapons of destruction. For such animals, no half-way measures will suffice."

Not even the national parks offered refuge to the outlaw cat. Yellowstone officials, after complaining of cougars that caused "a great deal of mischief," procured lion hounds in 1893 to help hunters eliminate the feline scourge; the scheme proved so successful that, within a decade and a half, the park sold its dogs for lack of cats. Elsewhere—at Sequoia, Glacier, Mesa Verde, Yosemite, Crater Lake, Rocky Mountain, and Grand Canyon National Parks—government agents routinely gunned down cougars (and wolves, and coyotes, and foxes) as vermin to protect more "desirable" species.

Residents of Boulder and nearby towns enthusiastically participated in the frenzy of killing. Colorado enacted its first cougar bounty just five years after statehood; by a vote of thirty-six to zero in the house, the state set the price on a lion's head—literally, since to collect payment one had to turn in the scalp and ears—at ten dollars. (In the ensuing years, the reward for killing a cougar fluctuated between three dollars and fifty dollars.) For a while, the *Denver Post* pitched in, too, offering its own bounty—twenty-five dollars per adult lion, ten dollars per cub—and urging its readers to join the fight for the common good:

> Come on-n-n-n-n-n-n-n, you lion killers!
> Come on-n-n-n-n-n-n-n, you trappers and hunters and mountaineers!

The lions are loose and—

The Post has plenty of money and is not stingy. . . .

[I]t is the duty of every true Coloradoan to do his best to rid
the state of these beasts which kill so much game every year.
By no other means than hunting out the mountain lions and
killing them can the game be protected.

Boulder-area ranchers, annoyed by cougars that ate poultry and livestock, got their revenge. In the summer of 1891, James Walker—a homesteader who amassed a large spread in Boulder's foothills for his cattle,
horses, mules, chickens, pigs, wife, and son—killed a mountain lion and
turned it in for the ten-dollar bounty. Almost six decades later, Walker's
son, William—the then elderly inheritor of the family ranch—proudly
told the *Daily Camera*, "Fortunately for us, we don't have any mountain
lions. I haven't seen one for years." The campaign of killing had had its
intended effect. By the middle of the twentieth century, the Boulder area
was largely free of cougars. Except for the occasional stray that wandered
through the region—such as an eighty-five-pound lioness glimpsed west
of town, and promptly shot, in 1944—Colorado's remaining cougars were
holed up in the rugged south-central and northwestern portions of the
state, more than a hundred miles from Boulder.

It is impossible to give an accurate body count in America's war against
the cougar, since most deaths went unrecorded. But if one sums the official statistics—lions killed by state and federal trappers, those hunted with
permits, carcasses turned in for bounties—the toll for about *half* of the last
century in the United States and Canada has been tabulated at 66,665. More
significant than the flood of lions killed was the trickle that remained. By
the early 1960s, the United States was home to as few as 4,000 cougars,
and Colorado's lion population had fallen, by one estimate, as low as 124.

Then, once the lions were gone, people wanted them back.

America's remarkable change of heart toward mountain lions can be
traced, more than anything, to a conservation fiasco that resulted from
good intentions.

In 1906, President Theodore Roosevelt created a million-acre game
preserve on the forested Kaibab Plateau along the North Rim of the Grand
Canyon. At the time, preserving game (i.e., deer) meant slaughtering predators, which the government did with great zeal. Lion hunter Uncle Jim

Owens killed or captured at least six hundred cougars on the Kaibab in about a dozen years, with a little help from celebrity guests: Zane Grey, the author and romanticizer of the American West, in 1908, and former President Roosevelt and his two younger sons in 1913.

As the lions were killed off, deer proliferated. This is, of course, what biologists had hoped would occur. Soon, however, abundance led to over-abundance; in ecological terms, the deer "irrupted." (The word's meaning approximates that of its geological homonym.) In less than twenty years, a starting population of about four thousand deer ballooned into a throng estimated to be as large as a hundred thousand. The results were disastrous, as the National Park Service reported:

> By 1924, deer had increased until more than seventeen hundred were counted in one meadow in one evening. Winter came, deer died, and those that lived ate every leaf and twig till the whole country looked as though a swarm of locusts had swept through it, leaving the range (except for the taller shrubs and trees) torn, gray, stripped, and dying.

With little left to eat, the deer population collapsed, and the vegetation was left so denuded that scientists estimated it could take fifty years for the forest to recover fully. The lesson seemed clear: cougars had helped keep the Kaibab ecosystem healthy by holding prey numbers in check; paradoxically, deer *benefited* from the presence of an animal that ate them.

Although revisionist thinkers have questioned whether lion hunting really caused the Kaibab irruption, the debacle provided a strong circumstantial case for keeping cougars around, and the incident changed minds—none more profoundly than that of Aldo Leopold, America's prophet of ecology. Early in his career, Leopold served as an enthusiastic combatant in the war against predators; he was a disciple of the great wolf and lion hater William Temple Hornaday, worked with esteemed cougar hunter Ben Lilly, and urged "going out after the last lion scalp, and getting it." But after seeing what happened to the Kaibab and other forests robbed of predators, Leopold—then a distinguished professor at the University of Wisconsin and president of the Ecological Society of America—began proselytizing for the *protection* of carnivores with the passion of a convert. "By killing off all species having predatory tendencies we may have been doing a greater damage to our game species than ever did the

predators," he wrote in 1935. Leopold argued his case to the general public in a book that would become a sacred text of the environmental movement, a collection of nature writings published posthumously under the
title *A Sand County Almanac*. In simple, eloquent language, Leopold's little book, which eventually sold millions of copies, urged Americans to
think like a mountain—to look at nature from a holistic perspective—and
that meant valuing all of the parts, predators included.

Another book, *Silent Spring*, captured global attention in 1962 with a
doomsday message about pesticides and a more general warning about
humankind's hubris. ("The 'control of nature' is a phrase conceived in arrogance, born of the Neanderthal age of biology and philosophy, when it was
supposed that nature exists for the convenience of man," Rachel Carson
wrote.) Meanwhile, nuclear annihilation became a realistic fear, Ohio's
Cuyahoga River ignited, and the public came to see *humans* as humanity's
biggest threat and nature as Earth's savior. Predators, as symbols of the
wilderness, were no longer considered evil and destructive, but noble and
beneficial. (By 1976, an opinion survey in Canada found that the most popular adjectives used to describe cougars were "beautiful" and "fascinating.") In this new atmosphere, a movement coalesced to halt, for practical
and ethical reasons, the poisoning and trapping and hunting of mountain
lions and other carnivores.

The author and champion of wilderness Edward Abbey, who enjoyed a
rock star–like following in Boulder, praised cougars and urged their protection in an article for *Life* magazine. "We need mountain lions for the
same reason that we need more bald eagles, golden eagles, Gila monsters,
alligators, redtailed hawks, coyotes, bobcats, badgers, wild pigs, grizzly
bears, wild horses, red racers, diamondbacks, sacred datura, wild grapes and
untamed rivers," he wrote. "How to say once more what has been said so
often? Who is listening?" Abbey ended the article on a reassuring note. He
pointed out that despite America's brutal treatment of the mountain
lion—despite the butchery, the savagery, the humiliation people had
heaped upon the cougar—the cats did not respond in kind. "Apparently
they bear no malice toward us," he wrote. "There is no authentic record of
a lion actually attacking a human being." It was a nice sentiment, but
Abbey was wrong.

During this time, in Colorado, a chorus rose against the government
bounty on cougars. By the mid-1960s, the *Denver Post*, which had once

eagerly offered a bounty of its own, editorialized against the state law because it could cause "the careless extermination of an animal as interesting and graceful as the mountain lion." Biologists urged an end to the bounty because it impeded rational game management. State officials disliked the fact that it encouraged fraud; a black market had developed in which cougar hides harvested in neighboring states were smuggled to Colorado to claim the generous fifty-dollar reward. As a result, in 1965 the state legislature repealed Colorado's bounty and declared the cougar a game animal. (Colorado was the second western state, just two months behind Nevada, to grant game status to the mountain lion; within eight years, every western state but Texas would follow suit.) Under the new law, lions could still be hunted, but the harvest was highly regulated—subject to quotas, bag limits, seasons, and restrictions on the killing of cubs and mothers with cubs. Colorado's new goal was to maintain a healthy population of cougars, and the numbers started to rebound.

Although counting cougars is a notoriously difficult exercise (how do you census an animal whose expertise is hiding?), Colorado wildlife officials estimated by the mid-1970s that the state's cougar population had risen to between 1,100 and 1,500, a reasonably healthy level. By the 1980s, the lions had slipped—quietly—back into the Boulder area. The big cats began to subdivide the land, defining home ranges and squeezing into the interstices of human life. They walked ridges and saddles and cliffs to learn the contours of a terrain that had once been theirs.

The large cat on South Boulder Peak veered south and climbed a tongue of hillside jutting into Eldorado Canyon. A tall ponderosa held its arms to the wind. From this high ridge, a community came into view below. The houses—sparse and small, along dirt roads—blended into the forest, but new home sites were being platted and foundations poured for architectural showplaces with grand porches, picture windows, and satellite dishes. A road sign read "Couger Drive" [*sic*], homage to a creature many residents assumed had been relegated to the region's past.

The lion had come to reclaim its ancestral home, but the land had changed since the end of the previous feline dynasty. Humans had not only built homes and roads; they had altered the flow of streams and the growth of forests. They had irrigated the once bare plains and made them bloom. They had modified the deer's migration patterns and daily rituals. They had exterminated the lion's natural enemy, the wolf, and replaced it with a more timid race of canines. And the humans themselves were different. Unlike the Native Americans who once hunted the cougar for its skin and meat, and unlike the miners and ranchers who killed the cougar out of hatred, these people would seek to live in peace with lions.

The cougar descended toward the houses, traveling as silently and invisibly as a whispered breeze. Mountain lions are masters of stealth, "natural sneaks" some have called them, creatures whose modus operandi is to observe without being observed. "Only the very lucky ever see this beautiful monster in the wild," wrote Edward Abbey.

No one saw the lion that traversed South Boulder Peak five days before Christmas in 1987. All that was found were its tracks in the snow.

3

HAPPY TIMES

Two days after the old year yielded to the new, on a frigid Saturday morning at the dawn of 1988, Professor William B. Krantz was at his home in Boulder Canyon, six miles west of downtown. Krantz, a whiskered and bespectacled chemical engineer at the University of Colorado, had acquired his Ph.D., beard, and ecopolitics at Berkeley in the 1960s. Like many of Boulder's inhabitants, he was an ardent environmentalist; he counted Henry David Thoreau, Rachel Carson, John Muir, Paul Ehrlich, and Aldo Leopold among his intellectual influences, and he proudly supported the Sierra Club, Friends of the Earth, Save-the-Redwoods League, League of Conservation Voters, and Zero Population Growth. (Fearing that ZPG's policies did not go far enough, Krantz also gave money to *Negative* Population Growth.)

That morning, Krantz was working at his computer in a windowless, ground-floor study paneled in walnut. He was alone. "I heard a *tap-tap-tap-tap*," he recalls. "I thought somebody was knocking at the door. And we had a doorbell, so I'm wondering, you know, *Why are they knocking?*"

The Krantz home, which Bill shared with his wife and daughter, stood along a narrow strip of relatively flat ground tucked between Boulder Creek and a steep, wooded hillside that climbed to meet the Roosevelt National Forest. The site, surrounded by undeveloped land, would have felt secluded if not for the constant traffic on Highway 119, the two-lane road through Boulder Canyon, which passed just fifteen yards away, across the creek. The house, dressed in marine-plywood siding, rose three stories and boasted several decks that looked over the creek. At the west end of the property, Mrs. Krantz tended a flower bed that had become an unintended food patch for deer that ate the delphiniums, marigolds, bleeding hearts, verbena, and chrysanthemums, but generally left the zinnias untouched. At the east end, cut into a cleft in a lichen-covered cliff, was an old gold mine in which someone had placed an upholstered couch, its floral design and plump cushions an odd sight in the dank cave.

Bill Krantz left his study to investigate the source of the tapping. He headed down a tiled hall toward the front of the house, which faced north onto a small yard that bordered a gravel driveway. The drive led to a short, thick-planked bridge across Boulder Creek—the only way on and off the property. A wooden archway framed the bridge like the entrance to a ranch, and a plywood sign dangled from the top. Bill had constructed the sign in the shape of a schoolhouse clock, but where the numbers should have been, he had placed letters spelling out the name of the family homestead:

The sign, the archway, the bridge, the house were all barn red, a hue that would appear grayish yellow through the eyes of a mountain lion.

In the standstill universe of the Happy Times clock, it was always 7:00, but in reality it was about 10:00 A.M. when Bill reached the carpeted family room at the end of the hall. He tilted his head toward a casement window that looked into the front yard. "And it was like one of those things where you don't believe what you see at first," he recalls. "I see four faces looking in, like kids with their noses pressed up against the glass in a candy store or in a toy store. But they weren't human faces." They were lion faces.

Bill had lived in Colorado for twenty years, and he had never seen a cougar. Now he had a quartet at his window. The group appeared to be a family; he guessed they were a mother, two small kittens, and an older, larger cub from a previous litter. Such a grouping would be unusual—adolescent lions generally leave home before new siblings are born—but rare cases have been reported of females with cubs of two sizes. The smaller kittens, bigger than adult house cats, stared through the glass with sapphire eyes. Their coats were spotted, pale gold dappled with umber. (The kittens must have been quite young. By six months of age, a cougar's baby blue eyes darken and its spots begin to fade.) Bill Krantz was dazzled—"I wanted to *share* the experience with somebody"—but his wife and daughter were in town, shopping.

The Krantz property might appropriately have been called a compound, in a rustic sort of way. Across the driveway from the main house stood the family's "cabin," comprising two stories and two bedrooms, which was being rented by two young men for a reasonable $375 a month. Bill Krantz picked up the telephone and called the cabin. Bill Held—a twenty-something, outdoorsy, not-so-serious-student tenant—answered.

"[Bill Krantz] called over and said, y'know, 'Look outside. There's four mountain lions out in the drive,'" recalls Bill Held. "And there, between my house and his house, they were out in the middle of the drive kind of frolicking around, the little ones. At first, it kind of seemed like they were playing. It was really cool. We're goin', *Whoa.* We're checkin' it out. And then, uh, he's like, 'Oh, *no,* it looks like the one has a trap on her back foot.' And I'm like, 'Yeah, sure enough, she *does* have a trap on her back foot.' And then we realized why or what they were doing. These kits were, like, trying to pull the trap off. It turned out to be kind of a pretty sad scene."

What had at first seemed a beautiful natural spectacle took on a tragic cast. The frighteningly handsome, immensely muscular, presumably mother cat was in obvious pain. She limped and dripped blood in the snow.

Back at the main house, Bill Krantz stepped outside, peered into the stricken animal's eyes, and saw supplication. He believed that the lion had consciously tapped on his window seeking help. "She knew that trap was due to man and only man could take it off," he says. "And I honestly thought of Saint Francis of Assisi and the wolf of Gubbio." (Francis, whose rapport with wildlife resembled the perfect relationship between man and animal in Eden, called out, "Come hither, Brother Wolf," and negotiated a peace accord between the dreaded beast and the terrorized people of Gubbio.) For a moment, Bill considered approaching the lion, Androcles-like, to remove the source of injury to its paw. Then reality set in. He had no experience handling wild animals. This was a job for a professional. Bill retreated into his home and called the Boulder County Sheriff's Department to report a wildlife emergency.

Meanwhile, the leonine family ambled over the small bridge spanning Boulder Creek, passed beneath the Happy Times sign, crossed the double yellow line of Highway 119, and vanished among the ponderosa pines on the northern slope of Boulder Canyon.

Michael Sanders was not involved in the pursuit of the injured cougar. In his new job as resource specialist for the Boulder County Parks and Open Space Department, he was busy counting geese and organizing a Christmas-tree recycling program. Michael collected hundreds of de-tinseled trees and tied them together with chicken wire attached to cinder blocks; he then sank these artificial reefs in the county's artificial lakes to provide habitat for artificially introduced fish. By the time Michael read about the Krantz lion incident in the pages of the *Daily Camera*, the tragic saga had already played itself out.

A lengthy search involving a dozen people—state game wardens, city park rangers, lion hunters—scoured Boulder Canyon's hillsides for the wounded cat. The searchers looked for tracks in the deep snow. They ran hounds, which located the two young cubs, but not the large cat. They hung a dead fawn from a tree, as a lure, but the carcass went untouched. Finally, one week after the initial sighting, a driver spotted the lioness on Sugarloaf Road, and a gang of wildlife officers rushed to meet her.

The cougar sat on a ledge. As the people approached, the lioness snarled and hissed but did not move; she seemed weak. A tranquilizer dart was launched and stuck. Once the cougar was anesthetized, the human helpers found that she had freed herself from the trap but had lost two toes in the process. They washed and bandaged her wounds, injected penicillin, carried her to a truck (one of the cat's bearers noted how sweet she smelled, like sage), and drove her a short distance away to place her beside a road-killed deer so she would have a ready meal when she revived. The humans watched the lioness until the sun set, and they saw her stir. The *Daily Camera* reported the joyful news of the lion's rescue.

By the following morning, however, when wildlife officers returned to check on the cougar, they found her dead; apparently her injuries had been too severe, and the attempts at first aid had come too late. A postmortem examination revealed that the muscles of the injured leg had atrophied, suggesting that the lion may have struggled with the trap for as long as a month. Biologists also determined that the lioness could not have been a mother; she had never lactated. They guessed that the *other* large cougar seen by Bill Krantz—which he had assumed was an older cub—had actually given birth to the kittens, but the relationship of the four cats and why they were traveling together remain a mystery. "It's a pretty unhappy end to the story," a state wildlife official told the *Daily Camera* in announcing the lioness's death, "but I think now she was in shock and wouldn't have made it anyway."

The tale of the Boulder Canyon lion had several effects on the community at large. First, given the prominent coverage in Boulder's newspaper of record, the incident acted as an official coming out—a sort of puma cotillion, if you will—announcing the return of cougars to the area. Lions became a topic of conversation. Furthermore, the circumstances of this incident reinforced the new, prevailing view of mountain lions—as victims, not villains. To the people of Boulder, the injured lioness was not, in the words of Theodore Roosevelt, "the destroyer of the deer, the lord of stealthy murder . . . with a heart both craven and cruel." This animal, wounded by a callous human being, was the cougar of Edward Abbey, who wrote, "Humanity has four billion desperate advocates, but how many has the mountain lion . . . ?" and "A world without mountain lions I wouldn't want to live in." A woman, quoted in the *Daily Camera*, seemed to speak for all of Boulder when she said, "I am appalled that there are still people trapping in Boulder County. I think the public should know the circumstances under which that animal died."

The incident, finally, had another effect, which would, in time, prove important. It piqued Michael Sanders's interest in the large cats. "All of a sudden this brought a *whole new* definition to what I was doing," he recalls. "It was a big, charismatic megafauna, you know. A *lot* more interesting than prairie dogs. It was something that could eat you."

A month later, Jim Halfpenny stood in front of a chalkboard before a small audience of rangers and volunteers with Boulder's parks departments. Jim had a rugged face and dry demeanor, and he conveyed a surprising message: the recent sighting of mountain lions in Boulder Canyon was not a freak incident; it was to be expected, and it was likely to recur. "Our deer population has gone up in recent years, and I think that the lion population has gone up, too," he said.

From a distance, Jim appeared earless. His hair, dark and straight and shiny (it almost looked shellacked), draped down his temples where it covered his ears and, merging with thick sideburns and a heavy beard, outlined his face with a ring of black. The dark features, the deep-set eyes, the hirsute chest through the open collar of a flannel shirt, gave him the look of a mountain man, albeit one who cleaned up nicely.

Jim paused, sipping Mountain Dew from a can. "I'm not a lion biologist," he explained. "I'm a tracker, and that puts me in close proximity to a lot of different animals a lot of the time. And over the last five years I've gotten to spend a lot of time thinking about and working with lions."

Jim Halfpenny was not just a tracker; he was a renowned naturalist with a Ph.D. in mammalogy. Michael Sanders, sitting on the right side of the room toward the front, was starstruck. He was well acquainted with Jim Halfpenny's accomplishments: research in Antarctica, expeditions to Greenland, participation in a Sino-American trek through Tibet to collect animal specimens for museums. Jim taught ecology and tracking courses for the National Outdoor Leadership School, Yellowstone Institute, Teton Science School, and Aspen Center for Environmental Studies. He had helped investigate the bizarre and tragic killing of Colorado's last known grizzly. And he was a published author. Michael owned a copy of Halfpenny's *A Field Guide to Mammal Tracking in North America*, which Jim had inscribed—"Mike, Here's to the great Colorado Outdoors. James C. Halfpenny"—when the two men had met briefly, at a conference, the preceding year.

Jim Halfpenny worked in Boulder as a research fellow at CU's Institute of Arctic and Alpine Research, and the city Open Space Department had asked him to conduct a seminar on identifying mountain lion sign. Hence this gathering, at seven-thirty on a Wednesday evening in February, in a bleak second-floor classroom on the CU campus.

"Someone want to get the lights there in back?" Jim asked. The room darkened. Jim switched on a slide projector, and images of animal prints in snow appeared on the screen. Each track had been photographed beside a comb, pen, ruler, or pocketknife to provide scale.

To Jim, tracking was detective work. "When you're tracking, you never make a judgment based on one track," he told his audience. "You gather every single clue that you can before you venture an educated deduction.

"It's incredibly easy to mistake dog tracks for lion tracks. It's *incredibly* easy," he cautioned. "People say you can tell cat tracks from dog tracks by claws. Dogs usually show claws. Cats usually do *not* show claws. But those are not absolute rules by any means." Jim advanced the carousel on the slide projector with a remote control and gestured at the changing images on the screen, pointing out various characteristics that can distinguish canine prints from feline: toe position, gait, the shape of the heel pad, the overall geometry of the track. He explained that a dog track looks somewhat rectangular—longer than it is wide—whereas a cat print gives "an overall impression of that track being round, or wider than it is long."

Jim had begun tracking at age eleven, inspired by a library copy of Ernest Thompson Seton's *Animal Tracks and Hunter Signs* (Seton called tracks "the ancient script of the woods") and aided by an unending supply of plaster of Paris from his parents' store, the Halfpenny Hobby Shop, 2022 Avenue B, Scottsbluff, Nebraska—"Unpainted wall plaques (our specialty)," read the cover of the 1954 catalog. He spent his youth along the muddy banks of the North Platte making plaster casts of raccoon and muskrat and mouse and coyote tracks, some of which he still had, now at age forty-one, in his cluttered, peach-hued trailer home along with skulls and antlers and legs of elk and grizzlies and moose, plus frozen rats in plastic bags in his refrigerator. ("You gotta have *somewhere* to keep specimens," he explained.)

Jim was also a professional scatologist. Celestial Seasonings had once hired him to help workers recognize trace fecal matter in bulk herbs purchased from overseas; the firm had suffered an embarrassing episode some years back when the Food and Drug Administration found excessive amounts of excrement and insects in Egyptian chamomile that had been blended into Sleepytime and other herb teas. The ability to identify excrement could be valuable not only to herbal tea makers but, as Jim explained, to anyone searching for evidence of lions in Boulder County.

Jim squeezed a button on the remote control, and an image of feces, enlarged to the size of his arm, appeared. "Scat of the predators come in cords—long thick areas," he said. "What do you look for on any cat scat? Cat scat tends to be broken cords where segmentations, *here*"—he pointed at the screen—"are about equal to the diameter of the scat. So a given piece is sort of kind of squarish." Indeed, the image looked like a parade of over-sized morsels of Mini-Wheats cereal.

Lions eat mostly deer, Jim explained, so if one finds a partially eaten deer carcass, that may suggest the presence of lions. Of course, other animals—coyotes, dogs, raccoons—kill deer or scavenge them. "When you find a suspected kill, you want to check the kill out for signs of what may have killed the animal," Jim continued, pacing and gesturing as he spoke. "If the animal's fairly fresh, try to determine where it might have been bitten. Cut the skin open. Pull the skin back. If you can find puncture marks, measure the distance between them. Lions on the average, a good-size female or male, will have four and a half to five centimeters between the [centers of the] canine teeth on the upper skull"—Jim jutted out his upper jaw and pointed to his eyeteeth—"and three to four centimeters on the canine teeth on the lower skull." If the animal had been killed rather than scavenged upon, he added, one will find massive hemorrhaging at the location of the bite. "When you pull that skin back, there'll be all sorts of black blood clotted all over. If the animal was scavenged, you won't find blood. So blood indicates active predation." Mountain lions rarely scavenge.

"Look for a broken neck," he added. "The lion is the only one of the animals around here that will break a neck." Jim scanned his notes. "Oh," he said, realizing he had forgotten something. "Lions are really possessive about a carcass that they've got. If you get yourself a fresh carcass, be sitting on it the next morning." The lion will likely be there, too.

Some in the audience were skeptical that Boulder County could sustain a lion population of any significance, given the rapid, suburban development and the intense recreational use of parcels of land that remained undeveloped. Mountain lions were generally considered a wilderness species; according to a 1965 state publication, they "shun close association with man, his buildings and fences."

Jim responded with a mischievous smile. "That's been a traditional thought. If you have people, you can't have these wild predators—lions, bears, and so on. I don't buy that. Once somebody isn't out there killing them, I think we'll find that predators, with a few notable exceptions—say, grizzly bears—they're quite content to live with people.

"I think lion are *perfectly* content to live right here in Boulder," he continued. "This is ideal lion habitat. This is great. They couldn't have any-

thing better. You've got lots of caves, ledges, trees—ponderosa pine trees—
and plenty of deer. There's everything they want."

In fact, Jim said, he *knew* that there were quite a few lions around. During the preceding year, with the help of an undergraduate named Kristin McGrath, Jim had solicited lion sightings from Boulder-area residents through public service announcements and a notice in the *Daily Camera*. ("Seen a mountain lion lately?" it began.) Dozens of people had phoned in reports: a woman said she'd glimpsed a lion as it crossed Highway 119 through Boulder Canyon; a man claimed to have witnessed a cougar eating a buck on the south side of Gross Reservoir; a pair of women reported that, while on horseback in the foothills, they'd surprised a lion and watched it run off. Most observations were made in the early morning or late evening—times when mountain lions are known to be most active, but also times when, in the dim of twilight, a bobcat, golden retriever, or large house cat might look like a cougar to an excited layperson. Jim and his student assistant had interviewed each observer to weed out obvious cases of mistaken identity, and they judged eighty-two sightings to be reasonably credible. Six were within city limits.

To Michael Sanders, who had followed Jim's talk with great interest, this was exciting news. *Mountain lions in town.* As the presentation concluded, with the lights back on and the audience rising, Michael spoke up. "Uh. One other thing is," he said haltingly and with a dab of Memphis in his voice. "Would those, uh, records of sightings be open?"

Jim nodded slightly. "Mm-hmm."

"Could I take a look at those?"

"Mm-hmm."

"Where, um, where might I—who might I contact?"

Jim poked his right thumb at his chest. "I think we can arrange that."

4

CITY OF NATURE

Boulder's passion for nature, so evident in the late 1980s, was an integral part of the city's identity. Residents heated their homes with solar energy, recycled their trash, and ate organic produce. (An old Safeway supermarket had been converted into a popular health foods store named Alfalfa's.) It was fitting that the city should be home to Celestial Seasonings, a company started in 1970 by friends who harvested wild herbs in the mountains, packaged the leaves and flowers and berries in hand-sewn muslin bags, and sold the concoction as a healthful tea. Although the firm had since become a multimillion-dollar business, owned briefly by Kraft Foods (and later to merge with the Hain Food Group), it retained a homegrown feel with psychedelic boxes offering inspirational aphorisms—"little spiritual quotes," founder Mo Siegel called them—that promoted a philosophy of "people living happy with nature."

Boulder's love of nature was not a fad; it far predated the "hippie invasion" of the late 1960s. Since its early days, Boulder felt so possessive of its natural surroundings that it decided actually to possess them. In 1898, by a margin of thirty-five to one, Boulderites voted to spend $20,000 to purchase a seventy-five-acre ranch at the base of the Flatirons and to convert it into a park. (Complete with a dining hall, auditorium, and cottages, the

park was created to host a summer program of recreation and high culture—known as a chautauqua—and eventually became known as Chautauqua Park.) Soon, the city acquired the Flatirons themselves, and then
the entire mountain backdrop from Sunshine Canyon to South Boulder
Peak, as a way to block development and preserve the scenery.

The drive for preservation took on added force when a group of concerned citizens hired landscape architect Frederick Law Olmsted Jr.—son
of the famed designer of New York's Central Park and the U.S. Capitol
Grounds—to draw up a beautification plan for Boulder. His prescient and
incisive 1910 report, *The Improvement of Boulder Colorado*, urged the city to
shun heavy industry, ban billboards (the city council did not act upon this
recommendation until 1971), and create even more parks as a way of safeguarding Boulder's most precious asset, its view. By 1928, the city's parklands had swollen to more than six thousand acres, one acre for every two
residents.

Boulder's accumulation of undeveloped land accelerated in 1967. With
the city experiencing unprecedented growth that threatened its small-town
character, residents voted to tax themselves to purchase additional open
space. A new dedicated sales tax, amounting to four cents per ten-dollar
purchase, provided the city with millions of dollars of extra revenue, and
Boulder began to buy more land: 227 acres the first year, 830 acres the
next, 667 acres the following year. By 1988, Boulder controlled parks and
open space lands spanning an area larger than the island of Manhattan,
and a similar *county* parks and open space department controlled almost half
as much acreage again. As land passed from private hands to public, cows
were evicted from some former ranchlands, forests once logged were left to
regrow, hunting grounds became wildlife sanctuaries, and, most important, development was prohibited. Piece by piece, Boulder was surrounding itself with a moat, a buffer from the outside world.

The Front Range and adjacent plains became Boulder's chessboard. The
city strategically purchased parcels of land to scuttle developers' plans,
block highways, and hem in nearby towns. To some, Boulder was the
neighborhood bully; to others, the city was a savior. Environmentalists
nationwide hailed Boulder as an exemplar of how to combat suburban
sprawl. Boulder had created a greenbelt—although, given the semi-arid
climate, it was often brown—that allowed a community of plants and animals to thrive on the edge of civilization. The city that loved nature was

now the city *of* nature, a village surrounded by a wilderness under its own protective care.

But Boulder's landscape was not as natural as most residents imagined. The city and its environs were less a wilderness than a garden. As Frederick Law Olmsted Jr. had recommended in his 1910 report, Boulder's surroundings were preserved in such a way that "Nature should appear to be in full command." "Appear" was the operative word. Boulder was a complex blend of nature and artifice, not unlike the elder Olmsted's masterpiece of park design in the heart of New York City.

Boulder's urban forest was a human creation. At the time of its founding, the city sat on a treeless plain; the lush greenery evident by the 1980s resulted from a century of ambitious landscaping, begun by early residents to, as an 1871 editorial read, "take away the barren look, and give us an air of thrift and comfort." (Human hands eventually planted more than three hundred thousand trees.) And much of what had been planted—the apple, maple, and chestnut trees, the tulip gardens, the Kentucky bluegrass lawns—was alien to Colorado and would have shriveled without irrigation.

The city's water traveled in unnatural ways. Boulder Creek had been dammed in its higher reaches to even out its erratic flow. Irrigation ditches and pipes carried moisture away from stream channels to farms and fields. Much of Boulder's drinking water came from across the Continental Divide; water flowing toward the Pacific Ocean was diverted thirteen miles through the Rockies to Boulder and other Front Range cities, where it then entered the South Platte, Platte, Missouri, and Mississippi Rivers on the way to the Atlantic. Boulder's lakes were artificial, created as reservoirs, excavated for flood control, or fashioned from abandoned gravel pits.

Even the rugged foothills above town were unnatural in character. The forests of ponderosa pine and Douglas fir grew much denser—some scientists estimated the overabundance of trees at ten- to twentyfold—than in the days prior to European settlement, the result of wildfire suppression that saved houses but allowed a riot of seedlings to flourish that would otherwise be scorched every decade or so. Meadows, too, displayed evidence of human disturbance; foreign plants, such as spotted knapweed and leafy spurge—alien invaders from Europe, legally classified as "noxious weeds"—had spread voraciously, displacing ecologically valuable native grasses. And hidden within the tangle of trees and weeds remained the scars

from gold and silver mining: crumbling mineshafts and tunnels that per-
forated cliffs, and giant piles of tailings the shape of anthills and the color
of greed.

By the late 1980s, the garden that was the city of Boulder was beginning to show signs of strain. Viele Lake, an eight-acre artificial lagoon surrounded by a broad lawn amid ranch-style homes, had recently acquired a
vast gaggle of Canada geese. More than a thousand of the waterfowl had
descended on the lake, attracted by ice-free water in winter (thanks to a
bubbler installed by the Kiwanis Club), handouts of bread and grain from
a well-meaning public, and the perpetually green, irrigated bluegrass lawn.
The geese grazed the turf in great herds like buffalo, their heads held low,
occasionally honking, depositing truckloads of olive turds the size and
shape of a puffed cheese snack. Some residents, complaining about piles of
excrement and waddling gangs that encircled cars and chased people, urged
that the geese be hazed or physically removed. Others rallied in defense of
the birds. "What's with these Boulder residents who want to get rid of the
geese?" one woman wrote to the *Daily Camera*. "If they don't appreciate
nature, then why are they living in Boulder?"

A similar, and more serious, problem concerned Boulder's deer. As the
city's greenbelt expanded and lands once hunted and grazed became
wildlife sanctuaries, mule deer (a species so named "because of its great ears,
which rather detract from its otherwise very handsome appearance," wrote
Theodore Roosevelt) multiplied and spilled into town. Many of the animals
preferred the unnaturalness of the city—with its lush, sunlit gardens and
lawns—to the unnaturalness of the foothills, where unpalatable weeds had
replaced nutritious grasses, and overabundant trees had crowded out low-
growing shrubs. By the early 1980s, Boulder's urban deer herd had grown
large and pervasive. Bucks and does feasted on tulips and apples and sod,
climbed onto back decks to gobble potted plants, copulated and gave birth
in front yards, and died on city streets. About every third day, a vehicle
struck a deer, killing it instantly or mangling it so badly that it had to be
euthanized. Wildlife officials became expert at dispatching injured deer
with a single shot from a .22-caliber rifle, the barrel aimed behind the top
of the jaw so the bullet would simultaneously sever the windpipe, carotid
artery, and spine. Other deer impaled themselves on fence posts or were
killed by packs of dogs, but few residents witnessed the gruesome reality
firsthand. Like litter collectors at Walt Disney World who hide the detri-

tus of daily life, wildlife officers quickly removed the bloody carcasses and dumped them in remote fields or shoved them into the Humane Society's crematorium, keeping the city pleasant and serene.

Although some homeowners complained about deer nibbling their roses and sunflowers and aspens, Boulderites generally appreciated their antlered neighbors. When biologists conducted a study that involved capturing deer and fitting them with colored ear tags and radio collars, residents protested that the bright yellow, orange, and red accoutrements degraded the deer's aesthetic value, and activists staged nocturnal raids to liberate the animals from traps. When state wildlife officials urged Boulder to cull the burgeoning deer herd with a hunt on open-space lands, locals responded as if the state had recommended shooting puppies. The city struggled to find more "humane" methods for controlling deer—among the proposals: build an eight-foot-high fence between town and the foothills, place salt licks in natural areas to draw deer from urban neighborhoods, implant birth control drugs in does—but even these ideas were discarded. Residents wanted the deer left alone. So the city distributed pamphlets on how to deer-proof gardens and, in a quixotic effort at reducing deer-vehicle collisions, installed roadside reflectors designed to repel wildlife. After the reflectors were installed, in 1986, the number of road-killed deer *increased* 57 percent.

Boulder's answer to the "deer problem" was tolerance, and the animals settled into a comfortable, urban life. Many residents lured deer into their yards, despite a city ordinance forbidding the practice; homeowners put out salt blocks and, during harsh winters, bales of hay. And when the deer came around, people spoke gently to them. "You can have the apples," one resident informed a buck, "but don't eat the daisies." Instead of scattering at the first sight of people as their wild brethren would, Boulder's deer paced the streets and glanced nonchalantly at passing pedestrians. The animals were tame.

Enos Mills, an early Colorado naturalist and author who lobbied for the creation of Rocky Mountain National Park, about thirty miles northwest of Boulder, once wrote, "The mountain lion is something of a game-hog and an epicure. He prefers warm blood for every meal, and is very wasteful." The wastefulness of cougars is largely myth, but mountain lions do possess a gourmet's palate.

Cougars feed off an extensive menu. They have been known to eat grasshoppers, snails, mice, rats, lizards, turtles, snakes, squirrels, rabbits, bats, gophers, weasels, prairie dogs, skunks, beavers, raccoons, opossums, armadillos, marmots, porcupines, turkeys, chickens, geese, grouse, badgers, foxes, bobcats, coyotes, bighorn sheep, domestic sheep, pigs, goats, cows, horses, elk, moose, alligators, bison, bears, and other cougars. But a mountain lion's favorite meal, by far, is venison. In one study, scientists dried, washed, and sifted 239 cougar droppings collected in Utah and found hair or bone from mule deer in 80 percent of the scats. In another study, researchers took a more direct approach; they looked inside the stomachs of lions killed by California hunters and similarly found that "34 out of 43, or 80 per cent, contained deer."

Wildlife biologist Starker Leopold called deer the cougar's "bread and butter." Texas writer and folklorist Frank Dobie referred to venison as "the lion's staff of life." A single cougar may eat forty deer in a year, four hundred in a lifetime, a toll that can exert a significant evolutionary force on its prey, as National Park Service biologist Ben Thompson argued:

> How much part the cougar played in developing the deer into an animal with its particular type of fleetness, grace, alertness, and cunning—the very characteristics which make the deer a deer and not a cow and hence desirable for recreation and game—we can only conjecture. We do know this, however, that in areas where deer have had the predatory menace entirely removed, they have largely lost both the game and the aesthetic values.

Cougars sculpt the deer, and deer sustain the cougar. Where deer thrive, lions prosper. When deer dwindle, lions diminish. Should deer migrate—for instance, from summer mountains to winter valleys—lions follow. As a classic text on cougars from the 1940s put it, "the puma 'goes with the deer.'" In Boulder, in 1988, with prey residing among homes, biology and hunger dictated that predators would soon do the same.

5

LION SEARCH

Michael Sanders grabbed a stack of posters, loaded them into his Boulder County truck—a green Jeep Comanche—and drove to where people often congregated. He stopped at Alfalfa's, the health foods store, and tacked one of the signs to the community bulletin board that displayed ads photocopied on colored paper. ("Housemate wanted"/"Guitar lessons"/"Yoga workshop"/"Spiritual Energy Healings"/"HypnoBirthing"/"Bikes for sale.") He placed a poster in the window of Dot's Diner, a popular eatery on Pearl Street, and at Rob's Hot Tubs, on the next block. He displayed signs at Gart Brothers Sporting Goods on Arapahoe Avenue, the Millsite Inn on the scenic Peak-to-Peak Highway, and a gas station in Lyons, north of Boulder. He drove up Flagstaff Mountain to Walker Ranch, the large spread once owned by homesteader James Walker and now a county open space area, and posted one by the trailhead.

The posters—measuring eleven by seventeen and printed on heavy, cream-colored cardstock—featured, in the center, sketches of an adult mountain lion and black bear along with images of their cubs and tracks. In bold, black letters the signs read,

LION AND BEAR
INFO SOUGHT

Have you seen a Mountain Lion or Black Bear recently? These elusive animals are rarely seen, but chance encounters by residents can provide important information on the size and location of these large mammal populations.

If you have observed either species or if you have noticed their signs (tracks, scat, etc.):

Please contact:
Michael Sanders, Resource Specialist
Boulder County Parks and Open Space

At the bottom, the posters provided Michael's phone number.

It was the summer of 1988, and in the half year since Michael had first learned about Boulder's cougars from Jim Halfpenny's winter tracking workshop, the two men had become scientific partners. It had started when Michael visited Jim at his university office, a jumble of books and animal traps and plaster tracks and maps and piles of paper stuffed into a double room with a jade linoleum floor and the underfunded look of academia. Michael stood in the doorway, on the threshold of Jim's mayhem, clean-cut and eager and asking for information about Jim's study of cougar sightings in the Boulder area. The young Tennessean, intimidated by the diplomas and awards hanging on the walls, felt like a student coming to meet with a professor, although the difference in age between the two men was not great—less than seven years. Jim explained that the Boulder Lion Search, as he called his study, was a temporary project that was soon to end. His job at the university involved research on arctic and alpine ecology; the lion study was outside the realm of his usual duties and had been made possible by help from his student assistant, who was soon to graduate. When Michael suggested that *he* take over the role of collecting sighting reports from the public—after all, his job with Boulder County focused on human-wildlife relations—Jim enthusiastically accepted.

In a series of follow-up meetings at the university and others over coffee and pastry at *Pour La France!*, the two formalized their collaboration. Jim described the pitfalls of conducting a study that used laypeople to provide data; not every citizen could be relied upon to accurately identify a mountain lion, especially when the sighting might consist of little more than a glimpse. Jim thought it best to take the approach of a police detective questioning an eyewitness: ask broad questions about the animal's appearance and behavior, and don't "give people a prompting of the answer we want, but get them to talk to us in their own words." Based on the witness's description of the animal (for instance, if someone neglected to mention a long tail, the creature was probably *not* a mountain lion) as well as an examination of any physical evidence (tracks, hairs) at the scene, Michael and Jim would then judge if the sighting was valid and assign it a letter grade. An A ("definitely a lion") required incontrovertible proof, such as a clear photograph or, in some cases, a dead cougar. Any sighting so questionable that it earned an F would be discarded from the database.

With the Boulder Lion Search now his responsibility, Michael printed the new signs—which included a request for bear sightings, as long as he was asking—and posted them around town. He designed an official Observation Report Form to be filled out for each sighting, and he put a stack of blank forms in his soft-sided Lands' End briefcase, a black canvas bag with leather handles, which he took wherever he went. The *Daily Camera* ran a notice about the new collaboration ("Boulder County and the University of Colorado are stepping up their efforts to identify and track mountain lions in the area") and gave Michael's telephone number for people to call with reports.

Meanwhile, the city was in the midst of its golden season. Summer meant sweet corn and peaches (organic, of course) sold by local growers at the downtown farmers' market. The warm weather brought laughter from children splashing down Boulder Creek on inner tubes and music from fiddlers entertaining tourists along the Pearl Street pedestrian mall. Summer was a tranquil hike in a meadow of columbine, the refreshing coolness of an afternoon thunderstorm, and the rainbow that appears when the clouds pass.

It was Michael Sanders's first summer in town, and he joined the crowds of spectators at annual festivals and athletic contests: the Bolder Boulder, a Memorial Day road race so popular that its mass of running legs (almost 43,000 of them in 1988) seemed to rival the great wildebeest migration of the Serengeti; the Boulder Creek Rubber Duck Race, a charity event in which 1,300 lemon-bodied, orange-lipped plastic waterfowl braved rapids past a roaring crowd to earn one lucky sponsor a trip to Mazatlán; the Colorado Shakespeare Festival, which in 1988—its thirty-first season—featured Val Kilmer as Hamlet; and the Coors International Bicycle Classic, widely considered America's premier cycling event, which brought world athletes to Boulder and Boulder athletes to world attention.

Sunday, July 17, provided another reason for Boulderites to congregate outside. A gray banner across Fourteenth Street declared "mini classics usa," and, below that, "Celestial Seasonings." Orange traffic cones and cheering parents lined the streets around the Pearl Street Mall, along a course that described a deformed figure eight. Children on bicycles sped past while onlookers, along the curb, pressed against a yellow-and-black nylon rope. Little girls bejeweled in plastic necklaces clutched pink balloons. Crimson petunias sprouted from hanging baskets. Cumulus clouds floated in a lapis sky. It was a perfect Boulder day, celebrating athleticism, family, and alternative modes of transportation.

The Red Zinger Mini Classic, sponsored by Celestial Seasonings, served as a Tour de France in miniature for boys and girls age ten to fifteen. The Zinger, as participants called it, attracted more than two hundred bicyclists from as far away as South Dakota and Missouri. The series consisted of twelve stages, including time trials, road races, hill climbs, and criteriums—races in which competitors ride a predetermined number of laps around a relatively short course on closed roads. The first stage had been held in Fort Collins ten days earlier; this day's stage, the Boulder Mall Criterium, was the last.

Michael Sanders, who had the day off from work, stood among the onlookers on the pedestrian mall. He was not acquainted with a young racer who was about to compete, but these two people, the man embarking on a study of mountain lions and the boy obsessed with cycling, would become intimately connected, their lives sewn together with feline thread.

At 4:15 P.M., the race for the oldest group of boys—the fifteen-year-olds—was about to begin, and the six top-ranked competitors took their places at the starting line. "That's the first line this afternoon," a race official announced over a public address system. He then called the next six boys: "Russell Lewis, Luke Miller, Kevin Fairlie, Brendan Dallas, John MacDonald, and Scott Lancaster."

Scott Lancaster, a small boy with shoulder-length sandy hair billowing from his black helmet rode up and took his place along the left curb, the last spot remaining in the second line of racers. He leaned forward on the handlebars, his left foot on the ground and his right foot resting on the pedal. With his shaved legs, black Lycra shorts, white Gitane bicycle, Bell V1 Pro helmet, and Oakley Factory Pilot sunglasses—the same style worn by Greg LeMond—Scott looked like a young version of the professional racers he admired. (A framed photograph of LeMond, the first American to win the Tour de France, hung in Scott's bedroom.) Scott's number, 30, was safety-pinned to the sleeves and back of his T-shirt.

Scott lived near the blue-collar mountain town of Idaho Springs and had just completed his freshman year at Clear Creek High School (beside the granite marker that commemorated prospector and lion slayer George Jackson's discovery of gold), but his temperament was that of a Boulderite. Having grown up in the shadow of two high-achieving older brothers, Scott distinguished himself by shunning conventionality; he favored tie-dyed shirts and Birkenstocks, played the harmonica, and was an academic slacker. Scott's passions were skiing and cycling, and he had been encouraged in the latter by a high school English teacher, Mike Dallas, whose son Brendan was also competing in the Zinger. Brendan and Scott had hung out earlier in the day, anticipating this race—the final stage of their final Zinger, since both would be too old to compete the following year. The pair had performed above average in the series—Brendan in tenth place and Scott in twelfth out of forty-one racers on the "Boys 15" roster—but they wanted to do better. This was their final chance to excel. "It's our last race, our last Red Zinger," they told each other. "Let's try going out with a bang. Do or die."

A man with a bullhorn in one hand and a pistol in the other called, "Riders set!" Then a gunshot, and the boys were off.

Scott made a strong start. He stood on his pedals and pressed forward, quickly moving toward the front. In a criterium, you don't want to fall behind early on, or you might never catch up. As the field of riders slows on corners and then sprints on straight segments, it compresses and expands like a rubber band, eventually breaking into separate packs. A good rider will make sure he's in position to be in the lead pack when the split occurs. Scott had positioned himself well.

By the end of the second lap, Scott was not only in the lead pack; he was in second place overall. He was racing in good form. At each corner, he pulled out wide and then dove in with his bike leaning over, coasting through the turn with his inside pedal up so it wouldn't scrape pavement. Immediately out of the turn, Scott straightened his bike and stood out of the saddle to accelerate back up to speed.

Lap after lap, Scott remained near the very front, an impressive showing but not necessarily smart. Lead riders work extra hard; they provide a windbreak for those immediately behind. A wise criterium rider will hang back a little and draft off those in front, conserving his energy until the final laps. But Scott wasn't strategic; he often wasted his energy early and faded toward the end, and this race would last a tiring fifteen laps.

As the racers completed their fourteenth go-around, a boy rang a hand bell to announce the start of the final lap. Nearing the finish line, the riders sprinted. Those who had hung back began to push toward the front, and Scott couldn't keep up. A few strong riders broke away from the pack entirely, sped around the final turn, and crossed the finish line to the roar of the crowd. Scott finished just six seconds behind the leader, but that put him in eleventh place.

If Scott was disappointed, he didn't show it. He cultivated what friends described as a healthy "fuck you" attitude. He did what he wanted, and if that meant receiving low grades or finishing far off the front in a race, so be it. Scott did things his own way, on his own terms. That was one of the traits Scott's classmates admired: his seeming lack of concern for what others thought of him. Scott was hard to faze, generally cool, with a catlike independence.

Meanwhile, in the hills above town, wild cats were multiplying. Although cougars do not adhere to a defined breeding season, births tend to peak in summer, and in that season in 1988, in the vicinity of Boulder, in hidden dens among thickets and rocks, a new generation of lions emerged, the result of amorous liaisons three months earlier.

Cougar reproduction is a bawdy business. Exactly how the reclusive, solitary creatures hook up for sex in the wild is unclear, but evidence from captivity suggests that a lioness will advertise her receptiveness with odors and caterwauls. "Zookeepers generally agree that a female in estrus screams repeatedly for hours at a time and for several days," according to Australian-Canadian author Lyn Hancock, who has written of her adventures raising cougars in captivity:

In my own experience such vocalizations drew my attention to the animal's estrous condition. When no male was present the female sought a close association with her owner, purred, crouched on her back legs, and scraped her anus along the ground. Vaginal fluid was observed. When a male was present the female walked beside him even while he defecated. She rubbed against his neck then while he was sitting or lying, she stood in front of him, tail up in his face, her back legs spread apart to lift her whole rear on top of him. Her head was held trance-like, her eyes almond-shaped and rather "inane" in expression. During these movements she made loud whine-like sounds like a sustained gargle.

Thus seduced, the male mounts the female from behind and, while biting her nape, inserts his barbed phallus. (Felid penises are tipped with backward-directed spines, perhaps to aid in stimulation, perhaps to secure the sexual coupling.) The encounter is brief—cougar intercourse usually lasts less than a minute—but is repeated with stunning frequency; a breeding pair may engage in coitus seventy times in one day. After perhaps a week of marathon lovemaking, the female then dismisses her consort with snarls and spits and jabs.

Following a thirteen-week pregnancy, the lioness delivers her litter, usually twins or triplets, in solitude—a wise choice, as adult male cougars are prone to infanticide and cannibalism. In the safety of her den, the mother licks her newborns clean and eats the afterbirth, thereby recycling valuable nutrients and calories. In their first days, the cubs do not look very feline; they approximate a russet potato in shape and size, an overripe banana in coloration—black spots on a background of yellow-brown fur. Although the kittens cannot see, cannot even urinate or defecate without help, they can already spar. They grapple for their mother's nipples, swatting each other with tiny, razor claws, such mammary squabbles sometimes proving fatal for the weaker sibling.

Fueled by their mother's supercharged milk, which contains almost six times the fat of cow's milk, the cubs grow rapidly. Within two weeks, the youngsters have more than doubled in size and their eyes have opened a Mediterranean blue. Now unmistakably cats, with whiskers fanning out from a button nose, they walk unsteadily, wrestle and play, purr and growl, nurse and burp. Mother and cubs communicate with a vocal repertoire that sounds more avian than feline. The lioness summons her brood by pulling back her lips and issuing a high-pitched *caw*. The cubs chirp for attention.

By one month of age, the kittens scamper on oversized, padded feet, running like demons. Each day, they grow braver, more coordinated, more purposeful in their actions. They climb trees and leap from rocks. They stare with fascination at moving objects: grasshoppers, butterflies, swaying grass, mother's tail. They chase.

At two months, the young cougars—weanlings now, the size of full-grown house cats—begin following their mother to kills to share her adult repast. With tiny teeth, they tug and gnaw at the flesh of disemboweled deer, their lips and tongues and muzzles smeared scarlet. While the lioness moves on to find new prey, her young stay behind, romping around the half-devoured corpse. "The kittens play a great deal with the kill, and pieces of skin and bits of bone may be found at some distance from the carcass," observed lion hunter and researcher Frank Hibben. "At one such place in the Mogollon Mountains [of New Mexico], the kittens had had the dried-up head of a fawn for a plaything, and the ground was tracked and marked where they had tumbled and rolled the head in their play."

As summer of 1988 waned, Boulder's young cougars began learning to hunt for themselves. They crouched in the grass, stalking bluebirds and gophers. They practiced their killing technique on mice. In Boulder's verdant, welcoming, deer-filled landscape, the cubs grew and thrived.

By mid-September, Michael Sanders's request for lion sightings was paying off. People had seen the posters and newspaper articles describing his Lion Search, and they were calling in reports at the rate of several per week. The Maish family, who lived in Boulder's Table Mesa neighborhood below the Flatirons, phoned to say that late on a June night a cougar had broken into a chicken-wire cage to eat their daughter's pet rabbits, Anabell and Snowball; lagomorph body parts were found the next morning strewn around the yard. Jerry Dickinson, a local construction worker, reported that while hiking in Boulder Canyon one afternoon in July he had spotted three cubs near Castle Rock. In August, an out-of-state visitor claimed that, while on a sunrise hike at Chautauqua Park, he had stumbled on a lion beside a deer carcass; the cougar, he said, had crouched, growled, and made a "coughing-bark" noise.

Then came a report from Pat and Eugene Kayser. "We heard sort of a clanging, bumping sound on the roof," Pat recalled. Eugene remembered the noise a little differently; it was a clicking, he said, "like tap dancing. You know, *ch-k-ch-k-ch-k*, on the roof, just walking." The married couple—he an engineer, she a schoolteacher—lived in the foothills behind the Flatirons in a two-story house with a metal roof and an unobstructed view south, providing a sweeping vista of peaks and canyons and giving the home so much sunshine that it was amply heated by solar energy. One-inch planks of cedar sided the structure, and flickers had an annoying tendency to peck holes in the boards, causing considerable damage. In an attempt to frighten away the woodpeckers, Eugene had purchased a decoy at a hardware store and placed it on the roof. The make-believe bird—a plastic great horned owl with brown folded wings and wide golden eyes—stood sentry on a vent pipe above the master bedroom, where it spun in the wind, watching the world incessantly.

The Kaysers had been disappointed by the owl's job performance; it had not repelled flickers. And when the couple awoke to the strange noise coming from the roof after midnight in mid-September 1988, they realized that the plastic bird was now *attracting* wildlife. "We could tell that something was playing with the owl," Pat says, "which we thought was sort of funny. So I got up, I opened the window, I looked out. It was dark, but I could see a big furry ball of cat sliding down the house. It was definitely bigger than a domestic kitty cat, and it looked furrier to me than a bobcat." Pat was pretty sure that the yellowish creature was a young mountain lion. Eugene was positive that it was a cougar cub. "The next day, the owl had bite marks all over its head," he says.

When Michael Sanders heard the story, he laughed. *You've got to be kidding me*, he recalls thinking. *A lion was up on your roof?* (Such incidents have been reported historically. In nineteenth-century Pennsylvania, "panthers often leaped on roofs of shanties at night, frightening the female occupants considerably," according to author Henry W. Shoemaker.) Michael arranged to visit the site to search for physical evidence. On a morning soon thereafter, he drove his county truck west on Baseline Road by Chautauqua Park and began the steep ascent of Flagstaff Mountain. The narrow road rose two thousand feet in five miles of sharp switchbacks, passing picnic areas and scenic vistas as it traversed city parkland, then circled behind the Flatirons, entered an area of rural homes, and dipped into a high valley that cradled the old Walker Ranch. Michael followed the road as it curved sharply left, and then, as the pavement veered right, he pulled into a gravel driveway and drove fifty yards through the woods to the Kaysers' home.

An open forest of ponderosa pine and blue spruce surrounded the house, which sat on a slope overlooking the spectacular landscape. Michael raised his eyes to the roof and saw the plastic owl, still staring at the scenery from its high perch. He examined the cedar siding for claw marks, but found none. He scanned the ground for tracks, but a vast carpet of pine needles provided a poor surface for recording prints. Although he could find no proof of a lion's presence, Michael considered the Kaysers' report credible. City parkland, county open space, and national forest known to harbor lions encircled the rural neighborhood. And whatever the animal was, it must have been an extraordinary athlete. The creature, which probably first climbed on the Kaysers' woodpile or shed to launch its attack on the plastic owl, must have leapt some ten feet vertically to reach the roof—an easy feat for a lion, a near-impossible task for most other Colorado mammals. Michael graded the observation a B, a probable lion.

In the following weeks, Michael continued to receive phone calls, and to fill out Observation Report Forms, at an astonishing rate:

- September 15: Two people reported a cougar on Boulder's popular Mesa Trail in the late afternoon.
- September 20: A man spotted a cougar by Gross Reservoir in the early morning. "Observer was in vehicle," Michael noted on his form. "Lion walked toward car—ran into woods."
- September 21: A man discovered paw prints in a mountain meadow. Michael wasn't convinced they were lion tracks, so he gave the report a C.
- September 28: A Boulderite watched two lions cross in front of his car while he drove in the foothills at 10:30 P.M.
- September 29: Two sightings—at dawn, a lion sprinted across the road near the old mining settlement of Jamestown; at dusk, a couple on the west side of Boulder spied a lion sitting on a rock.
- September 30: A resident of Boulder's Table Mesa neighborhood spotted a cougar around 6:45 P.M. and reported that the animal had exhibited "no fear."
- October 15: Two reports of a lion "stalking thru grass"—one, in Boulder, at 5:40 A.M.; the other, in Lyons (twelve miles north), at 3:00 P.M.

- October 18: A man in the mountain community of Allenspark saw a lion walking through the woods at a campground in the early morning; it "looked up," then "ran."
- October 31: At 11:00 P.M., a woman who lived a few miles west of Boulder saw a lion chase a deer across the road.

The number of lions sighted surprised Michael, but their behavior did not. The cougars were acting the way textbooks said they should. The animals were seen mostly on the outskirts of town and were therefore avoiding areas of dense human settlement. And the lions were most active between dusk and dawn. (Cougars tend to hunt and move during periods of low light; they are often termed "crepuscular," active around morning and evening twilight.) This spatial and temporal pattern of behavior was comforting. The lions were most active where and when most people weren't. There was little danger of humans and cats crossing paths in a hazardous way.

6

THE DAY SHIFT

The reverend and pious Thomas Gouge, a seventeenth-century British minister and philanthropist, devoted his life to spreading the gospel. Gouge established, in Wales, hundreds of schools to teach English and the catechism, and he produced a series of books—*The Principles of Christian Religion Explained to the Capacity of the Meanest*, *A Word to Sinners and a Word to Saints*, and *The Young Man's Guide through the Wilderness of this World to the Heavenly Canaan* among them—to convey the basics of Christianity to the masses. In simple question-and-answer form, Gouge explained fundamental concepts: faith, sanctification, repentance, sin. "Wherein consisteth the providence of God?" he asked rhetorically in one book, then replied,

> Multitude of passages in the World do clearly evidence the same: as, That wild Beast[s] should not be so fruitful as the tame, lest the World should be over-run with them. . . . And that the wild Beasts, whose nature is to prey, should lie in their Dens all the day long, when men go abroad to their work; and in the night time only should go abroad to seek their prey, when men lie down to rest. . . .

It is, indeed, a fortunate thing that many carnivores—cougars and tigers, leopards and wolves—tend to hunt at night, when humans are in bed. To scientists, the nocturnal activity of predators is easily explained by evolution and adaptation; the animals can often enjoy greater hunting success under cover of darkness. But if, as Gouge suggested, the behavior was a sign of God's handiwork, then Boulder had entered a perilous condition in the autumn of 1988; sometime around the first weekend in November, the Lord had left town.

That weekend, the last before the presidential election, saw both major-party candidates visit Colorado for last-minute campaigning. George Bush held a breakfast rally in conservative Colorado Springs, while Michael Dukakis, flanked by Hollywood celebrities, spoke to supporters on the outskirts of Denver. Liberal Boulder was, of course, rooting for the Massachusetts Democrat. In a mock election at the city's Casey Junior High School, Dukakis won the student body in a landslide, 126 to 26. At the same time, a nationwide poll of high schoolers gave Bush the victory by a two-to-one margin, providing additional evidence of Boulder's outsider status in the twilight months of the Reagan era.

Ponce Gebhardt would normally have been out campaigning for Democratic candidates in the days before an election, but with two young children to care for she spent the weekend at home. Ponce—whose real name was Linda ("My middle name is Penserot, an old family French name, so people coined 'Ponce'")—had worked in Governor Dick Lamm's office back in the 1970s, where she met her husband, Richard, a man deeply involved in Democratic politics. In the 1960s, Rich Gebhardt had been Boulder's state representative—in which capacity he had voted enthusiastically to repeal the state's mountain lion bounty—and had served as a manager of Bobby Kennedy's presidential campaign. A black-and-white photograph of the young Kennedy, signed "With Christmas love" by the widowed Ethel, hung in the Gebhardt family room.

Rich now sold life insurance and worked as a lobbyist, and Ponce was a full-time mother. Though forty-one, she remained almost girlish in stature and enthusiasm; she approached life with optimism and an open, genuine smile beneath her brown permed coif. Ponce loved animals, and a typical day found her on her back porch outside the sliding glass door from the kitchen, sipping herb tea and taking in the activity in the yard.

Ponce lived in what she considered the most perfect spot in this most beautiful city. Her property lay along the very dividing line between plains and mountains, just west of Fourth Street, where the level ground suddenly pitched. The house, a two-story ranch of brick and brown wood, sat on a cul-de-sac below a sloping front lawn in a subdivision called Knollwood, a community of winding streets, modern homes, and elegant yards. The neighborhood was within walking distance of Boulder's restaurants and shops on the plains side, and it abutted open parkland toward the mountains. Knollwood was quiet and safe, a good place to raise a family.

The Gebhardts' backyard, shady and overgrown, sported a profusion of trees, shrubs, and weeds: box elder, chokecherry, cottonwood, wild mint, rhubarb. A stream ran through the middle, above which towered two giant willows. The property was not large—about one hundred feet separated the Gebhardts' home from their nearest neighbors behind them—but the small forest felt like a jungle to Ponce's six-year-old son, Michael, who spent hours playing among the trees and in the stream with his friend Nicholas, who lived a few houses to the south. In Ponce's yard, robins nested, magpies chattered, foxes roamed, squirrels leapt, raccoons climbed, and the Gebhardts' twelve-year-old orange tabby cat, George, watched the commotion from his lookout, a redwood picnic table beside a flagstone patio lined by geraniums in large terra-cotta pots.

Deer also grazed the yard, and Ponce had come to know them so well that she could recognize individuals. She was particularly fond of a doe that sported large ears, a dark face, and a deformed left front hoof that curved upward like an elf's shoe. The doe had recently given birth to twins, and her fawns—tan, with white spots, big brown eyes, and dark noses—seemed in perpetual motion: nibbling grass and buds, sipping water from the creek, bouncing around the yard. They would prance over to their mother, lower their front legs, bow down beneath her belly, and raise their heads to reach her nipples. As they nursed, their stubby tails stuck out straight. Soon, the doe would break away, walk a short distance, fold her legs, and lie down. The twins would do the same while their mother kept a lookout, turning her head occasionally, pivoting her ears to catch distant sounds, alert to potential danger.

The Saturday before the election, the deer family spent all day by the flagstone patio in Ponce's yard. A buck appeared as well. On the Gebhardts' property, it was common for deer to feed during the day, but this behavior was not natural. It was yet another trait of Boulder's deer that deviated from the norm, an activity pattern not seen in more wild settings.

In the early 1980s, at a state park forty miles north of Boulder, wildlife biologists placed radio collars around the necks of twenty-two female mule deer to learn how the animals allocated their time. The collars enabled scientists not only to trace each doe's movements as it wandered among the rock outcrops and ponderosa pines and grasslands but also to determine what the animal was doing (feeding, resting) based on the position of the deer's head (tilted up or down). The researchers took 4,365 readings on the deer over three winters, and they then correlated the animals' behavior with the time of day, weather, even lunar phase. Air temperature, wind velocity, and fullness of the moon had no apparent effect on how the deer spent their time, but the hour did. "They fed most during sunset, night, and sunrise periods and least during the day," the team concluded. "Deer rested most during daytime and night periods."

Many studies suggest the same thing: deer forage mostly at dawn and dusk and rest during the day. Like cougars, they are crepuscular. When the sun is high, mule deer bed down in thick vegetation to ruminate (the rumen, the first and largest chamber of the species' four-chambered stomach, acts as a fermentation vat in which swarms of bacteria break down hard-to-digest cellulose) and to hide—from insects, from the heat, from predators. In Boulder, however, by the late 1980s, the deer had developed a more cosmopolitan lifestyle. Among the yards and homes, mule deer actively fed in daylight, in the open. Perhaps the town's irrigated vegetation provided such nutritious forage that the ungulates had little need to conserve energy by taking an afternoon siesta. Perhaps the homes offered shade from the midday sun. Perhaps the urban deer felt protected from predators. Whatever the reason, the deer seemed to shift their activity from periods of low light to times of bright light. This diurnal adjustment would produce ripple effects.

"Predators are known to synchronize their predatory activity with the main activity of their prey," German biologist Eberhard Curio has written. In other words, predators hunt when prey is available, and if prey animals shift their behavior, predators will change in kind. "Many 'nocturnal' feeders among marine fish will readily feed in the day if and when food becomes available," Curio cites as an example. Similarly, now that Boulder's deer had shifted their activity to be more in line with that of humans, Boulder's cougars would do the same.

Monday morning, the day before the election, Ponce Gebhardt stayed home alone with three-year-old Christina. Her husband, Rich, was at work, son Michael was at school, and Ponce was tidying up the house. As she washed dishes, cleared the kitchen counter, and sifted through a stack of mail on the dining room table, she listened to election news on talk radio and watched, through the sliding glass door that led to the back porch, half a dozen deer grazing in the Morelands' yard next door. As she recalls it, around nine-thirty, "I heard this growl." As if shaken by a thunderclap, the deer bolted, birds screeched, squirrels scattered, and Ponce—wondering at the source of the noise—stepped onto the porch.

At the far end of the deck, a sled leaned against a wooden railing, the balustrade braced by x-shaped supports. Looking beyond the sled and railing, Ponce saw—at the base of one of the giant willows beside the creek, about twenty-five feet from her house, in full daylight—a lion. The giant maneless cat was impressive and imposing, its sinewy ocher body finished by a tail that seemed to stretch forever. Ponce struggled to comprehend the surreal scene. *Where am I?* she thought. *Am I at the zoo?* Then the cat eyed her, and she stepped back inside.

Ponce wasn't sure what to do; she had never imagined having to face such a situation. She reached for the phone and began dialing. She called Rich to tell him about the large cat. She notified her neighbors. She telephoned the Boulder County Sheriff's Department, hoping they could send someone to remove the lion and return it to the wilds. The Sheriff's Department referred Ponce to the Colorado Division of Wildlife.

As implied by its name, the Division of Wildlife was the state agency responsible for Colorado's wild animals. Like fish and game departments elsewhere, the division's funding came largely from the sale of fishing and hunting licenses, and the agency was run largely for the benefit of sportsmen and anglers. Since the late 1800s, the division and its predecessor agencies had operated fish hatcheries to stock lakes and streams, developed and enforced hunting regulations to keep elk and deer abundant (but not too abundant), and spread game birds (pheasants, quails, partridges, turkeys) around the state for sportsmen to shoot. To the division, wildlife was a resource to be managed and exploited—a philosophy that placed the agency solidly in the conservationist, "wise use" camp of Theodore Roosevelt.

Boulder's attitude toward nature tended more toward the preservationist, "leave it alone" school of John Muir, and this philosophical split had caused a rift between the state and the city. Boulderites wanted their wildlife wild—*un*managed, *un*manipulated, *un*hunted. From the division's point of view, Boulder's hands-off policy was harmful and wasteful, for it had produced an unnaturally large herd of garden-destroying deer that were being killed by cars. (*Why not allow sportsmen to kill the deer?* the division argued; hunting could provide recreation, generate revenue, and reduce damage to vehicles and shrubbery.) But the city refused to alter its no-hunting stance on open space lands. The result, as some described it, was a "cold war" between the division and Boulder.

Kristi Coughlon had only recently stepped into this minefield, when the lion appeared in Ponce Gebhardt's yard that November. Kristi was the division's new field representative in the Boulder area, a position other states called a game warden but Colorado labeled a district wildlife manager. The silver-colored badge on her gray uniform revealed her rookie status. (Kristi's number, 872, signified that she had entered the division's training program in 1987 and was the second person, alphabetically, in her class.) Just three years out of college, Kristi proved enthusiastic but inexperienced, unprepared for the fierce politics and overwhelming demands of her job. As a district wildlife manager, Kristi was part cop, part wildlife biologist, part park ranger. She oversaw an area that spanned more than three hundred square miles, from the plains east of Boulder to the high mountains, and within that vast region she was responsible for arresting poachers, advising local governments on habitat issues, talking to school groups, and taking calls from frantic homeowners with wildlife problems, such as a mountain lion in a backyard.

By the time Ponce got through to Kristi, it was already six o'clock and the lion had spent the entire day near her house. At three, Ponce had watched the cougar on the property next door, springing forward as if attacking something. At three-thirty, the cat had walked southward along Ponce's back fence. Half an hour later, it had moved northward again. Ponce told Kristi of the loitering lion and expressed concern for the safety of the neighborhood children.

"What do you want me to do?" Kristi asked.

Ponce did not want the lion hurt or killed. As an animal lover, she couldn't even bring herself to swat bees trapped in her house; she'd capture the insects in a pair of cups and admonish them, "Don't sting me, I'm trying to help you," as she'd move them outside. Ponce hoped the Division of Wildlife could take the same approach to the cougar. "Couldn't you tranquilize it and move it?" she asked Kristi.

Kristi said no. "It's Boulder's problem," she explained, "because of its lack of policy on deer." Kristi said that with all of the deer in town, a lion showing up in a backyard "had to happen sometime." The division would take action "only if someone were threatened" or "if it were injured." "The bottom line is that I have to prioritize the important calls to go out on," Kristi commented later. "I cannot be setting a precedent that every time a skunk walks across somebody's driveway or a lion is merely *sighted* that I need to do something about it." Besides, there was no easy way to capture a lion; doing so generally required the use of hounds, and Kristi couldn't run dogs through an urban neighborhood.

Ponce was not pleased with the answer, and she indicated as much.

"You know, you *chose* to live there," Kristi replied. She argued that Boulderites who lived on the edge of open space had to accept responsibility for coexisting with wildlife; they couldn't feed the deer one day and then expect the division to come bail them out when a lion showed up the next. If residents didn't want that burden, they could move to Denver. (Kristi's argument resembled a legal doctrine known as "coming to the nuisance," which contends that a person who knowingly takes up residence beside a potential annoyance—a smelly farm or noisy factory, for instance—bears responsibility for accepting his neighbor's bothersome ways. However, when Ponce moved to Knollwood in 1980, she had no inkling that lions lived next door. In fact, lions probably did not inhabit the neighborhood at that time.)

Kristi saw the situation in Knollwood not as a lion problem but rather as a human one. People had inadvertently lured the cougar in, and those same people were now overreacting to its presence. Kristi saw no cause for alarm. She considered the risk to public safety minuscule, and she expected that the animal would not stick around long. Kristi assured Ponce that the lion would "go away in a couple of days." Until then, she advised Ponce to keep pets indoors.

The next morning, election day, Ponce scanned her backyard. She saw deer but no evidence of the lion.

The preceding evening, after talking to Kristi, Ponce had been careful not to let her cat George outside, but now he was pleading. The orange tabby stood at the glass door to the back porch and stared at Ponce. Ponce cringed. *Well*, she thought, *he's always been outside here, I just can't stop his habit*. At 8:00 A.M., she relented. "Here goes," she said as she slid the door open. "Now, you come back." George darted out. Although Ponce thought of George as her child, on this morning the distinction between pets and real offspring was stark; under no circumstances would she allow son Michael outdoors alone with a lion nearby.

That afternoon, Ponce's mother visited. The women often chatted over Red Zinger tea, donuts, and sweet rolls at the kitchen table, its circular top of blond wood covered with toys and books. Daylight filtered through the sliding door from the deck and brightened the otherwise dark room, with its walnut cabinets, brown floor and refrigerator. At 3:27, Ponce's mother—who, with her back to the stove, could see through the glass door—looked up and said, with all casualness, "Oh, look, dear. There's a lion on your porch."

As Ponce turned, she glimpsed the enormous cat crawling through the x-shaped opening beneath the deck's railing and jumping down toward the south. Ponce grabbed her Minolta camera and tiptoed onto the porch. She found the lion in the neighboring yard, beyond a split-rail fence, walking through leaves and high grass. The cat, moving away, stopped, swiveled its head back over its right shoulder, and stared. Its tail hung calmly and its face expressed nothing discernible—not fear, not ferociousness, not even curiosity. The lion seemed as unfazed by Ponce as her mother had been by the lion. Ponce raised her camera. One, two, three clicks of the shutter, and she retreated inside.

For Ponce, a nightmare had returned. She called the city, she called the county, she called the Division of Wildlife, she called an old friend at the governor's office, but no one would come to remove the lion. (The city did send an animal control officer, a ruggedly handsome man named Clay Leeper, who briefly combed the neighborhood but couldn't find the cat.) Ponce was heartened when, finally, she gained a sympathetic ear at Boulder County's Parks and Open Space Department; a "very pleasant woman" explained that a biologist named Michael Sanders would be interested to hear about the lion for a study he was conducting. The woman said Michael would call back.

In the meantime, the lion made the rounds of the subdivision. Barbera Moreland, the Gebhardts' neighbor, checked to see why her dog was barking and found the big cat on the concrete walk just ten feet in front of her split-level home. Across the street, Marge Black was sitting at her dining room table when the lion appeared on her deck and stared through the window. ("We just stood there and looked at each other for a while," Marge recalls. "I was just thrilled.") Vicki Cherner, one block west, reported the cat dozing outside her live-in housekeeper's apartment. A little to the south, the lion dragged its claws down a back entry to Wally and Miriam Allen's Tudor home, leaving parallel, vertical slits in the screen door outside their son's bedroom. To the east, on Fourth Street, Anne and Steve Dubovsky found scratch marks on their back deck.

Although residents were nervous about the lion in the neighborhood, they were protective of the animal. With the notable exception of Bud Zorichak—an olive-eyed native Coloradan who disdained "tree huggers" and "fish kissers" and was fond of rifles ("Just go blow the son-of-a-bitch up," was his suggestion for dealing with the lion)—no one wanted to see the cougar harmed. And that included Ponce. "We wanted everything," she recalls. "We wanted the lion to be okay, but we wanted us to be okay, too." The cougar became Knollwood's celebrity guest. Each sighting triggered an outbreak of phone calls as residents notified each other of the cat's current location. Eyes peered from windows for a view of the magnificent creature. At one point, while the cat walked along the creek behind Ponce's house, Wally Allen and his son Larry approached the animal. When the lion growled, they retreated.

"Beasts of prey have no history," the philosopher Martin Buber once wrote. "A panther can indeed have a biography and a colony of termites even State annals, but they do not have history in the great distinguishing sense which permits us to speak of human history as 'world-history.'" As such, the Knollwood lion could not appreciate the context in which it found itself, did not know of bounties or past persecution or the societal shift in attitudes toward wildlife. Unaware of social trends and changing mores, the lion did not grasp the novelty of the human behavior it was witnessing. But cats figure things out; they learn by observation and have excellent memories. The Knollwood lion watched the bipedal beings who inhabited large dens, who came and went in boxes on wheels, who stared from a distance and exhibited no threatening behaviors. The cat understood that the humans meant no harm, and it soon determined that where people lived, food could also be found.

Mountain lions must kill to survive. Unlike bears and coyotes, which eat as much fruit as flesh, cougars are obligate carnivores; they consume only meat. And unlike African lions, which hunt cooperatively, mountain lions are solitary predators, able single-handedly to take down prey as large as seven times their size, a skill that requires tremendous strength, precision, and stealth.

A cougar on the prowl moves like a fugitive, creeping from one hiding place to another, its head and body held low against the ground. Mountain lions possess great speed but poor stamina, and therefore must ambush their prey. When a puma identifies its victim, it sneaks up slowly from behind. Daniel J. Singer, a hunter and author of the early twentieth century, once witnessed a cougar stalking deer in Sonora, Mexico:

> **So light, silent and cautious was his every move that he might be said to drift light as a wisp of smoke toward his prey before making the death-dealing spring. Now crouching with fierce aspect, fore paws extended, head laid between them, while his lithe tail oscillated at its extreme tip with a gentle waving motion, his pale gooseberry eyes glared malevolently upon his unsuspecting victim.**

With its prey in striking distance, perhaps fifty feet, the lion tenses its body—head stretched forward, ears up, mouth slightly agape—then shifts its hind legs back and raises its heels off the ground, preparing to spring. In an instant, potential energy becomes kinetic as the cougar launches itself with a leap followed by a bound. A puma's rear legs are significantly longer than its front legs, enabling it to jump tremendous spans—as much as eighteen feet vertically, forty feet horizontally. As the big cat pounces toward its prey, small flexor muscles in its feet contract, causing retractable, sickle-shaped claws to snap out like switchblades. Grabbing its victim by the back and thrusting it to the ground, the cougar quickly bites the throat, to sever the windpipe and jugular vein, or the nape, to break the spinal cord. A cat's fangs slip easily into the gaps between vertebrae, wedging them apart and snapping the spine with a single bite.

Once its quarry is dead, a cougar will drag the carcass to a secluded spot—a grove of trees or a thicket of bushes. It won't eat immediately; first, it prepares the meal. The cat will often shave the fur off its prey's belly with its incisors, as if readying the body for surgery. The cougar will then cut the carcass open—chest to abdomen—bite through the sternum and ribs, open the thoracic cavity, and push aside the stomach and intestines. With powerful jaw muscles and scissorlike teeth called carnassials, the animal slices through flesh as if using freshly sharpened kitchen shears. Cougars do not chew. They cut meat into strips and swallow the chunks whole.

A mountain lion's first meal on a carcass will often consist of the organs: heart, liver, kidneys, lungs—rich in blood and fat, protein and vitamins. It will then scrape leaves or pine needles or twigs onto the body, as if to mark the cache as its own, until it is ready to eat again.

On election night, as Americans watched George Bush accept victory and pledge to work toward a "kinder, gentler nation," Ponce Gebhardt stood on her porch and beckoned for her own George, the cat, missing since morning, to return. He did not. Two days later, Ponce's neighbor Miriam Allen stepped into her backyard and noticed a large mound of twigs and leaves tucked between a pair of willows near the northeast corner of her property. *What is that?* she remembers thinking. *That wasn't there yesterday.* Miriam moved toward the pile of debris, keeping a cautious eye peeled for the lion. She passed beneath her children's tree house and beside the teeter-totter. The lawn dipped and rose. Miriam rounded a small garden in which she grew string beans, squash, peas, and horseradish. The creek along the back of the yard burbled. As she neared the jumble of brush between the twin willows, Miriam gasped. Within the mound of twigs and leaves, partially concealed, was the bloody, lifeless form of a deer. The animal's head had been snapped back, and a hole cut in its belly. The purple abdominal cavity, devoid of organs, showed through gnawed ribs.

Miriam noticed one of the doe's front legs protruding from the brush. The foot was deformed, almost silly looking. The hoof curved upward in the front, like an elf's shoe.

———

"What was the lion doing when you saw the lion?" "Did the lion see you?" "After the lion saw you, at that instant the lion saw you, what did the lion do?" "How *long* did it look at you?"

Michael Sanders stood in the Gebhardts' dining room, by an ornate walnut table beneath a framed photograph of the Flatirons, and asked Ponce a series of questions about what she'd observed. There was no doubt that what she had seen was a cougar—she had photographic proof—but Michael was interested in details of how the lion had reacted when it saw a human being. He was polite, but persistent, in his questioning.

"And during the time it was looking at you, what did it do? Was it dead still? Was its ears up? Back? Did it just look at you and just go on its way?" Michael jotted down her responses. On an official Observation Report Form, at the line labeled *Reaction of animal when observed*, Michael wrote, "WALKED AWAY—NO CONCERN."

Eight days had passed since Ponce's original cougar sighting, and it appeared that the animal had now left the Knollwood subdivision, just as District Wildlife Manager Kristi Coughlon had said it would; no one had seen the lion for the better part of a week. Still, Ponce was bothered by the Division of Wildlife's refusal to do anything about the lion.

Michael was similarly upset with the division's inaction. He found the behavior of the Knollwood lion worrisome. Like Yellowstone's Bear 59, the cat exhibited no fear of people. Michael believed that the agency should have made an effort to track the animal—tranquilize it, affix an ear tag to it, release it in the high country, and see if it came back. "They were doing nothing like that," he complained later. "There was no way to identify the problem again." Michael was also concerned that the lions were "changing their trend of behavior from dusk and dawn to middle of the day. These were time periods when kids were pretty active."

But Michael didn't share his political opinions with Ponce. He looked around the back porch and yard, asked some additional questions, and mentioned that in a few weeks he would be traveling to Arizona for a national convention of scientists and wildlife managers who work with mountain lions. He asked Ponce whether he could make copies of her cougar photos to show around. Ponce reached on top of the refrigerator and handed Michael the negatives.

Ponce had also given copies of her photos to the *Daily Camera*, and the newspaper printed one of them on the front page beside an article head-lined, "Young lion prowls area in Boulder." The story contained a com-pelling mix of ingredients—charismatic wildlife, worried parents, good visuals (Ponce's photograph showed a massive cat stalking through the grass)—so it was no surprise when Denver's TV stations decided to pick up the story. Reporters and cameramen descended on Knollwood to interview residents, and the result was mostly lighthearted coverage. "Ponce Geb-hardt may have traded her nice little house cat for one of the big cats," reported Channel 4. "Her kitty named George has been missing, and a mountain lion showed up in her backyard."

The news fed on itself, generating even more coverage. Boulderites were now on the lookout for cougars in yards and on trails, and a hiker thought he spotted one on a Sunday morning while climbing Flagstaff Mountain with his dog; Dick Martin saw a tawny animal about twenty-five feet away, its eyes "greedily fixed" on his five-year-old sheltie, Kip. "I thought [Kip] was going to be lunch," Martin told the *Daily Camera*. Again, Denver TV stations picked up the story, and this time they had visuals that surpassed Ponce's photographs. Martin had videotaped his encounter.

When Michael Sanders saw the broadcast, he thought, *Oh, my God. You've gotta be kidding me.* The pointy ears were a dead giveaway; it was not a lion, but a fox. Officials with the Division of Wildlife reached the same conclusion. "If I'm wrong about that picture, I need a new job," said divi-sion biologist Kathi Green. The agency notified news outlets about their taxonomic misidentification, and Channel 7 and the *Daily Camera* retracted the story, declaring a "false alarm."

During this flurry of news coverage about lions, both real and imagined, an uncomfortable dynamic developed between the Division of Wildlife and Michael Sanders. In speaking with the news media, state wildlife offi-cials tried to quell public fears. "I would feel lucky to have seen a moun-tain lion," District Wildlife Manager Kristi Coughlon told the *Colorado Daily*, a free Boulder newspaper directed largely at the CU campus. Michael Sanders believed that the division was too dismissive of the threat lions posed. "We've received reports of where people have gotten within 30 or 40 feet of cats, where they've let people come that close," he told the *Rocky Mountain News*. "If that trend continues . . . it could be a problem down the road."

But Boulder remained enthusiastic about the lions. A survey of American attitudes toward wildlife, conducted in the late 1970s, had found that while many segments of the public were still reluctant to embrace predators as desirable animals, the demographic groups most likely to hold positive views of carnivores included "wildlife enthusiasts, persons of higher socioeconomic status, non-livestock producing Westerners . . . and those under 35 years of age," which perfectly described the typical Boulderite. The city approached cougars the way it did the Soviets, seeking friendship and understanding. Paul Danish—a former city council member, prominent growth-control advocate, and future county commissioner—welcomed the cougars to town in a column, slightly tongue-in-cheek, for the *Colorado Daily*:

> Ain't nature wonderful?
>
> Without so much as a by-your-leave to City Hall, it seems to have come up with an elegant, natural, ecologically sound solution to what is delicately referred to as "the deer problem."
>
> Cougars.
>
> Mountain lions started moving into City of Boulder open space a couple of years ago, for the same reason practically everybody moves here: Boulder's great environment and laid back, New Age life style. They particularly liked the part about not killing Bambi. They saw it as the next best thing to a free lunch. Sister cities, hell. This was Food for Peace.
>
> And after a while, they discovered what so many shy newcomers find out, which is that in Boulder folks don't hassle you. They give you space to be yourself, and that means you can come out of your shell and realize your full potential. A cat can dig it.
>
> Which is why folks are suddenly reporting mountain lions in places like Chautauqua and the Knollwood subdivision—in the act of taking a deer to lunch. Indeed, the word is that three of Knollwood's deer are missing and are unlikely ever again to grace Maggie Arden's garden on Fourth Street.
>
> In other words, the cats are doing what the city fathers and mothers have been unwilling to do, which is cull the deer herd.

Ah, the food chain. You gotta love it.

Still, there is a troubling question here that Boulder should give some serious attention to early on.

Boulder has a "deer problem" because it is full of people who do not believe in frightening the animals. That is a wonderful thing; a community in which animals can safely walk the streets will have no trouble in adapting to a kinder, gentler America.

Cougars are predators, and they can weigh more than 100 pounds. If they are allowed to take up residence in the greenbelt, and if people refrain from frightening them, a certain number of pets are going to get eaten along with the deer; homeowners are occasionally going to find lions knocking over their garbage cans or crapping in their yards; and sooner or later someone is going to have an encounter in which he or she is mauled or killed.

What the city needs to think through is whether it wants to treat cougars the same way it treats deer (and raccoons and skunks)—which is to say give them run of the place.

Personally, I hope the answer is yes. Yeah, I know having an occasional cougar in town will make the streets marginally more dangerous, but you would still be a lot more likely to be attacked by a mugger than a mountain lion.

The fact is most wild animals who move to town are reasonably well behaved, and if they are not always polite, well, the same can be said of plenty of dogs—and of Homo saps.

To be sure, you can't be as chummy with a cougar as you can with a deer, but I think their presence enriches the community, even if there is a chance of getting scratched or bitten. Besides, if they get too far out of line, you can always shoot 'em. Bambi would understand.

The following week, Boulder shifted its focus back to more commonplace concerns—the upcoming holidays. Christmas lights once again adorned the Pearl Street Mall, St. John's Episcopal Church planned its annual *Messiah* sing-along, and shoppers returned to the stores. On the day after Thanksgiving, in a ceremony broadcast on the radio, the traditional holiday star—a five-pointed constellation of four hundred forty-watt bulbs—was illuminated on Flagstaff Mountain, where it had shined above the city every Christmas for four decades. But the landscape below had recently and fundamentally changed. Carnivores had returned.

Part Two

BORROWED TIME

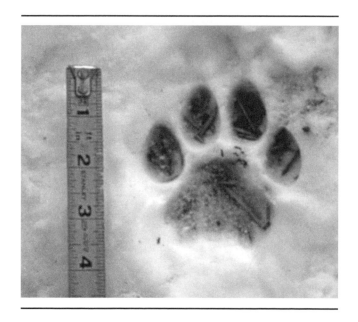

STERKFONTEIN REDUX

In the deep recesses of ancient caves in South Africa's Sterkfontein Valley, amid the rolling, grassy hills of the Transvaal highveld forty minutes west of Johannesburg, scientists have unearthed evidence of humankind's deep and disturbing connection to cats.

The bone-filled limestone caverns are prehistory's killing fields. The cave deposits, laid down as long as four million years ago, contain disarticulated, fractured, and gnawed skeletons of thousands of creatures both extant and extinct: antelope, wildebeest, warthogs, zebras, porcupines, buffalo, baboons, hyenas, foxes, mongooses, lions, leopards. And within the jumble of bones, which has solidified into rock the consistency of concrete, lie the jaws and skulls and teeth of early humans.

Researchers first thought that these primitive hominids (australopithecines, or "southern apes") had caused the carnage in the caves. In 1953, paleoanthroplogist Raymond Dart theorized, on the basis of studies of the ancient bone yards, that our apelike forebears were cannibalistic hunters "that seized living quarries by violence, battered them to death, tore apart their broken bodies, dismembered them limb from limb, slaking their ravenous thirst with the hot blood of victims and greedily devouring livid writhing flesh." But scientists now believe Dart's bleak reading of the evidence was wrong. Humans were not perpetrators of the violence in South Africa's limestone caves; they were the victims, the prey.

The animals that ate our ancestors were probably cats: large ones, with big teeth. Paleoanthropologist C. K. "Bob" Brain, who wrote about the Sterkfontein Valley deposits in his 1981 book *The Hunters or the Hunted?*, found among the remains an ancient child's skull that had been pierced by two holes thirty-three millimeters apart, a spacing that exactly matched the fangs of a fossil leopard found nearby. Based on this find and on the overall assemblage of bones, which looked a lot like the leftovers of a carnivore's meal, Brain argued that the caves had been lairs into which big cats had dragged their victims for consumption. Brain further suggested that one variety of cat had specifically targeted our ancestors. This specialized predator of primates, he contended, was an extinct, jaguar-sized, false saber-toothed cat ("false" because its fangs were not as long or as curved as those of the "true" saber-tooths) known as *Dinofelis*. "One may visualize *Dinofelis* biding its time in a concealed position while a troop of baboons or hominids passed," Brain wrote. "[S]electing a straggler, the cat would then overpower its prey, holding it down with its powerful forelimbs while killing it silently and quickly by a throat bite."

Like most paleontologists, Brain was prone to weave elaborate stories from cryptic evidence, and he and colleague Elisabeth Vrba saw clues to perhaps the greatest tale of all in the upper (i.e., younger) layers of one of the Sterkfontein Valley caves. In these more recent deposits, they found abundant stone tools and other signs that humans had come to occupy the cavern once controlled by the cats. In other words—perhaps through the use of fire, or the development of weapons—our ancestors had ended the feline reign of terror and had thereby taken a major step toward becoming modern humans. Brain wrote, "The tipping of this balance represented, I think, a crucial step in the progressive manipulation of nature that has been so characteristic of the subsequent course of human affairs."

English writer Bruce Chatwin, enthralled by Brain's theories (Chatwin called *The Hunters or the Hunted?* "the most compelling detective story I have ever read"), took the argument a step further. In *The Songlines*, his fictionalized travelogue and discourse on human nature, Chatwin speculated that humankind is haunted by an ancestral memory of being prey to big cats. Our tendencies toward war and violence, he suggested, stem not from an innate aggressiveness but from a defensiveness—a deep-seated fear of being devoured by a beast in its lair:

> Could it be, one is tempted to ask, that *Dinofelis* was Our Beast? A Beast set aside from all the other Avatars of Hell? The Arch-Enemy who stalked us, stealthily and cunningly, wherever we went? But whom, in the end, we got the better of? . . . Compared to this victory, the rest of our achievements may be seen as so many frills. You could say we are a species on holiday. Yet perhaps it had to be a Pyrrhic victory: has not the whole of history been a search for false monsters? A nostalgia for the Beast we have lost?

In modern times, with *Dinofelis* just a crumbling fossil, humans are no longer the staple of any feline species' diet. But neither can it be said that man-eating by big cats is entirely obsolete.

During the early twentieth century, tigers killed on the order of a thousand people annually in India, and some of the cats took to the sport with great enthusiasm. The infamous Champawat Tigress, driven from Nepal in 1905 after devouring an estimated 200 people, killed another 236 in India's Kumaon region before Jim Corbett, the famous hunter of man-eaters, shot her dead. (Upon the tigress's demise, Corbett discovered that her canines had been broken by a previous gunshot wound, which he speculated "had prevented her from killing her natural prey, and had been the cause of her becoming a man-eater.") Today, despite dwindling numbers of tigers in the wild, man-eating remains more than an occasional nuisance in the Sundarbans, a vast mangrove forest on the Bay of Bengal, which supports a healthy population of aggressive cats that routinely prey upon woodcutters, honey collectors, and fishermen who enter the watery realm. (One scientist has blamed the ferociousness of the tigers on the estuarine forest's brackish drinking water, which may put the cats in a perpetual foul mood.)

African lions, too, have been known to seek human flesh. History's most notorious leonine duo, the "man-eaters of Tsavo," descended upon a railway construction camp in British East Africa (now Kenya) in 1898 and, as Britain's prime minister at the time put it, "conceived a most unfortunate taste for our workmen." For more than nine months, neither thorn fences nor pit traps nor fires could stop the cats from raiding workers' tents to snatch human meals, racking up a death toll that may have exceeded 130. The maneless male lions—eventually shot by a railroad engineer, Colonel John H. Patterson (portrayed by Val Kilmer, Boulder's Hamlet, in the 1996 movie *The Ghost and the Darkness*)—now reside, stuffed, at Chicago's Field Museum, where one can purchase souvenir mugs, posters, and T-shirts displaying the killers in an innocuous, colorful, *Lion King*–style graphic.

Leopards, though small in relation to tigers and lions, can be equally deadly. In 1936 and 1937, a leopard reportedly killed 67 people in Zambia before making the fatal mistake of jumping a man carrying a large fishing spear; the cat impaled itself on the weapon, and thus ended its murderous career. Between June 9, 1918, and April 14, 1926, northern India's world famous "man-eating leopard of Rudraprayag" claimed 125 official victims and likely many more off the books. That same region of India still suffers frequent leopard attacks—"once every 10 days on average, though not all are fatal," according to a 1998 report in *Asiaweek*.

Compared with its Old World cousins, the mountain lion is a veritable pacifist. Despite being as large and powerful as a leopard, cougars will almost invariably turn tail when confronted by a person, and no puma has ever been known to eat humans habitually. "The least dangerous to man of all the big cats" was Theodore Roosevelt's description of the mountain lion. Legendary mountain man James Capen "Grizzly" Adams called the American lion "a cowardly brute, which dare not stand face to face and fight with a man." Artist John James Audubon, in his 1851 book *The Quadrupeds of North America* (co-authored with naturalist John Bachman), stated reassuringly, "We do not recollect a single well authenticated instance where any hunter's life fell a sacrifice in a Cougar hunt." Tracker and author Ernest Thompson Seton similarly concluded that "under no normal circumstances will a Cougar declare war on man personally, and under no circumstances, normal or otherwise, will it turn on him the full measure of power and ferocity that it holds in reserve for such other fellow brutes as may cross its will." Such were the opinions of experts in the nineteenth and early twentieth centuries.

Among the general public, however, the mountain lion enjoyed a far more sinister reputation. Folktales, popular literature, and campfire stories—stoked by ignorance and a fear of the unknown—told of voracious, blood-thirsty cougars that leapt from high limbs onto unsuspecting travelers, snatched babies from mothers' arms, and possessed a special craving for the flesh of pregnant women. A pivotal scene in *The Cub of the Panther*—nineteenth-century southern writer William Gilmore Simms's final novel, set in the mountains of North Carolina—centers on this myth. When the beautiful but poor Rose Carter flees into a midnight snowstorm from the evil Widow Fairleigh, whose illegitimate grandson Rose carries in her womb, a cougar pursues the young mother-to-be with a "terribly ferocious appetite."

Newspaper and magazine accounts of the day similarly portrayed the mountain lion as a ruthless killer. Some early headlines from Colorado:

THE FIGHT IN A CABIN

In Echo Canon Between a Mountain Lion and an Unknown Man.

Evidences of a Desperate Struggle—
Man and Beast Found
Dead.

—(Leadville) *Weekly Herald*, April 11, 1885

MAN HALF EATEN BY LION FOUND WITHIN FIFTY MILES OF DENVER

Savage Beasts Rabid from Hunger, Spread Terror in Entire Community

Woman Looking for Lost Colt Discovers a
Human Corpse, Partially Covered by Dirt—
Victim, Known as 'Andy,' Ranch Hand.

—*Denver Post*, November 12, 1911

HUNTER SLAYS 3 MOUNTAIN LIONS IN DEATH BATTLE

Chicago Nimrod Limps Back Into
Georgetown Suffering From
Wounds After Hand-to-Hand
Encounter in Canon.

—*Rocky Mountain News*, July 6, 1914

Such stories, often boasting implausible claims (in one case, an attacking lion that measured "ten feet and nine inches from the tip of its tail to the point of its nose"), were considered blatant fabrications by naturalists and nature writers, who launched campaigns to clear the cougar's name. A leading crusader, managing editor J. A. McGuire of the then Denver-based sportsmen's magazine *Outdoor Life*, used his publication to rail against "the almost universal tendency among the newspapers of our country to publish fake and exaggerated stories regarding the habits of our wild animals—and particularly our carnivora." McGuire made it a practice, when he saw a published report of a fierce encounter between a human and a cougar, to attempt to verify the story. In some cases, he tried to contact people (victims, witnesses, reporters) mentioned in the articles, only to have his mail returned as undeliverable. In other cases, McGuire wrote to hunters and government officials near the site of reported attacks and received replies of the following variety: "My private opinion of the article is that someone had partaken of a little too much Fourth of July 'fire-water,' under which spell any kind of an article might come to life. . . . [I]t sounds like a gigantic fake." In a 1914 editorial, McGuire summed up the results of his inquiries. "In the seventeen years I have been editing Outdoor Life I have investigated fifty of these alleged attacks," McGuire wrote, "and insofar as I could learn, but one of them turned out true."

This one "true" attack occurred in Northern California on a July afternoon in 1909. Schoolteacher Isola Kennedy, while relaxing beside Coyote Creek near the town of Morgan Hill, saw a lioness jump from the bank and attack a boy wading in the stream. According to the *Morgan Hill Times*,

"Miss Kennedy ran to his assistance, when the animal jumped upon her, knocking her down." For fifteen minutes, Kennedy wrestled the lion— which chewed off her left ear and mangled her left arm while she attempted to stab the cat with a large hatpin—until a man arrived with a rifle and shot the cougar. Despite her severe injuries, Kennedy healed well in the following weeks and was considered convalescent, but she then suddenly fell ill and died, as did the young boy she had rescued. A physician who had treated both victims declared their deaths to have been due to rabies, a diagnosis that seemed to explain the cougar's bizarre behavior.

Thus, in his 1914 *Outdoor Life* editorial, J. A. McGuire acknowledged that, yes, mountain lions *do* kill people—but only under exceptional circumstances. "Let us put a stop to this nonsensical idea," he wrote, "that there are any [mountain lions] who take any interest in us from an edible point of view."

In the following decades, at least one mountain lion proved McGuire wrong by killing and partially eating a human being, but this incident, too, seemed aberrant and explicable; the victim was a child, and the offending cougar, according to some reports, was gaunt, old, and desperate. Nonfatal attacks were documented as well, some on adults. These maulings were also rare and were blamed on extenuating circumstances, as outlined in a 1953 book on mammals:

> In one instance, a man was mistaken for a deer. In a second case, a cougar was defending its kittens. In several other cases, the animal was undoubtedly mentally unbalanced. In another case, the cougar had been cornered and was in a badly wounded condition. In yet another case, the animal was suffering from rabies, possibly acquired indirectly from dogs. And in one other case, the cougar was found to be very old, starved, and unable to kill its normal prey; its teeth were broken and claws worn away.

Consequently, by the latter half of the twentieth century, biologists and hunters were forced to modify J. A. McGuire's theorem ever so slightly: *Healthy* mountain lions do not take interest in humans, and certainly not adult humans, from an edible point of view. In other words, predatory attacks were freak events perpetrated by sick individuals and were therefore inherently unpredictable.

Such was the consensus opinion of America's mountain lion experts on the first Monday of December in 1988, when most of those experts crowded into the elegant lobby of the historic Hassayampa Inn in Prescott, Arizona, to kick off the Third Mountain Lion Workshop, a three-day national conference on cougars. (The workshop was modeled after two previous gatherings that had been held in Nevada and Utah in 1976 and 1984, respectively.) One hundred fifty biologists, park rangers, conservationists, and hunters—many donning cowboy boots and jeans and nametags—drank beer and wine as they stood on the tile floor by the grand piano or sat on soft couches by the fireplace, renewing old acquaintances and making new ones.

On that evening, a few in the crowd, including Michael Sanders, who had flown down from Boulder, were tentatively discussing an unsettling question: Was McGuire's theorem obsolete? Were healthy cougars—some of them, in some places—beginning to consider people prey?

Michael Sanders had come to the conference in Prescott seeking advice. Having worked on the study with Jim Halfpenny for less than six months, he was no cougar expert, but he knew enough to realize that Boulder's lions were not behaving in the manner that they should. The scientific literature suggested that cougars were elusive, timid, frightened of humans and their dwellings, yet Boulder's cougars wandered through backyards in broad daylight and jumped onto roofs, seemingly unfazed by the presence of people. He and Jim feared for public safety. Should they?

Michael had brought along his Observation Report Forms, which provided details of recent sightings, and he carried Ponce Gebhardt's photos. "Here are some pictures of what we've seen in Boulder," he told attendees at the meeting, cornering them in hallways or over dinner or while drinking Budweiser and shooting pool at a bar on Whiskey Row, Prescott's famous saloon-lined street. "This is just one example of many different occurrences that are happening," he explained. "What do you think? How would you deal with it?"

Conference organizer Harley Shaw, a well-known Arizona cougar researcher with vast experience and a thoughtful, gentle manner, spoke at length with Michael. "I didn't think mountain lions would live near people," Harley recalls. "Most of us were a little surprised that this was happening." Still, Harley saw no reason for concern in Michael's observation reports. "I thought it was probably temporary, quirky. I think none of us really felt that this was going to be a major issue."

Actually, one man at the conference did think that Michael's observations could portend a major, frightening trend. He had come to the meeting from California, a state that had recently suffered two high-profile cougar attacks. Both had occurred south of Los Angeles, in Orange County, on the edge of suburbia.

The first attack had come almost three years earlier, in March of 1986, on a Sunday afternoon while the town of San Juan Capistrano celebrated the return of its famous swallows with a festival (the annual Fiesta de las Golondrinas) around the old mission. Susan and Donald Small avoided the crowds and took their children, nine-year-old David and five-year-old Laura, for a hike at Ronald W. Caspers Wilderness Park, a 7,600-acre county-owned preserve frequented by backpackers, equestrians, and picnickers in the nearby foothills of the Santa Ana Mountains. The family drove past the visitor center (where an interpretive display featured a photo of a cougar kitten with the caption "The Cougar or 'Mountain Lion' is quiet and secretive, with a healthy aversion to humans"), parked in a gravel lot, marched past a corral and playground, headed up the Nature Trail, and paused beside a shallow stream. Young Laura—blond and blue-eyed, wearing shorts and a sleeveless top—removed her sandals and waded into the water to catch tadpoles, when her mother glimpsed a muscular animal leaping from the bushes. It grabbed Laura by the head and vanished with her in its mouth. As Laura's mother, Susan, recounted later: "I was just standing next to her, then the next second there was total silence. I didn't hear any growling, Laura didn't scream, I didn't hear any dragging. They were gone. And I could see that they had gone behind me, but when I turned around there was no sign at all of them. There were no marks on the ground. There was nothing. I could hear the stream, that was all I could hear. . . . [A]nd that was when I heard Laura. . . . It sounded like moaning." While her son, David, ran for help, Susan and her husband searched the cacti and underbrush, eventually locating their child, still locked in the jaws of the large cat, squirming and covered with blood. Laura was badly injured: her scalp and nose and upper lip hung loose, her right eye had been sliced open (allowing the jelly-like vitreous humor to ooze out), her skull was crushed, and a portion of the brain beneath had been effectively liquefied by the trauma.

Laura was still alive, however. A brave, stick-wielding stranger, whose heroism would later earn him a medal and $2,500, persuaded the lion to drop the girl; Laura's parents, taking turns carrying her, rushed their daughter down the trail; a helicopter airlifted her to Mission Community Hospital; and, in a thirteen-hour emergency operation, doctors saved Laura's life. (Laura's medical ordeal had just begun, however; her initial hospitalization would last thirty-eight days, followed by years of reconstructive surgery and physical therapy that would still leave her blind in one eye and partially paralyzed.) The morning after Laura's attack, a government hunter killed the lion believed responsible, about a half mile from where the incident had occurred. The male cougar "appeared very emaciated and sick," according to an official incident report.

Initially, it seemed that the cougar attack—California's first since the mauling of Isola Kennedy by a rabid lion in 1909—was the sudden, unexpected, and desperate act of a sick animal. But that explanation didn't hold up for very long. A postmortem examination of the cat found no signs of serious illness, and park officials soon revealed that months of unusual lion behavior had foreshadowed the Smalls' ordeal. The preceding September, a mountain lion had reportedly stalked a family of four hiking through Caspers Park; the father threw rocks to drive the animal away. In November, a ranger and fourteen park visitors encountered a lion during an afternoon nature walk; the cat, about five feet up a tree, watched the large group of humans with seeming nonchalance. And in early March—less than three weeks before Laura Small was attacked, and on the same Nature Trail where that incident occurred—a lion approached a man and woman, circled them, and crouched as if about to leap; the couple pelted the lion with stones and ran to safety.

Then, seven months *after* Laura Small's attack and after the offending lion had been killed, a cougar struck again—also on the Nature Trail, also on a Sunday, also on a family hike. This time the victim was six-year-old Justin Mellon, snatched by the cat as he ran to catch up with others after tying his shoe. "When I saw the lion, it had Justin by the head," the boy's father, Timothy Mellon, told the *Los Angeles Times*. "At that point, I ran at it with a knife—I had a hunting knife with me. Right before I got to it, it released him." In a replay of Laura Small's rescue, Justin's parents rushed the boy down the trail to a helicopter that transported him to Mission Community Hospital. Justin's injuries were far less severe than Laura's; he had suffered multiple cuts, but the lion had not crushed his skull. Despite a massive search, hunters with dogs failed to locate the cougar that had mauled him.

The pair of attacks in close succession caused a sensation in the media. The Small and Mellon families sued Orange County, claiming that Caspers Park, a county facility, had not adequately warned visitors about the dangers. (A jury in the trial of *Small v. County of Orange* eventually sided with Laura and awarded her $2,018,638 in damages, later reduced to $1.5 million in an out-of-court settlement upon appeal. The Mellon family settled its lawsuit for $100,000.) Orange County erected new signs—"WARNING. MOUNTAIN LION COUNTRY. A RISK."—and imposed new restrictions: no children in most of Caspers Park, and no solo hikers in remote areas.

The attacks also fueled a smoldering political fight in California. In 1971, the California legislature had imposed a moratorium on mountain lion hunting, a temporary measure intended to give biologists time to evaluate the health of the state's cougar population. Initially planned to last four years, the hunting ban had been repeatedly extended by lawmakers and the courts; as a result, by 1988, California's lions had enjoyed almost two decades of protection. Sportsmen, who long fought for the resumption of cougar killing, blamed the recent attacks on the moratorium; they said that a lack of hunting had allowed the lion population to grow dangerously large and bold. (Despite this argument and further attacks in later years, California's lion-hunting ban continues, extended and upheld by ballot measures in 1990 and 1996.)

Even before the maulings in Orange County, Lee Fitzhugh had worried about the potential threat posed by mountain lions in California. In 1985, he had written to Governor George Deukmejian urging that the hunting moratorium be lifted: "In the past month at least three incidents of close contact between unsuspecting humans and mountain lions occurred in California, in residential areas. Mountain lion attacks on humans, especially children, are well documented. . . . The signs are reminiscent of warnings made about coyotes in 1980 and 1981, just before a child was killed in the Los Angeles area by a coyote." At the time he wrote the letter, Fitzhugh looked like a fear monger. After Laura Small's ordeal, his warnings appeared prophetic.

Square-jawed, fair-skinned, and middle-aged with slicked-back hair, Fitzhugh had the clean, conservative look of an insurance agent but was, in fact, a wildlife biologist at the University of California at Davis. He had been invited to speak at the Third Mountain Lion Workshop in Arizona, and on the first afternoon of the conference he took to the stage at the Elks Theatre, the venue for most of the talks and panel discussions. The theater, across Gurley Street from the Hassayampa Inn, had been constructed as an opera house in 1904, with elegant box seats and a graceful proscenium arch. Michael Sanders sat in a wooden chair in the audience. As Fitzhugh spoke, his words seemed directed toward Boulder.

Fitzhugh made a bold and controversial argument—that, under certain as yet ill-defined circumstances, healthy cougars can learn to view humans as prey. ("I knew there was a body of biologists that were still saying, 'This can't happen,'" he recalled later, "and I wanted to disabuse them of that thought.") Fitzhugh spoke of the attacks in Orange County and of the close encounters that had preceded them, and he described what witnesses had seen: the cougars had crouched and swept their tails while eyeing humans. "These traits indicate predatory, rather than defensive, behavior," Fitzhugh said. In other words, the bold actions of the cougars in Caspers Park could not be explained as the simple result of curiosity or fear or territoriality; the lions were sizing up park visitors as potential meals.

That cougars are capable of viewing humans as food really shouldn't come as a surprise, Fitzhugh contended. "Prey recognition is a learned behavior in cats," he told the audience, and he cited the experience of wildlife rehabilitators in California who successfully trained a young cougar to hunt animals that it had not previously considered prey. For instance, the rehabilitators had reported, "When we offered [the male cub] his first guinea pig, he did nothing more than play with it until he left. Several days of feeding him on guinea pigs brought a different response when he was presented with another live one." A cougar's idea of what is and isn't prey is malleable, "and knowledge of what constitutes prey may be gained in several ways," Fitzhugh explained.

"One lion may learn from another that a 'strange' animal is prey if the two are together at the time of an attack," Fitzhugh said, reading from his prepared remarks. "Another method of prey identification, according to a controversial theory, is that the drive for prey-catching, if interrupted or unsuccessful, must vent itself. So, if a human-lion encounter occurs just after an unsuccessful attempt to catch prey, the behavior could be transferred to the human." Additionally, Fitzhugh surmised that a lion might be prompted to attack a person if the human exhibited behaviors that mimicked the cougar's natural prey, "such as running, quick movements, and, probably for children in small groups, excited conversation."

Fitzhugh believed that before a cougar attacked a human, it first had to go through a phase of merely observing humans. "According to [German ethologist Paul] Leyhausen, it takes a fairly lengthy period of time for a cat to decide what a new animal is, and they'll be somewhat fearful of it until they decide," Fitzhugh says. "Once they make a decision whether it's prey or not, then they'll behave according to that decision. Lions that come into human-inhabited areas and begin to wander around, they're probably in that process of deciding. They've learned at that point that humans are not to be feared, so they're into that process a ways, and they're into it in the wrong way."

Therefore, on the stage of the Elks Theatre, Lee Fitzhugh made the following cautionary remarks: "An increase in the rate of lion sightings or any 'close encounter' is a warning sign that should stimulate analysis of the situation to assess the risk." And: "Any situation is potentially dangerous if the lion places itself in visual contact at close range with people, or remains in visual contact, without moving away, after being discovered by people." And: "Warnings should be direct and severe. Mountain lions are no animal to consider lightly, and people should be told forcefully that lions are dangerous." And: "People in responsible positions should not dismiss encounters between humans and lions as merely curious events."

To a large extent, the biologists in the audience were not buying it; they *knew* that mountain lions were not man-eaters. As philosopher Thomas Kuhn wrote in his landmark book *The Structure of Scientific Revolutions*, scientists are conservative, reluctant to accept evidence that runs counter to their accepted worldview, and "will devise numerous articulations and *ad hoc* modifications of their theory in order to eliminate any apparent conflict" when confronted by an anomaly in the data. That's exactly what attendees at the Third Mountain Lion Workshop did—they started making excuses. They dismissed Fitzhugh's talk as irrelevant; the Orange County lions *must* have been sick or deranged to act the way they did. Or perhaps there was something unique about the environment at Caspers Park that provoked bizarre behavior *there* but would not elsewhere. Many of the scientists saw no reason to rethink basic assumptions of how cougars relate to humans. Conference organizer Harley Shaw summed up his reaction to Lee Fitzhugh's talk: "This is not something we really need to be worrying about."

Yet Fitzhugh's words worried Michael Sanders immensely, and the two men spoke at length about the similarities between what had happened in Orange County and what was happening in Boulder. "I told him there was a problem there that needed to be dealt with," Fitzhugh recalls.

A third man joined the conversations, as well. Phil Koepp was chief ranger at Big Bend National Park, in west Texas. The vast park, tucked in a curve of the Rio Grande, had recently experienced its first serious cougar incidents. In August 1984, eight-year-old David Vaught had been hiking with his family on the popular Basin Loop Trail when a lion jumped him and tore off a patch of scalp. The following day, officials tracked down and killed a cougar within two hundred yards of the attack scene; the cat, which appeared healthy, had human hair in its stomach. In an official incident report, rangers conceded, "The reasons for the attack may never be known." Three years later, on the same trail, a cougar attacked thirty-one-year-old Linda Burt. According to Burt's husband, "The lion circled around towards my wife. . . . The lion then leaped on her back. I then threw a rock. We both began to yell. The lion was off after a few seconds." Burt's injuries were relatively minor: six punctures to the left thigh and two scratches to the right buttock. Park officials killed this second offending cat. It tested negative for rabies.

Phil Koepp could not explain what had caused the lions to attack, but it seemed obvious to him that Boulder was headed down the same path as Big Bend and Orange County. "You're just living on borrowed time," he told Michael Sanders. "Sooner or later, you're bound to have a human attack."

On a chilly Colorado morning one month later, Michael Sanders and Jim Halfpenny stood in six-inch snow, staring into a narrow slot in a secluded hillside west of Boulder. As they shined a flashlight into the cave, the beam vanished in the black void. "Do you see any eyes?" Michael asked with a nervous laugh.

Two weeks earlier, Michael had been summoned to the nearby home of Sondra Donovan, who lived with her husband and young daughter on a remote dirt road off Fourmile Canyon. It was the kind of house where, if one had a sense of modesty and any immediate neighbors, it would be unwise to walk around naked; a wall of sliding glass doors provided an unobstructed view of the scenery from almost every room and, conversely, allowed outside eyes to peer in. But the Donovans had no neighbors, so Sondra had no qualms about toweling off after her morning shower in front of the windows, which faced southward across forested canyons to the peaks behind the Flatirons. "It was a crisp, bright, no-clouds-in-the-sky morning with a fresh coat of snow everywhere," Sondra recalls, "and out of the corner of my eye, I saw something move." A mountain lion, perhaps twenty feet away on the other side of the large pane, was dragging a freshly killed deer across the driveway. Sondra gasped with excitement. *Oh, my God.* She tried to get her daughter to watch the natural scene unfolding outside the window—"Here!" Sondra shouted to Sara, "Look at this! Look at this!"—but the two-and-a-half-year-old was more interested in playing with bath toys, and the lion disappeared down a ravine.

When Michael Sanders arrived that afternoon to investigate, he could read the entire story in the snow. A disturbed area in the blanket of white just west of the house revealed where the lion had ambushed the deer. From there, a drag mark—a long, flat depression in the snow's surface that looked like the trace of a child pulling a plastic toboggan—showed where the lion had hauled its quarry. Cat tracks and specks of blood paralleled the drag mark. Michael followed the lion's trail for a quarter mile as it headed to the southeast across a snowy meadow, angled down a steep slope into a dense forest of ponderosa pine, dodged a rusting barbed wire fence, crossed a small gully, and ascended the opposite slope, where it vanished into a hole about the size and shape of an automobile windshield. Tracks entered the cave but none exited. Michael dared venture no farther. ("First rule of nature is: Don't screw with a lion while he's eatin'," says Michael.)

Contrary to popular myth, mountain lions do not maintain a single den or lair to which they return each day; rather, within its home range a cougar will use many different hiding places—cliffs, thickets, overturned trees—where it can eat, sleep, and rear its young in seclusion. This cave appeared to be a rest stop that the resident cougar used regularly. "The lion knew *exactly* where it was going," Michael concluded after following the path directly to the hidden site, which was surrounded by dense vegetation. He noted the location and, after a fortnight, returned with Jim Halfpenny to see what lay inside.

As the men stood on the threshold of the cave, the early morning sun and the scent of pine needles filtered down through the trees. The grotto's entry, topped by a ledge of rust-stained granite, rose only to thigh level. Michael and Jim had to stoop to peer into the opening. Jim was reasonably sure that the lion was not home—he saw no fresh tracks—but Michael remained anxious. He let Jim enter first.

Jim ducked beneath the granite overhang, hugged the soil, and slipped his body in sideways. Once inside, he scrambled down a dirt slope and found himself on a hard, flat floor. The cavern was surprisingly large; Jim could stand upright without bumping his head. He scanned the rock surfaces with a flashlight. Small, milk-colored stalactites hung like nipples from the ceiling. A slow trickle of water streaked the walls. Near the entrance, a clear pool filled a depression, and the area around it was sandy, a miniature beach. The cavern possessed its own, mild microclimate; despite below-freezing temperatures outside, it was warm enough in the cave for water to remain liquid. The air smelled musty, like that of a damp basement.

Michael followed Jim into the darkness, and the men quickly realized that the cave was not a cave, but a mine. (They had stumbled upon a section of the long-abandoned Monarch Mine, which had produced as much as twenty-five ounces of gold per ton of ore in 1886, its first year of operation.) The horizontal tunnel—an adit, in mining parlance—extended about forty feet into bedrock. Its cross section was triangular: flat bottom, vertical wall on the left rising about eight feet, and then a slanting ceiling that sloped down toward the right to meet the floor. The odd shape appeared to reflect the geometry of a vein that the miners had been working, which dipped from the upper left to the lower right at forty-five degrees. Cylindrical blasting holes pierced the walls. Looking back toward the entrance, Jim and Michael could see that the original opening was now almost entirely blocked by a century's worth of accumulated debris—boulders, sand, branches, pine cones—that had spilled down the slope outside.

Inside, evidence of recent lion activity was easy to find. To the left of the pool by the entrance: a pile of deer ribs, legs, vertebrae, and a head that was largely intact. (These remains, many of them still clothed in dry skin, appeared to be the leftovers from the kill of two weeks before.) Farther on: a cache of older bones, dry and dusty and broken. Everywhere: pugmarks in the sand.

Michael kept an eye on the entrance, where a shaft of light pierced the darkness, in case he should see the shadowy form of a large cat returning. Jim examined the recent deer remains. He picked up the head and sliced open the cheeks, which had hardened to rawhide, so that he could pry the mouth apart. He saw that the animal still had its milk teeth and that the adult molars had just started to erupt, which suggested that the deer was young, perhaps five months old. Jim grabbed a femur and, using a six-inch, coarsely serrated saw that he had brought along for the purpose, cut through the bone to examine the marrow. It was solid and looked like a marbled cut of raw beef, red and white intermingled. The color and consistency indicated that the animal had been well nourished; a starving deer will metabolize the fat inside its bones, leaving marrow that is red and gelatinous, like raspberry jam. Jim wrote in his field notes, "No signs of ill health." Everything about the lion kill and the lion's hideout seemed normal, with one exception. This lair was man-made.

Within the echoing confines of the mine, Jim and Michael remarked that this artificial cave—which offered shelter, warmth, and water—was the perfect hideaway for a lion. Michael called it "the Hilton of mountain lion dens." Jim wondered how many other mines, of the hundreds that dotted the Front Range, had become so-called cougar hotels. ("Those lions know every single mine up there," he speculated later, "and they use 'em a lot, I'll bet. And that makes that better lion habitat because of the mines.") It was a historical and ecological irony; the early miners, who killed countless cougars and destroyed wildlife habitat while raping the foothills for gold, had left a legacy that helped the lions upon their homecoming a century later.

In South Africa's Sterkfontein Valley more than two million years ago, our ancestors had wrested control of limestone caves from the Beast, *Dinofelis*, thereby taking command of the natural environment. Now, in Boulder, cougars were usurping the caves of humans. The balance of power was shifting, subtly, back toward the cats.

8

CATS AND DOGS

"It is one of the strange provisions of nature that nearly every living thing has a mortal enemy," Utah mammalogist Claude Barnes once wrote. "[T]he rattlesnake fears that agile bird called the road runner; the porcupine dreads the fisher; and even the colossal whale flees before the tenacious killer. Our puma is no exception to the universal rule. . . . So far as I know there is nothing quite so dreadful to a puma as a barking dog."

Cougars exhibit a deep-seated and enigmatic fear of the canine clan, a phenomenon long remarked upon by naturalists and much appreciated by hunters. (By far the most efficient way to hunt a mountain lion is with a well-trained pack of hounds, which will handily chase the cat up a tree and keep it at bay until a human arrives on the scene with a rifle.) "The panther always runs from the dog, no matter how small he is, and never turns to face him," wrote nineteenth-century biologist Livingston Stone, exaggerating slightly, since cougars have been known in rare cases to turn on their canine pursuers. "I could train a poodle to hunt cougars if he had the nose for it, and if he'd bark he would tree most of them," Canadian hunter John Lesowski once boasted. Naturalist and author Ernest Ingersoll added that dogs seem "to terrify [the mountain lion] to a degree comical when we consider the difference in size."

This trait of the cougar does seem bizarre—the equivalent of a prize-fighter's cowering before a schoolyard bully—and begs a deeper explanation. As cougar biologist Maurice Hornocker has speculated, "At some time in the lions' history, something barked and chased them, something that could cause them real harm." That "something" was, in all likelihood, the wolf.

Centuries ago, when cougars and wolves were abundant and ubiquitous, these top carnivores fought for terrain and prey. Nineteenth-century trapper Felix Michaud—a "most reliable" authority, according to author Franklin Welles Calkins—contended that "the great cat's worst enemy is the gray wolf." Michaud asserted that when wolves caught sight or scent of a lion, they invariably gave chase and sometimes succeeded in killing and devouring their quarry. Michaud further alleged that, during periods of extreme cold, wolves employed a clever battlefield tactic; they would chase a cougar into a tree and wait below until the cat's paws froze and the animal fell, defenseless, into the murderous pack.

In modern times, in areas where the large carnivores share habitat, wildlife biologists have chronicled numerous humiliations heaped upon lions by wolves. Wolves steal food from cougars, eat cougar kittens, and kill adult cougars. On December 8, 1990, researchers in Glacier National Park observed eight wolves that had killed an adult female puma. The members of the felicidal pack tore at the body of their victim but did not eat it; they treated the lion as if a vanquished foe. "One black Wolf was observed urinating on the Cougar's head," the scientists noted.

Until the last century or two, mountain lions could not escape their canine tormentors; wolves occupied almost every corner of the cougars' vast range throughout the United States and Canada. But the same farmers, ranchers, hunters, and trappers who butchered cougars showed even less mercy toward wolves and enjoyed greater success at eradicating them. Colorado, for instance, enacted a wolf bounty thirteen years before its first bounty on lions, slaughtered wolves at a faster pace (in 1891, a year when Boulder County recorded the death of just one lion, twenty wolves were killed within the county's borders), and by the mid-1940s—when Colorado's cougar population was reaching its nadir but surviving—the state's wolves had already been exterminated. As a result, when the protections afforded cougars in the 1960s enabled the species to rebound in the 1970s and 1980s, mountain lions returned to a more welcoming landscape, one from which their enemy had been eradicated.

It is reasonable to assume, therefore, that by 1989, no mountain lion in the Boulder area had ever encountered a wild wolf, nor had any of its forebears for more than twenty generations. The evolutionary environment that had molded the cougar into a "fraidy cat," as one federal trapper disdainfully called the species, had been altered. The stage had been set for Boulder's cougars to view dogs differently.

Wednesday, February 8, 1989. Bernice McCain's alarm clock sounded at 5:00 A.M., tuned to Denver radio station KOA. The major news that morning was the continuing arctic cold spell that had gripped much of the nation for more than a week, bursting water pipes, stranding motorists, and causing homeless shelters to overflow. Near Yellowstone National Park, trumpeter swans were dying from the cold. In Malibu, California, it was snowing.

In Lyons, Colorado, where Bernice lived with her husband, Merle, it was ten degrees below zero. The McCains' ranch-style home, avocado with ivory trim, sat at the end of a gravel road, in a suburban subdivision beneath a towering sandstone bluff called Steamboat Mountain. The setting was spectacular; deer, elk, and coyotes wandered among the homes. During severe winters, Merle often put bales of hay in the yard to help the deer survive.

On this particular morning, Merle was out of town—playing poker in Vegas—and Bernice awoke alone in the king-size bed, accompanied only by her "girls," two half poodles. Fifi, the cock-a-poo, was a nine-pound piñata of a dog with stubby legs, curly black hair (graying with old age), and oversized ears that she had inherited from the cocker spaniel side of her family. Fifi liked to sleep on her back, paws sticking straight in the air. Missy, a peke-a-poo—half Pekinese, half poodle—sported a pale coat and a short tail that curled upward. Both dogs were rambunctious and playful, but Fifi was the braver of the two. She liked to chase cats.

"Come on. Let's go out," Bernice said, swinging her legs from the bed as the dogs jumped onto the burnt-orange carpet and ran into the hall. Bernice, five feet two and blond, followed in her nightgown. The next day would be her sixty-third birthday, but this was a workday like any other. She had to be in Boulder at the Granville-Phillips electronics plant, where she soldered components onto circuit boards, by seven.

Bernice shuffled through the living room to a set of sliding glass doors that led to a redwood deck overlooking a small yard. Sunrise was still two hours off, and the world outside was black. After Bernice switched on the porch light and slid open the door, the dogs ran out, yapping as they descended the wooden stairs to the snow-covered yard below. A blast of cold air flowed across her feet.

As the dogs faded into darkness, Bernice turned back inside but left the door open a crack so Fifi and Missy could return to the warmth of the house. She headed into the bathroom, washed up, and dressed in blue jeans and a T-shirt. Suddenly she heard frantic barking and then a *thump* out on the deck, and she walked back across the living room to investigate. As Bernice exited through the open door to the porch, Missy ran past her legs into the house.

Bernice immediately spied the source of the commotion: a large animal climbing her deck stairs. Although she had never seen one before, she knew that it was a mountain lion. The creature was reddish brown and muscular. Its eyes glowed emerald in the electric light. ("Her eyes, they were just as green as green grass," Bernice recalled later of the cougar's mesmerizing eye shine, produced by a mirrorlike structure called the *tapetum lucidum*— literally "bright carpet"—which reflects light from the rear of the eye back through the retina, allowing the cat to see in darkness.)

The lion stood not ten feet from the door to the house. Bernice was stunned but not scared. As far as she could tell, the lion reacted similarly; it appeared surprised but showed no fear of the dog or human before it. Fifi, barking, held the middle ground between the big cat and Bernice.

Then Fifi lunged at the lion.

The cat extended its neck, opened its mouth, and snatched the dog with its teeth. In an instant, Fifi ceased barking, and her body went limp, her head and tail drooping from the lion's maw like a mouse in the jaws of a house cat. Excrement and blood dripped onto the redwood deck.

Bernice screamed, "Drop her!" The lion stared back. Missy barked frantically from the living room.

Immediately to Bernice's left, leaning against the house, was a sturdy push broom with black plastic bristles and a five-foot wooden handle that the McCains used to clear snow from the deck. Bernice grabbed the broom, heaved the large brush skyward, and swatted the lion's head. The cougar did not budge, nor did it drop Fifi. Bernice hit the lion again. The cat slowly backed up, maneuvered its large body sideways in the narrow space of the deck, turned toward the driveway, and sauntered alongside the house. Ber-

nice watched helplessly as the lion leapt over her three-foot split-rail fence—
Fifi still in its mouth—and vanished into the cold, black morning.

Several hours later, unaware of the cock-a-poo's demise, Michael
Sanders and Jim Halfpenny arrived at the Colorado Division of Wildlife's
Denver headquarters. The low, sprawling building, which sat in an industrial section of the city and had once housed a lumber company, resembled
a warehouse from the outside. Inside, the maze of cubicles and offices with
fluorescent lights and industrial carpeting could be mistaken for an insurance company, if not for the taxidermy animals (bald eagle, mule deer,
bighorn sheep, river otter) that stared down from the walls.

Michael and Jim had requested a meeting with state wildlife officials to
discuss the worrisome behavior of Front Range lions. In the half year since
the Boulder scientists had begun their collaboration, they had already accumulated more than fifty lion sightings. Mere observations of cougars did
not necessarily imply a problem, but the trend toward sightings in daylight and the frequency with which people reported cougars exhibiting "no
fear" suggested to Jim and Michael that Boulder's lions were habituating
to the presence of people. (**ha·bit·u·a·tion** *n.* "Stimulus-specific waning of
response; learning not to respond to something on finding that nothing
significant is contingent upon its occurrence. More roughly, getting used
to something to the extent of ignoring it, getting tired of it, becoming
inured to it.") The cats were becoming disturbingly comfortable around
humans, much as Yellowstone's Bear 59 had before she consumed photographer Bill Tesinsky in 1986.

But Jim and Michael could not diagnose the situation with any precision or certainty; their Boulder Lion Search was an admittedly crude
research project. The men relied on sightings phoned in by the public, and
that meant their study could reveal where lions were only when people happened to see them. The study could not answer many critical questions:
Where were lions when people *didn't* see them? How much time did
cougars spend near homes? Did the cats make brief forays into town and
then dash back into the foothills, or were they denning under porches? And
how many lions were people seeing? "We had no idea what numbers we
were talking about," says Michael. "We could have one cat. *Totally* unlikely,
but we could have one cat. We could have *fifty* cats, and they could simply
be taking turns coming in. We had no clue."

Jim and Michael decided it was time to take their research to the next level. In order to determine the extent to which lions were habituating, under what circumstances, and how big a threat the animals posed, someone would need to work directly with the cougars. The men wanted to track the animals' movements with radio collars, much as Michael had done with grizzlies at Yellowstone. "That way," Michael explained, "if every night we saw a lion that was basically hunting in and around an urban area, we could at least go in, trap the lion, and move it." But the Boulder researchers did not have the authority to take on such a project. Wildlife is the legal domain of the state, and if Jim and Michael wanted to handle cougars, they would need permission from the Colorado Division of Wildlife. It was with this purpose in mind that the men visited division headquarters on this February morning.

At 9:00 A.M., Jim and Michael entered a conference room and sat at a table, side by side, their backs toward the hall. The men had brought props: Michael's thick stack of observation reports, and a large topographic map of Boulder County—1:50,000 scale—to which they had affixed dozens of red and orange dots. Each sticker indicated the location of a lion sighting (red) or lion tracks (orange).

Facing Jim and Michael was an assortment of division personnel that could generally be divided into two camps: senior men and junior women. The former category included Deputy Director Bruce McCloskey and Chief of Wildlife Bob Tully, high-level administrators who had worked their way up through the ranks and now oversaw policy for the entire state. Among the women were Boulder's district wildlife manager, Kristi Coughlon, and Kathi Green, a biologist assigned to the Denver-Boulder-Front Range area.

Jim Halfpenny rose to speak. He told the wildlife officials about the growing incidence of lion sightings that he and Michael had documented in the Boulder area. He described the trend toward observations in daylight and lions that exhibited little fear of humans. He expressed concern that Boulder's cougars were becoming habituated to people. And he asked, ominously, "Are lions learning that people are normal prey?" (Kathi Green, jotting notes on a legal pad, wrote: *danger is sensational*. Then, below that: *danger probably real*.)

Jim outlined some questions that he believed should be answered. How many lions routinely moved among homes? How easily did the animals become habituated to humans, and did habituation require learning from a parent? Where should one draw the line between normal and abnormal lion behavior? "The only way to learn what lions are doing around people," Jim concluded, "is to track them in and around people." That meant conducting a radio-collar study.

The division officials were well familiar with radio telemetry; the agency frequently used the technique for wildlife research. In fact, the division had recently conducted an exhaustive study of Colorado mountain lions that involved radio-collaring forty-nine of the animals and tracking them for six years. That project, which addressed basic questions of lion behavior and population dynamics in a remote, rural setting—the Uncompahgre Plateau of west-central Colorado—had been costly and labor-intensive. Capturing cougars required hounds and a houndsman. Tranquilizing the cats and fitting them with collars proved difficult and occasionally fatal to the lions. Monitoring the animals' movements over their vast home ranges entailed use of an airplane. Deputy Director McCloskey questioned whether another study involving radio-collared cougars was worth the effort and expense. "What's it gonna tell ya?" was his reaction. "You've got x number of lions moving in this urban-rural interface, and they move at night, and they pass within so many feet of so many houses. So? What do you do with that? We've got better things to do with limited resources." (Kathi Green wrote on her notepad: *Priority setting. Is this indeed a big damn deal?*)

Jim argued that the study he proposed would not duplicate the recent research on the Uncompahgre Plateau; rather than examining wild cougar ecology, he wanted to explore urban cougar behavior—"what lions are doing at that interface of people and cats," as he put it. Without such information, Jim contended, any division policy toward urban lions would be devised blindly. The study, he added, did not have to be large or expensive. "I made the point that even one lion, radio-collared around people and interacting with people, was more information than anybody had anywhere," says Jim. Besides, he was not necessarily asking the state to pay for the study; he was willing to seek grant money elsewhere. What Jim and Michael needed was the division's cooperation. They sought the state's blessing.

Even that level of support, though, would prove difficult to obtain. Division officials doubted that Boulder's lions were really as brash as Jim and Michael portrayed the animals; the Boulder scientists had relied on observations made by laypeople, and wildlife managers didn't trust the public to identify cougars and cougar behavior accurately, especially in light of the infamous black panther scare of 1983. That incident had started when area newspapers ran a story about sightings of a large black cat south of Boulder. In the following weeks, the Division of Wildlife received dozens of calls from worried residents who swore they had seen a jungle cat in their yards or out on hikes, but when officials responded, they found merely house cats, black Labradors, or nothing at all. Agency personnel became convinced that the "black panther" existed only in the public's imagination, a creation of the media and mass hysteria. (Boulder's district wildlife manager at the time had told the *Daily Camera*, "If we reported that a circus train had overturned, I'm convinced we'd be getting elephant sighting reports within a couple of hours.") Similarly, wildlife officials suspected that many of the "lions" reported to Jim and Michael were really house cats, dogs, or foxes—as in the case of Dick Martin's embarrassing videotape—morphed into cougars by the mind's eye.

If one assumed, for argument's sake, that most of the lion sightings *were* legitimate, that cougars were routinely loitering around Boulder homes, that still did not warrant a study in the view of division officials. After all, widespread scientific opinion held that cougars were virtually harmless. And if lions *weren't* harmless, then radio-collaring the cats might put the division in an uncomfortable position. "Think about it for a minute," says Perry Olson, the agency's director at the time of the meeting. "If we would have allowed Jim Halfpenny to go band mountain lions, and one of his mountain lions was involved in a fatal accident, what do you think would have happened? I know damn well what would have happened. Halfpenny would have got his rear end sued." And the division, though insulated by Colorado statute—section 33-3-103: "The state shall not be liable for . . . injury to or the death of any person caused by wildlife"—would have faced a public relations disaster. (An embarrassing tragedy of this sort occurred in Nepal several years ago; a tigress radio-collared in Royal Chitwan National Park wandered into a nearby village, entered a home, and ate a man.) Handling lions implies responsibility for their actions.

Division officials did not give an absolute "no" to the idea of a radio-collar study, but Jim and Michael could tell that they were not going to get a "yes." The Boulder scientists sensed that the more senior people in the room, the men, resented that a couple of outsiders were trying to influence wildlife policy. Even worse, these outsiders were from Boulder, the city that had long frustrated the division's efforts to control deer with hunting. "It was almost as if, 'Who are you to come in here and tell us to do anything?'" says Michael. "It was a very cold meeting. At that point, I was like, 'Oh, this is futile. We can't go anywhere with this. Screw 'em.'"

Within twenty-four hours, the rift between the Boulder scientists and the Division of Wildlife deepened further when Michael Sanders learned of the attack on Fifi, which quickly became the subject of media coverage and widespread jokes. Even Michael couldn't restrain himself. "A little French food in the morning," he quipped, feebly attempting to roll his *r*'s like a Parisian. But Michael knew that the attack was deadly serious, representing another frightening escalation in the behavior of Boulder County's cougars. After all, lions were supposed to flee dogs, not chase them, and this cat was so bold that it had climbed the McCains' porch and confronted a broom-wielding Bernice.

Yet state wildlife officials, in their comments to the media, suggested that the mountain lion's behavior was not particularly noteworthy. "It might have just thought the poodle was nothing but a different (type of) rabbit," one division biologist told a newspaper reporter. "I wouldn't be too overly concerned about it. Definitely there is not any concern for humans— they are very afraid of people." Another division official added that mountain lions "aren't attacking any German police dogs or anything like that."

Michael Sanders clipped the article for his files and underlined the quotations. He shook his head. *They just simply don't get it.*

February melted into March. The foothills above Boulder bloomed with wildflowers (blue flax, lavender pasqueflower, golden banner) along an advancing front that marched up high meadows. In town, crocuses, daffodils, and tulips defined the edges of lawns, while crabapple, box elder, and cottonwood trees flowered overhead. Mountain bluebirds, their wings like sky, migrated from the south to greet the warmth, as a thaw settled over Boulder and the world.

The Cold War was easing. Improved relations between the superpowers were widely evident, including in the thriving friendship between Boulder and its Soviet sister city. With the arrival of spring, a group of local high schoolers arrived in the USSR on a student exchange, while Mikhail Gorbachev made startling news, announcing that his government would slash production of fissile material for nuclear weapons and suggesting that the Berlin Wall was not necessarily permanent. (Five months later, that physical manifestation of the Iron Curtain would indeed fall.) Boulder, meanwhile, basked in the glow of national publicity; *Outside* magazine declared the municipality "*the* sports town," America's premier locale for outdoor recreation, confirming what locals already knew, that they lived in a special, blessed place.

The city blazed green and lush, thanks to precipitation that came in profusion and variety in the spring of 1989. An April blizzard buried daffodils under a foot of snow. A May hailstorm triggered rockslides in Boulder Canyon. June began with a series of downpours. Then, suddenly, heaven's spigot turned off.

Summer commenced, dry and hot. Across the West crops withered, reservoirs fell, nerves frayed. By the Fourth of July, Boulder was breaking temperature records, and despite the *Daily Camera*'s demand for a change in the weather ("This newspaper stands unalterably opposed to 100-degree days"), conditions remained unbearably hot on the fifth, sixth, seventh, and eighth. The foothills turned brittle, brown. Sunday, the ninth of July, again dawned cloudless and blazing, but a breeze soon brought some relief and grew into a strong southeasterly wind. As one resident recalled afterward, "Little did I know that friendly wind would become an enemy just a short while later."

At approximately 12:35 P.M., according to an official reconstruction of events, someone discarded a lit cigarette along a bend in Highway 119, the road through Boulder Canyon, less than a mile west of Happy Times. The smoldering cylinder of tobacco—or marijuana, as the Sheriff's Department surmised—fell among dry grass in a gulch named Black Tiger, and it ignited a small ground fire that, fanned by the wind, climbed from grass to bushes, bushes to tree limbs, tree limbs to treetops, and soon erupted into a deadly crown fire.

Crown fires burn high in the forest canopy and can be devastating infernos, surging forward with a ferocious roar, "like a blast furnace" or "a train coming too fast around a curve," as witnesses describe. Uphill from Black Tiger Gulch, homeowners in the mountain community of Sugarloaf heard the train rushing toward them. They saw smoke boiling out of Boulder Canyon and the sky turning a sickly orange. They grabbed pets, valuables, and meaningful mementos while running to their cars, and as they evacuated, the fire belched its hot breath into their neighborhood, not just igniting homes but detonating them. Four days of intensive firefighting, aided by showers, finally brought the blaze under control, but by then the fire had burned almost 2,100 acres, causing an estimated $10 million in damage, and destroying forty-four houses and other structures. The inferno had transformed the meadows and forests into a seared landscape of charred trees like black toothpicks. As one resident described it, "The beauty of summertime had all been burnt away."

Late one night after the Black Tiger Fire had been tamed, Rob Altschuler stood guard at the base of Fourmile Canyon Drive where it intersected with Highway 119, two miles west of town. His brown-and-white Chevy Blazer, with flashing emergency lights, idled at a stop sign across from Boulder Creek. Even in the darkness, Altschuler—a big man with an auburn beard and a scarlet jumpsuit adorned with reflective tape on the cuffs and the words "BOULDER EMERGENCY SQUAD" on the back—was hard to miss, and that was intentional. The volunteer EMT and firefighter was manning a roadblock to prevent unauthorized people, such as potential looters, from entering the fire-affected area. When cars approached, Altschuler waved them down with a flashlight and checked identification.

Given the late hour, cars rarely passed. The canyon was quiet but for the muted sound of Altschuler's police radio, audible through the open window of his truck. He stood in the road, a little more than arm's length from the driver's door, and scanned the terrain. A lone streetlight on the northwest corner of the intersection shed a cone of yellow that fell in an ellipse on the ground. The lit area extended south across asphalt and illuminated the lower trunks of cottonwoods along Boulder Creek. To the east, the light shined on a small gravel parking lot where, on the edge of the darkness, a rocky, grass-covered berm emerged from the earth.

Around 2:00 A.M., Altschuler noticed a large, shadowy figure moving down the berm, and he could tell by the way the animal moved that it was feline. The cat stepped into the ring of light and showed itself to be a large cougar. "You're a really big kitty, really pretty," said Altschuler, thrilled by his unexpected night visitor. "Look how bright your eyes are," he added flatteringly.

The lion, ears erect, aimed its gaze and body at Altschuler, then walked forward. At first, Altschuler interpreted the animal's behavior as mere curiosity, as if the cat were trying to figure out what this creature in a jumpsuit was doing in the canyon in the middle of the night. But as the lion continued to approach, Altschuler felt a twinge of fright. *That's close enough*, he thought when the cat had neared to about twenty feet. Altschuler tried to appear calm—he didn't want the lion to sense fear—and began to step backward while keeping his eyes fixed on the cougar and continuing to talk to it as he groped for the truck's door handle. The cat stopped its forward motion and watched as Altschuler gently, slowly, smoothly opened the door to his vehicle and prepared to jump in, just in case. The cougar remained still, its eyes and the human's locked for perhaps thirty seconds. Then, apparently losing interest, the cat turned and exited the circle of light.

When Michael Sanders learned of Altschuler's encounter, he added another observation report to the growing pile and placed an additional red dot on his topographic map, which was at this point so covered with lion-sighting stickers that Boulder County appeared to have contracted chicken pox. In the time since Jim and Michael's meeting at the Division of Wildlife, Boulderites had continued to phone in cougar observations at the rate of several per month. Residents reported cougars lying in the grass, feeding on deer carcasses, crossing rivers and roads. (One man, who watched a cougar sprint in front of his car in Boulder Canyon on a March evening, told his calico cat upon returning home, "Honey, you've sure got some big cousins living here in Boulder!") Although none of the lions had acted threateningly, Michael's and Jim's concerns for public safety had not abated, nor had their anger at the Division of Wildlife. On many an evening, the men vented their frustration over drinks at a raucous, country-western bar that, despite changing hands and names several times, people still called by its original moniker: Peggy's Hi-Lo (so named, according to one version of the story, because of the owners' high expectations and low reserves of cash).

Peggy's—a long, low-slung concrete structure on the northeastern edge of town—appeared unremarkable on the outside, "but it sure was a shit-stomping place inside," recalls Peggy Moore, the establishment's namesake and onetime proprietor. Music blared constantly, from live bands that performed on a small stage and from the jukebox. (One jukebox favorite, by the Canadian band Showdown, began, "Well, it's forty below and I don't give a fuck, got a heater in my truck and I'm off to the *ro*-dee-*o*. . . .") Fights erupted by the billiard tables and were doused with a stern lecture from Ellie Halliday, the Hi-Lo's septuagenarian bartender, manager, mother figure, and bouncer. "You may be old enough to be in a bar," Ellie scolded one

rowdy patron, "but you aren't *mature* enough to be in a bar." Peggy's sponsored contests—wet T-shirts, arm wrestling, swing dancing, Elvis imper-
sonation—and was legendary for hosting crazy, good times. A customer
used to ride his horse in the back door and up to the bar for a beer, which
he shared with his animal. At Peggy's, ranch hands mixed with IBM exec-
utives on the crowded dance floor, mud-splattered Ford pickups shared the
gravel parking lot with BMW sedans, the Old West kissed the New.

To Jim Halfpenny, Peggy's was therapeutic, a place where the staid and
logical scientist could let loose. ("Kept me good and sane," he says.) Some
weeks, he'd go there three nights in a row, donning jeans, cowboy boots,
and a western shirt for hours of two-stepping and jitterbugging with any
woman he could entice to the floor. Michael Sanders, who liked Peggy's
because it reminded him of his home in Tennessee, played pool, swigged
Budweisers, ate the occasional hamburger (with extra pickles, always), and
chatted with Jim when Jim wasn't dancing.

Given the loud music, conversations at the Hi-Lo tended toward shouting matches, and given the deteriorating relations with the Division of
Wildlife, Michael and Jim tended to gripe. The men continued to butt
heads with state officials. A recent *Rocky Mountain News* article had quoted
Jim speaking candidly about his mountain lion fears: "We've had at least
three females with kittens on the edge of the city. They are habituating,
and the kittens are learning from their mothers it's all right to be around
people. . . . In the long term, I expect we'll see more encounters—not
because there are more lions, but because more lions are becoming habituated." Division officials chastised Jim for using terms such as "habituation" and "encounter," which they considered fear mongering. "They didn't
like the words that implied people were likely to get in trouble with lions,"
Jim recalls. "And that's exactly what we were saying. They were."

At heart, the dispute between the Boulder scientists and the Division
of Wildlife was over turf and ego. The state agency saw itself, rightly, as
the outfit responsible for mountain lions. Division officials resented
Michael and Jim for portraying themselves as cougar authorities and for
continuing to push for a radio-collar study. "These guys were using the
media in order to sensationalize things, in order for them possibly to get a
research program, in my opinion," says Gary Berlin, a former district
wildlife manager in Boulder. Berlin and others suspected that the true goal
of the proposed radio-collar study was not knowledge but rather money and

scientific prestige. "They were seeking additional compensation and recognition for themselves."

Michael and Jim, for their part, resented the Division of Wildlife for asserting its authority over cougar issues while showing no willingness to *do* anything about the worrisome animals. The Boulder scientists saw a growing problem that, as far as they could tell, the state had chosen to ignore. In this leadership vacuum, they were not going to stop talking to the media.

Such were the subjects of conversations at the Hi-Lo, between beers and dancing, while Michael and Jim sat at a table or stood at a waist-high wooden ledge where one could rest an elbow and a drink. Besides discussing lion politics, the men speculated on where the storyline they were chronicling was headed. Who would be the first victim of Boulder's bold cats? Where would the attack occur? Jim suspected that the lion would strike around Chautauqua Park, maybe along one of the trails beneath the Flatirons. Michael guessed that the attack would happen on the western side of town, perhaps near the university and frat houses. "What we're gonna see—somebody's gonna get drunked up in the bar one night," Michael told Jim. "It's gonna be two o'clock in the morning. The kid's gonna be walkin' home. He's gonna get to a place, and he's gonna be taken." The way Michael saw it, the attack would be unexpected and unseen. "They're gonna find him the next morning on the side of the road because nobody had driven through the road that night."

Music thumped. Michael gulped a Budweiser. Jim led a woman to the dance floor. And a cloud of tobacco smoke hung in the air, thick as a wildfire haze.

By October 1989, Michael Sanders's obsession with cougars had become evident to anyone who visited his office, at the Boulder County Parks and Open Space field station northeast of town. The station consisted of a pair of buildings—a two-story A-frame and a squat, rectangular structure that people called the B-frame—which sat on the plains among a cluster of cattail- and waterfowl-filled marshes known, ironically, as Walden Ponds. A lacustrine double entendre, named for former county commissioner Walden "Wally" Toevs as well as Henry David Thoreau's watery retreat, Walden Ponds constituted one of Boulder's most unnatural natural areas. The ponds were former gravel pits that humans had "reclaimed" by sculpting rock piles into peninsulas and islands, planting the banks with seeds and seedlings, and stocking the water (which percolated up through the ground) with largemouth bass and bluegill, fish that were non-native to the area. In the warmer months, a riot of birds—belted kingfishers, black-headed grosbeaks, red-winged blackbirds, great blue herons, ring-tailed ducks—flew among the reeds and cottonwoods. Michael's office, on the southwest corner of the B-frame, looked across the ponds toward the Flatirons and the Continental Divide.

On the sill of a window that framed the ponds and peaks, inside Michael's office, perched the end piece to an old fruit crate; its decorative label shouted, in orange and blue letters on a black background:

MOUNTAIN LION BRAND *Colorado Peaches*

On the wall opposite the office door, Michael had taped up the topographic map of Boulder County speckled with red and orange stickers showing where lions and lion tracks had been observed. And to the right of his desk, on a pair of corkboards where he had hung the patch from his old Yellowstone uniform and a Smokey Bear key chain, Michael displayed cougar paraphernalia: a picture of a yawning mountain lion, Ponce Gebhardt's photographs of the Knollwood cat, an assortment of cougar-related newspaper clippings. One recent article from the *Denver Post* reported on distant events that, to Michael, sounded like the rumble of approaching thunder:

MOUNTAIN LION APPARENTLY KILLS MONTANA BOY

By The Associated Press
 EVARO, Mont.—A 5-year-old boy last seen riding his tricycle near his home in rural western Montana apparently was killed by a mountain lion that later was tracked down and shot, authorities said yesterday.

The body of Jake Gardipe was found Sunday night just 30 yards from his home, said Missoula County Sheriff's Lt. Greg Hintz.

Rick Schoening, a game warden for the Montana Department of Fish, Wildlife and Parks, said tracking dogs later treed

a female mountain lion that was then shot. The animal had
blood in its mouth and claws, he said.

On the morning of Wednesday, October 11, Michael Sanders was at his
desk when a government official called from Montana. Mike Aderhold, an
information officer for the Department of Fish, Wildlife, and Parks—Montana's equivalent of the Colorado Division of Wildlife—explained that his
state had recently suffered its first fatal cougar attack. (By now the five-
year-old boy's death had been conclusively linked to the mountain lion; bits
of human skin, lung, hair, ribs, and clothing were recovered from the
cougar's stomach.) A postmortem examination of the offending lion—a
young, fifty-two-pound female—turned up a dozen porcupine quills
lodged in its hide and evidence of past frostbite on its ears and tail, but the
injuries did not appear serious and there was no sign of disease. The cat
tested negative for rabies. The fatal attack shocked and perplexed the state
wildlife agency since, as Aderhold said, mountain lions "just were not
regarded as any kind of a threat to humans." He was now scrambling to
learn all he could about cougar attacks, what caused them, and how to prevent them. The inquiries had led to Lee Fitzhugh of UC Davis, who had
spoken about lion attacks at the workshop in Arizona, and Fitzhugh had
recommended that Aderhold call Michael Sanders.

Similarities quickly emerged between western Montana, where the boy
had recently been killed, and the Front Range of Colorado, where Sanders
feared an attack was imminent. Both places had experienced a recent boom
in the deer population (in Montana, the animals had proliferated because
of a string of mild winters), and the rise in deer had likely caused a con-
comitant increase in cougars. And both places were seeing a significant
influx of humans building new homes in wildlife habitat. In Montana,
Aderhold says, "people were wanting their ten acres out away from their
neighbors, and so people kept expanding in these valleys and moving to the
edges of these valleys in a way that they hadn't done before. And at the
same time lions are moving to the edges of *their* traditional habitat. So we
had an expanding lion population, and we also had an expanding human
population. And the people and the lions were intersecting." It was the
same story in Boulder.

Aderhold explained that officials probing the Montana attack had
uncovered one other possible contributing factor. A couple of weeks prior

to the child's death, the boy's family had lost a pit bull, which, investigators concluded, had likely been a victim of the same cougar; lion scat found near the boy's body contained white dog hair and nylon webbing, apparently from a pet collar. Biologists speculated that the family pet may have lured the lion to the house, and after eating the dog, the cougar came to view the property as a good hunting ground. (Paul Leyhausen, renowned researcher of feline behavior, has written, "Cats possess an exceptionally well-developed memory for places, and after only one positive experience they will often, and repeatedly, seek out the particular place in a room or on a certain piece of land with astonishing precision in order to 'look for more'. . . .") Mike Aderhold told Michael Sanders, "In the wisdom of hindsight, if everybody had been sensitive to the killing of that dog, maybe the incident with the child could have been prevented." But, the Montana official conceded, "we weren't sensitive to it."

Meanwhile, the following item appeared in the October *Mountain Messenger*, a community newsletter distributed to homes in Coal Creek Canyon, a residential area in the mountains seven miles southwest of Boulder:

Dear Friends,

Seems to me something pretty bad is going on up here. I hadn't realized how many cats have vanished in this area until I started to search for Alexander. What's happening? A Satanic coven grabbing our pets? Some creep with a profitable business supplying research animals? Wild predators, completely unafraid of dogs or human homes?

I think no one realizes the extent of the problem — we're not just talking a few pets missing. Please call me if your cat has vanished, so I can get some solid figures, and please, please call me if you know where all our pets are vanishing to. (And if you find a cat, please let me know. I know a lot of people looking for theirs!)

Shari Owen

Michael Sanders did not see this letter.

Teresa Overmyer did read it, but she didn't know what to make of it. *Gosh*, she thought. *That's kind of strange.*

9

TROUBLE IN THE CANYON

In early November, a system of high pressure moved inland from the Pacific and settled above Nevada and Utah while, to the east, a low deepened over Lake Superior. In the skies above Boulder—between these opposing, spinning forces—isobars compressed, the pressure gradient steepened, and the air became unsettled. On the western flank of the Front Range, strong winds collided with the Rockies and ascended the Continental Divide. As the air rose, it expanded, cooled, and shed moisture. Then, falling down the eastern slope, the mass of atmosphere accelerated and compressed into a warm, dry gale known as a chinook.

Chinooks bring rapid and welcome relief from winter cold—they've been known to raise the ambient temperature thirty degrees in three minutes and to melt a foot of snow in a few hours—but they also bring disorder. The howling winds can exceed hurricane force. Garbage cans tumble, tree limbs snap, windows implode; occasionally trains derail and roofs take flight. (Chinooks also produce more subtle and mysterious effects; ghostly tendrils of air infiltrate houses to puff out pilot lights, set hanging plants swaying, and, in at least one Montana home, flush toilets.)

The chinooks that arrived on the night and early morning of November 8 and 9, 1989, caused sporadic damage throughout the Boulder area.

On the north side of town, the winds toppled a two-story house under con-
struction and left it a pile of lumber. To the south, they flipped a bus bench
beside Highway 93.

In the foothills southwest of Boulder, the river of air gusted to more
than one hundred miles per hour as it rushed from the peaks to the plains
along a sinuous path through Coal Creek Canyon. The wind knocked down
the sign at the Copperdale Inn (known for its Wiener schnitzel, bratwurst,
and other Austrian and German specialties) and rattled the windows at the
Coal Creek Canyon Improvement Association hall, where the community
often gathered for pancake breakfasts, Thanksgiving dinners, the Miss Coal
Creek Pageant, Boy Scout meetings, and square dances. The blast of air
skipped across the top of Coal Creek Elementary, a one-story brick school
with a gently sloping roof designed to deflect frequent, fierce gusts. (The
school looked down a mountain valley that locals called "Windy Gulch.")
The chinooks flowed past the Conoco station and Kwik Mart and shook the
trees that sheltered the home of the Overmyer family.

The Overmyers, Rick and Teresa, had arrived in Coal Creek Canyon in
1986, young parents seeking a better life. "We always took our vacations
in the West," says Rick, a lanky engineer of German extraction with a
bushy blond mustache and a haircut reminiscent of the early Beatles. He
and Teresa had been living in Illinois but preferred the Rocky Mountain
region—its weather, scenery. "We like the nature," Rick explains. "We
both like wildlife." So Rick requested a job transfer to his company's
Denver office.

"One of the things that we decided on was if we were going to move out
here, we wouldn't move to the suburbs," adds Teresa, a homemaker with
dark Italian features who stands a foot shorter than her husband. "We might
as well stay in Chicago for that." The couple found the ideal mix of city
and country in Coal Creek Canyon.

Forested, secluded, and pastoral, the canyon sat at the intersection of
three counties—Boulder, Jefferson, and Gilpin—and at the confluence of
several national trends. The once rural area, settled by gold miners and
ranchers, had seen a surge of residential growth in the 1950s, spurred in
part by the Cold War. Rocky Flats, a Department of Energy plutonium-
processing facility that sat on the windswept plain near the canyon's
mouth, had brought jobs to the area (as well as a legacy of contamination

that would last long beyond the plant's closure; the site, which at one time harbored radioactive rabbits, is now the subject of a multibillion-dollar cleanup and is slated to become a wildlife refuge). By the late 1980s, a new phase of development had begun in Coal Creek Canyon, triggered by large demographic shifts. Americans, tired of the stress and traffic of old eastern cities and the uncontrolled sprawl of California, flooded the Rocky Mountains in a torrent reminiscent of the Pikes Peak Gold Rush. (*Time* soon noted this trend with a cover story that shouted, "BOOM TIME IN THE ROCKIES.") These newcomers—engineers, architects, writers, and lawyers from New York, LA, Chicago, and Boston—sought not mineral wealth but intangible riches: fresh air, broad vistas, sunshine. Many of the new arrivals bought modern homes on gravel roads within commuting distance of cities. Others telecommuted from mountain retreats.

Meanwhile, the Old West, a region that had defined itself by the extraction of natural resources, was dying. The western mining industry shed one-third of its jobs in the 1980s. Logging had begun such a sharp decline by 1989 that one industry magazine warned, "Crisis looming in western timber supply." Ranchers, plagued by low beef prices and high interest rates, were "giving up and getting out," as the *New York Times* reported, selling their spreads to developers who subdivided the land into bite-sized parcels. These changes in the landscape and in the economy reflected and propelled a change in attitudes. In the Old West, trees were to be cut, mountains mined, animals used for work and for meat. In the New West, trees and mountains were scenery, animals were pets and wildlife, nature was a postcard view.

By late 1989, Coal Creek Canyon was well into this transition. State Highway 72, which ran through the canyon, followed the route of a nineteenth-century toll road that once provided access from the plains to gold mines in the mountains; now it transported people in the opposite direction. Rick Overmyer and other white-collar commuters descended the two-lane road each morning to reach jobs in flatland cities from homes in the hills.

The Overmyer residence, a two-story affair, sat tucked in the woods on a patch of level ground along a winding dirt road. The house looked rustic from the outside, with rough-hewn cedar siding and a roof of shake shingle. A wooden walk led from a U-shaped drive to the front door. Inside, the home proved modern and cozy: dark paneling and brown wall-to-wall carpeting, a sunken living room below a vaulted ceiling, a large moss-rock fireplace beside a stack of logs. Rick and Teresa hung moose antlers on the wall. And they imported suburbia.

Out back, in an open, weedy area where nature had deposited pine needles and rocks, the Overmyers installed a lawn of trucked-in dirt and sod. Beside it, they erected a swing set from Sears and built raised beds out of two-by-sixes. Teresa planted peas, potatoes, spinach, carrots, zucchini, broccoli, beets, turnips, string beans, and onions, and then battled hungry deer and squirrels at harvest time. The girls—Jennie and Christie, blond like their dad—threw backyard picnics and tea parties to which they invited friends and Teddy bears. Beside the house and drive, Rick constructed a large dog pen by stretching a roll of wire field fence around trees and attaching it to metal posts. He made sure the fence was high enough, about six to eight feet, that Thor and Barney could not escape.

Thor—a Great Dane, all black but for a diamond-shaped white patch on his chest—loomed over Barney, a tiny West Highland white terrier. The dogs made a mismatched pair and rambunctious playmates. "Barney would jump up and grab hold of [Thor's] throat, or his lip, and just hang there" until Thor shook him off, recalls Rick. "And then Thor would open his mouth and put Barney's head in it." It was all in good fun. The canine friends slept curled together in an insulated, plywood doghouse that Rick had constructed and placed in a corner of the pen.

The Overmyers' first few years in the canyon were filled with neighborhood get-togethers and outdoor recreation. In summer, Jennie and Christie rode tricycles and roller skates along the back deck. In winter, Thor—harnessed to a sled—pulled the girls through snow. Teresa thrust herself into community affairs; she organized food drives and the annual Easter Extravaganza, and she volunteered at the elementary school. They were innocent times. As Teresa recalls, "We had no clue that there were lions."

In early November, around the time of the great wind, the Overmyers returned home one day to find blood on Barney's face. A prompt visit to the veterinarian turned up a deep wound on the terrier's forehead. Rick and Teresa surmised that the dogs' roughhousing had gotten out of hand and one of Thor's teeth had accidentally pierced Barney's skin. If not that, then perhaps Barney had snagged himself on the wire fence of the pen. Or maybe the little dog had had a run-in with a wild animal. "We thought it might have been a raccoon," says Teresa. But the wound was not serious, and Barney had healed by the day after Thanksgiving, when the Overmyers put up their Christmas tree.

The tree required assembly. While carols played on the hi-fi—*Here comes Santa Claus, here comes Santa Claus, right down Santa Claus Lane . . .*—Jennie and Christie removed metal branches from a box and laid them on the floor to their mother's approval. "Boy, you're good helpers," Teresa commented. "Look at the nice straight line they're making." Rick inserted the limbs into the wooden trunk, and the artificial shrubbery came to life. "Looks like a little tree, doesn't it?" Teresa said to the girls, who—wearing shirts that displayed Mickey Mouse dressed as Santa Claus—twirled on the living room carpet to the music. . . . *Peace on earth will come to all if we just follow the light. . . .* To trim the tree, the girls stood on tiptoes and carefully hung the family's collection of Hallmark ornaments. Teresa completed the decoration by draping strings of ruby-colored beads, purchased at Hobby Lobby, on the limbs. . . . *Let's give thanks to the Lord above 'cause Santa Claus comes tonight!*

The artificial Christmas tree that now adorned the Overmyers' living room had been flocked—covered with fake snow. Outside, in the dog run, real snow blanketed the ground. Thor and Barney usually ate a dinner of dry kibble in the outdoor pen, but Rick gave the pets a special holiday treat on the weekend after Thanksgiving; he invited them into the warm laundry room and fed them leftover turkey. Before eating, the dogs performed their usual ritual; little Barney stood before Thor's bowl and yapped for a few minutes. ("It was like, 'It's my food. I'm eating first,'" says Teresa. "Then Barney would back off and let Thor eat.") After the dogs ate their turkey, Rick returned them to the outdoor pen, and he and Teresa tucked the girls in bed. Later, in the master bedroom, Rick and Teresa undressed and slipped beneath their quilt, colored beige and cream, decorated with flowers and ruffles.

A few nights later, in the early-morning darkness of Thursday, November 30, Rick awoke to the sound of barking. He recognized the loud, bass *woof*. It was Thor. The Great Dane rarely barked in the middle of the night; when he did, it was usually for good reason. (One time, Thor's late-night vocalizations alerted the Overmyers to a thief pilfering a neighbor's ATV.) Without waking Teresa, Rick grabbed his glasses from the night table, pulled back the quilt, and slipped on a robe and moccasins. He walked down the carpeted hall to the kitchen and laundry room on his way to the back door, which he opened. In a muffled yell, Rick called through the screen of the storm door, "Thor, be quiet!"

Thor continued his refrain, which had an abnormal, timid quality. "Usually he would be a dominating type of bark, like he's the boss," says Rick. "And this one was like he wasn't quite sure of himself." Rick could see Thor pacing in the pen. Sometimes Barney would lie in the opening to the doghouse and block Thor's access, and Rick thought perhaps that was the cause of the commotion. He shouted, "Barney!" but the little terrier didn't answer. Rick switched on an outdoor light and stepped onto the back porch and into the cold. He spotted Barney, motionless, on the ground inside the pen. The terrier's white fur was red with blood. *Did the dogs get into a fight?* he wondered.

Rick ran inside to dress and then exited through the attached garage. As the automatic opener lifted the roll-up door, creaking and clanging, Rick grabbed a flashlight and stepped into the driveway. Floodlights popped on—triggered by a motion detector—and revealed Thor standing just inside the gate to the dog pen. Rick unhooked the latch, entered the pen, and walked with the Great Dane over to Barney's crumpled body. He could see cuts and puncture wounds (and would later discover that one of Barney's feet was missing), and he noticed that the terrier's body was twitching. Rick, baffled, kneeled for a closer look. Then he heard a snarl.

The events that immediately followed take longer to describe than their actual duration. Rick rose and shined his flashlight at the corner of the pen, toward the source of the noise. There, twenty-five feet away, a cougar stared back. Rick was stunned; he had no idea there were mountain lions roaming Coal Creek Canyon. The cat, too, seemed alarmed. It snarled again, took two steps, crouched, leapt over the six-foot fence, and melted into the dark forest. Rick had no time to experience fear. The entire encounter, from first snarl to the lion's disappearance, lasted perhaps four seconds. "*Boom. He was gone,*" says Rick. But that was ample time for the Overmyers' idyllic existence to crumble.

Moments later, Rick was back in the master bedroom, where the digital clock on the nightstand displayed 3:29 in red LED numerals, and he was telling Teresa what had happened while excising details that might alarm her. "Something attacked Barney," Rick said, adding that he was going to take the injured terrier to Boulder's emergency veterinary clinic.

Rick suspected that Barney was dead, but he couldn't be sure; the slight twitching left him hopeful that the dog was just in shock.

"*What* attacked Barney?" Teresa asked with concern.

"Something big," Rick answered cryptically.

"Thor?"

"No, no. It wasn't Thor."

"What was it?"

Rick ignored the line of questioning. "I just need to take him down," he said.

"Well, what was the big thing?" Teresa persisted. "Another dog?"

"Call the emergency clinic, and tell them I'm coming down," Rick said. "Barney's pretty bloody. I don't know if he's gonna make it." Teresa grabbed a couple of towels from the bathroom and handed them to Rick, who wrapped the little dog and carried him toward the family Jeep. Teresa asked one last time. "Well, what got him?" Rick relented. "A mountain lion."

As Rick sped down the canyon, Teresa suddenly found herself alone in a quiet house with the girls asleep, with Thor still in the pen, and with the knowledge that a killer lurked outside. She began to panic. Teresa vaguely recalled reading somewhere that mountain lions will return for their prey. She feared that the lion would come back looking for Barney and, not finding the terrier, would make Thor its next victim. But she didn't dare venture out to the pen to bring the Great Dane in.

Instead, Teresa carried a chair to a locked bedroom closet and, after opening the door, climbed up to reach Rick's .22-caliber semiautomatic rifle on the top shelf. Teresa had never fired the weapon, but Rick once showed her how to load it. With trembling hands, she grabbed the rifle, unscrewed the magazine, and inserted lead bullets—*one, two, three, four, five*—into the slot. Each round made a click as it entered. Teresa went through the motions in a dreamlike state. *Am I doing this?* she asked herself. *Am I loading a gun?*

Teresa carried the loaded rifle and a baby monitor to her sewing room, which overlooked the dog pen and driveway. She paced from window to window, firearm in hand, and stared into the night while praying that the mountain lion would not appear. As stars crawled across a silent sky, the young suburban housewife—recently of Chicago—stood guard, listening to the electronic sound of her daughters breathing, waiting for the cat to return.

"Sorry about the loss of your dog."

Jim Halfpenny, dressed in dungarees, stood before the Overmyer home. A *Rocky Mountain News* reporter had recently told him about Barney's death (the terrier was DOA when Rick reached Boulder's emergency veterinary clinic), and Jim explained to Teresa that he had come to investigate the incident for the Boulder Lion Search, a study of area cougars that he and colleague Michael Sanders were conducting. Jim wished he had known to come sooner—more than a month had now passed since the incident in the dog pen, ample time for snow and sun to erase the cougar's paw prints—but he believed there was still evidence to be found. Jim asked if he could look around. Teresa said, "Sure."

Teresa showed her guest to the dog pen and told him of Rick's encounter. Jim absorbed the words and the scene with the seriousness of a cop solving a crime, which is how he saw himself. (At his tracking seminars, Jim taught students to consider themselves "detectives in the court of natural history, with the judge Mother Nature.") Jim paced the pen. He examined the ground, the trees, the insulated doghouse. He walked the enclosure's perimeter, inside and out, and peered at the fence. Along the pen's backside, toward a neighbor's house, a section of the wire mesh had been warped inward, as if a large object had pressed against it. Jim looked closely at the fence and, using tweezers from a Swiss Army knife that he kept in his pocket, plucked hairs that he found lodged in the twisted wire. They were short, light brown, black-tipped—apparently from a cougar. He placed the hairs in a Ziploc sandwich bag, which Teresa kindly retrieved from the house, so he could transport them to his lab for later analysis. (Under a microscope, cougar fur is easily distinguished from that of a dog; the inner structure, or *medulla*, of cat hairs appears as if filled with bubbles.)

Jim asked Teresa some questions. The conversation proceeded approximately as follows.

Jim: "Did your dogs sleep outside?"

Teresa: "Yes. In the pen. Every night, except when it's too cold."

"Okay. What about outdoor lights? Do you leave them on?"

"We have a light in the driveway that's on a motion detector. It turns on if something walks by."

"Anything unusual you noticed in the weeks before the attack? Noises? Maybe tracks in the snow?"

"No. Actually, yes. There was this strange wound we found on Barney's forehead about a month before he was killed. We never did know what caused it."

What Jim then told Teresa stunned her. As he saw it, Barney's fatal encounter was no sudden, bolt-from-the-blue attack; the lion had cruised the neighborhood, possibly for weeks, planning strategy. The cat had learned the routines of the Overmyers—when they came and went, where the dogs slept. The lion became familiar with the lights on the house and determined they were nothing to fear. The cougar may even have made a preliminary attempt on Barney's life several weeks before the fatal attack; it pressed up against the back of the dog pen, stuck a claw through the wire mesh, and swiped the terrier's forehead—which would explain the warp in the fence, the collection of hairs in the wire, and Barney's mysterious injury. By the night of the fatal attack, the cat had become familiar enough with the dogs and their routine that it felt confident entering the enclosure and confronting Barney. Jim explained that a six-foot fence was no obstacle for a cougar. He told Teresa about the lion that leapt onto Pat and Eugene Kayser's roof to attack their plastic owl.

Teresa was shocked. Had the lion really been watching her family for so long? *Was it out when my kids were playing?* she recalls thinking. *Was he in the rocks?* What's worse, the lion was *still* watching her family. A week after Barney's death, she and Rick had found tracks in the driveway. The paw prints looked like those of a house cat. They were the diameter of a grapefruit.

"It frightens me," Teresa told a visitor a short time later. "I'm frightened for the kids. I really am. I'm upset because it has altered our lifestyle. It *has*. I go outside, and you have to look around. Lots of times I carry an ax with me. If I don't have the ax, I have something else that I carry, especially when I go in the pen area where the dogs are. And the kids—I can't put them outside by themselves anymore. They just started going out last summer by themselves, and feeling that freedom that children should *feel*. They can't. It's just like if your house was robbed, you wouldn't feel comfortable going in your home after that's happened to you. Just like I don't feel comfortable going outside lots of times."

Teresa wasn't the only member of the household visibly shaken by recent events. The girls, saddened by Barney's sudden demise—which came shortly after Teresa's grandmother had passed away—asked extensive questions about death, a concept that three-year-old Jennie found especially confusing; she continued to search for Barney and repeatedly asked, "Is he coming back again?" Older sister Christie coped by playing with dolls. (Barbie lay on a table while a make-believe doctor proclaimed tragically, "She's dying." Christie then added, lifting a toy dog, "Barney has to go with her.")

Thor, too, was not himself. The Great Dane seemed sluggish and depressed, and refused to eat. Teresa tried feeding the dog by hand, but he just moped and turned away. The hunger strike continued for some time, until Teresa remembered Thor and Barney's ritual: *They used to always bark at each other.* Unsure of what else to do, she placed a bowl of kibble in front of Thor, faced him, and tried to imitate Barney's yap. Hesitantly, the big dog moved forward. He began to eat.

Animals, like people, can develop eating patterns that are idiosyncratic and ingrained. Dining habits and food preferences are not innate but are shaped by upbringing and experience. Arctic explorer Vilhjalmur Stefansson once remarked that his Eskimo dogs, raised on the flesh of polar bear, seal, and wolf, would almost starve before accepting a meal of beef or fish; lack of familiarity with those foods made them unpalatable to the dogs. Cougars, too, have been known to develop peculiar dietary preferences. In the 1920s, California state lion hunter Jay Bruce killed a puma near Fresno that had acquired a costly taste for domestic pigs. "There was no doubt that it was the pork lover," Bruce concluded, "for the hog-killing ended with his death." A decade later, in the vicinity of Prescott, Arizona, cougar researcher Frank Hibben discovered a lion subsisting largely on porcupine; the cat left behind a trail of quilled hides that had been removed with such "clean precision" that they appeared the work of a man and a knife. Now, as 1989 gave way to 1990, it was becoming clear that a cougar in the Coal Creek Canyon area had developed a more than casual interest in *Canis familiaris*, the domestic dog.

Nine days after Barney's fatal run-in with a cougar, and seven miles northwest of the Overmyer abode, Bill Pierce was home alone in the Aspen Meadows subdivision—a cluster of rural residences on a high plateau near the old gold-mining settlement of Magnolia (where, among the collapsing tunnels and shafts, lay the remains of the once productive Mountain Lion Mine). Bill was an aerospace scientist and urban refugee who had traded the crime and noise of Los Angeles for a secluded showplace with a twenty-four karat view; from the vast living room, beneath a vaulted ceiling paneled with aspen, a quartet of picture windows faced west toward the snowy peaks of the Continental Divide. By late 1989, his kids had grown and his marriage was dissolving—his wife had recently returned to California in advance of their divorce—but Bill continued to preside over his twenty-eight acres of woods and meadow. Deer, coyotes, and hawks inhabited the property, and elk occasionally mustered by the hundreds. "People spend thousands of dollars so that they can visit a place like that one week out of the year," says Bill, who felt blessed to live among such beauty and solitude every day.

On Saturday, December 9, 1989, as an unseasonably warm day cooled into evening, Bill walked toward the back door to give his Doberman pinscher a quick bathroom run in the woods. The dog—eighty-five pounds of fur-covered muscle and sinew named Lance—followed Bill to an enclosed porch, then exited into the eight-o'clock darkness through a rickety storm door that opened into the trees. As Bill turned back inside, he heard a sharp yelp and immediately switched on the backyard light. Peering into the halogen glow, Bill saw Lance splayed on the ground just three feet from the porch with an immense cat ("Made my dog look tiny") gnawing on the Doberman's head. A surge of adrenaline gave Bill momentary courage. The ex-urbanite—who had previously seen cougars only at the zoo—stepped outside, yelled, waved his arms, clapped, and banged the feeble door open and shut, hoping to scare the lion away; when the cougar instead raised its head and bared its teeth (the snarl reminded him of the MGM lion), Bill's courage waned and he retreated to the safety of the porch. By the time Bill looked outside again, both animals had vanished, but within five minutes Lance returned—whimpering, bleeding, and so riddled with puncture wounds that, as the Doberman's veterinarian recalled, "He looked like a well-worn pincushion from his head all the way back to his tail."

Five weeks later, in the dawn twilight of Coal Creek Canyon, John Bennett stepped into his yard to feed his horses when he noticed that the family dog was missing. (John and his wife, Barbara, originally from Ohio, worked at office jobs in town but enjoyed keeping animals—including chickens, cats, and a black Labrador named Pepper—on their twelve acres.) "I remember it was cold and there was light snow," says John. "I was calling for the dog, and I looked up the hillside and I saw [Pepper] laying there. The body was still steaming." John ran a hundred feet up the open pasture to reach Pepper's remains; her throat had been torn out and large animal prints surrounded her body. The Bennetts buried Pepper in the frozen ground, among aspens beside Coal Creek, and they telephoned wildlife authorities. Michael Sanders visited the following day. On an Observation Report Form, Michael noted, "Found possible tracks . . . good possibility of lion."

Then, on the following Monday—almost one year after a lion ate a poodle named Fifi and an official from the Division of Wildlife downplayed safety concerns by telling a reporter, "[Cougars] aren't attacking any German police dogs or anything like that"—Boulder police officer Steve Headley walked to his backyard dog pen to check on his German shepherd, Katie. Steve's home, squat and cedar-sided, looked down on the Walker Ranch open space area just north of Coal Creek Canyon. The dog pen sat off the driveway and was built into the slope, a cinder-block retaining wall bounding the enclosure on two sides and a high fence of wood and chain link forming the rest of the perimeter. Steve entered through a gate and was confronted by a pile of German shepherd. Katie, lifeless and mangled, lay in the northeast corner of the pen, her neck snapped and her chest open. "She looked like she had a very painful death," says Steve's then girlfriend, Mary Miller, who still cries when recounting the fate of her beloved pet. "Her eyes were open, and she had this really anguished look on her face." A band of red snow from the doghouse to Katie's body, and what one observer described as "ooze and goo" streaking up the inside of the cinder-block wall, suggested that the attacker had tried to carry the seventy-pound shepherd out of the run. Tom Howard, the Division of Wildlife's officer responsible for the district just south of Boulder, responded to the scene and found lion prints leading up the driveway to the pen. When Tom backtracked, he saw that the pugmarks traced a straight line for hundreds of yards. "This lion didn't just amble along and stumble on the dog," Tom concluded. "He made a beeline like he'd been there before and knew what he was after."

———————

COAL CREEK AREA ON COUGAR ALERT

A front-page headline in the *Rocky Mountain News* at the end of January signaled that the canyon's cougar problems were ballooning. "Concern for the safety of children and pets is growing by residents in Coal Creek Canyon where a mountain lion killed three dogs and seriously wounded another in the past two months," the article began.

The anxiety of residents exhibited itself in diverse ways but for the most part focused on kids. Susan Fields, who lived down the road from Coal Creek Elementary, advised her daughter Alysha, "If you want to ride your trike, be sure you do it in the garage." At the school, teachers instructed students to hang out in groups and to make noise when walking outside. The Boulder County Sheriff's Department patrolled morning bus stops to monitor children standing by the roadside at hours when cougars typically hunt. Some locals dealt with the stress through humor. A joke made the rounds: "What do you call a dog on a leash?" Answer: "A meal on a string." A cartoon in the *Mountain-Ear*, a weekly paper in the nearby town of Nederland, depicted a woman reading a letter beside her rural mailbox. "Why, it's for you!" she says to her shaggy dog, its tail wagging. "It's from a Mr. Cat and it says 'Welcome to the Food Chain!'"

The Overmyers coped by organizing.

Rick, the engineer, organized data. After neighbors learned of Rick's frightening encounter in the dog pen, they began calling with news of worrisome things *they*'d observed in recent months: a lion crossing the road, large cat tracks in the mud, a trash can found shredded. One family reported three house cats missing. A jogger told of hearing a growl in the bushes. Rick collected the reports, entered them into a computerized database, and plotted them on a map of Coal Creek Canyon. He marked track sightings with a T, lion sightings with an S, and missing pets with an M. Dogs that had been killed—Barney, Pepper, and Katie—were indicated by a K inside a circle. By early February, Rick's map displayed a constellation of fifty symbols so tightly clustered that it implied a logical conclusion: a single, rogue lion was going from house to house, terrorizing the neighborhood.

Teresa organized people. She spread the word of Rick's findings and coordinated a community response. "With all the sightings, all the trackings, more dogs being killed, passing so close to our houses, I feel that it has become a problem, a *real* problem, that needs to be dealt with," she said. "This cat is different, a different type, a different breed of cat. An *urban* cat. And I have no problem with seeing it being killed." Many of her immediate neighbors agreed, and they lobbied the Division of Wildlife to come remove the offending lion. The division refused.

"We're not going to solve the problem by just going out and eliminating the animal," said District Wildlife Manager Kristi Coughlon. "For one thing, we aren't certain it's only one mountain lion. For another, we believe it's the increase in deer in that area that attracts the cats, and if we removed one cougar, it simply would open up a territory for another cat to come in and take its place." Kristi said she shared the residents' concern for children, but she contended that the solution lay in changing the behavior of people, not cougars. "We want to make residents aware of how to protect themselves—and to protect the lions as well," she told the *Rocky Mountain News*. "We hope to give them ways of dealing with their fears before there is an accident, because none of us, ever, wants to have to investigate the death of a child."

Michael Sanders watched the unfolding drama with growing frustration. "I thought it was *totally* wrong for the Division of Wildlife to say, 'We're not gonna do anything. We're not gonna trap it or kill it,'" Michael recalls. While he agreed that Coal Creek Canyon's lion problems ultimately stemmed from human actions—people moving into lion habitat, attracting deer into yards, leaving pets outside unprotected—he vehemently disagreed with the division's hands-off approach to what appeared to be a dangerous cougar. "It was absolutely no enforcement of showing human dominance over the lion," says Michael. After all, if authorities didn't remove or otherwise punish a cougar that had crossed the line of acceptable behavior, the cat—and perhaps others—might be further emboldened.

10

THE HUNT

America's historical persecution of cougars was never based so much on a fear for human safety as on a concern over money. "The mountain lion . . . is apparently of no economic benefit to the human race," argued California state lion hunter Jay Bruce in 1925. "[It] is of practically no value as a fur bearer, game animal, or source of food, but is simply a liability which probably costs the state a thousand dollars a year in deer meat alone to support each member of its lion population. . . ." The federal government estimated that the average cougar cost society an additional thousand dollars in lion-killed domestic stock annually, and while this figure was surely an exaggeration, ranchers and farmers in the early twentieth century had good reason to despise the cats. In some areas, at some times, lions ate significant numbers of sheep, pigs, calves, and colts. (Hence the name given to the cougar's Rocky Mountain subspecies: *hippolestes*, horse thief.) Financial losses understandably bred anger and vengeance.

In Boulder in early 1990, the economics of predation remained unaltered. Although the dog-eating lion of Coal Creek Canyon had triggered concern for the safety of pets and children, anxiety didn't yield to action until the cat killed something of more than emotional value.

In mid-January, while the feline menace continued its neighborhood rounds, two former schoolmates from CU were launching a small business that sat, inadvertently and imprudently, within the cat's territory. The young entrepreneurs opened a game ranch on a rented portion of the vast property owned by Bill Pierce, whose Doberman—Lance—had miraculously survived his cougar mauling. (Immediately after the December attack, Lance's injured head had ballooned to the size of a basketball. By January the physical wounds were healing, but emotional scars remained; the Doberman had turned paranoid, neurotic, timid.)

The would-be ranchers had no stock-raising experience. Mark Malan, a mustachioed general contractor on the verge of thirty, had become inspired to change careers while honeymooning in New Zealand, where a prosperous game-farming industry had grown from an environmental debacle. In the 1800s, New Zealanders imported European red deer, a close relative of North American elk, and released the animals into the wild, a decidedly bad idea given the islands' lack of large predators. Like the mule deer of Arizona's Kaibab Plateau after the massacre of its cougars, New Zealand's red deer irrupted, producing swarms of ungulates that denuded vegetation and spurred erosion. The government tried to control the deer by slaughtering them, but by the 1970s farmers had devised a better plan: they rounded up the abundant animals, raised them in pens, and exported the pricey venison to a booming world market for gourmet meats. The industry proved so lucrative that American ranchers soon began raising red deer in the United States. Mark Malan, having learned the tale on his down-under honeymoon, returned home with entrepreneurial ideas. He pitched the game-farming plan to his friend Matt Miller.

"[Mark] was just all fired up about it, and I'm like, *Yeah. Right*," Matt says with sarcasm. "He couldn't stop talking about it, just on and on and on and on. So I started making calls to butcher shops and meat markets to say, 'How much could I sell this stuff for, and is there really a demand?' And everyplace I called said, 'We would buy everything you had for the next twenty years. We cannot keep it in stock.' I put the numbers to it, how much it would cost to buy 'em, how much it costs in feed. And I ran numbers every which way—I'm an engineer, that's what I'm taught to do. And it was like, you can't lose money on this business. The only way you'd lose money in the business is if you were absolutely stupid."

Unaware that red deer are natural prey to large cats (Amur tigers feast on them in Russia's Far East) and that Bill Pierce's property was part of a large cat's home, Matt and Mark invested everything they had in the scheme, and then some. During the summer of 1989, at considerable effort and expense, the men erected a paddock using high-tensile Cyclone fence topped with three strands of wire, rising eight feet high. The pen enclosed seven acres of meadow, a pond, and an aspen grove, and around Thanksgiving Matt and Mark filled it with a dozen red deer purchased from a breeder in Arkansas. The collection of animals, worth several thousand dollars each, represented the young ranchers' entire savings.

"We joked about it. We did the thing you're not supposed to do. You put all your eggs in one basket," Matt recalls. "But our attitude is, we've got all the eggs in one basket, and it's sitting right down there at the end of the meadow, and we're gonna sit here and watch it. And we're gonna make sure it's safe."

Twice daily, Matt and Mark walked the fence line to check its integrity. Each evening, they fed and counted the deer. By mid-January, operations were running smoothly. Several females were pregnant, and the men could see profits growing in the swollen bellies of their deer.

On January 16, 1990, at 7:30 P.M., at the conclusion of a warm, sunny Tuesday, the men conducted a routine check of the paddock. All animals were present and accounted for. The next day's dawn, however, revealed a new state of affairs. The deer were anxious, skittish ("They were freakin' out," says Matt), and a quick count turned up one animal, a five-year-old female, missing. Searching the enclosure, the men discovered that a section of the eight-foot fence had been deformed, pressed down as if by a heavy object. Inside, they found a patch of disturbed snow—kicked up, blood-soaked, imprinted by hooves and giant feline feet. Nearby, they located the deer's body, cached among willows, resting on her left side, legs outstretched, head back, chest open, ribs gnawed, organs gone. The abdomen had been cut, too, and the deer's uterus protruded. It contained a perfect male fetus. Matt Miller's stomach sank. "I just wanted to curl up in a ball and make the whole world go away. We had everything we owned in the animals."

Anger, fear, and money are powerful motivators. Matt Miller did not hate mountain lions—in fact, during college he had helped train captive cougars for a man who displayed big cats at shopping malls—but he and Mark wanted *this* mountain lion dead. The ranchers butchered the dead deer and dangled its parts from trees as lion bait, then waited with a rifle for the cat to return. But the cougar was not easily tricked. "We were trying to figure out what to do," says Matt. "And then Mark made some calls and found out about Don Kattner."

Don Kattner—a.k.a. the Cat Man—lived far across the Continental Divide from Boulder, on the Rockies' western flank. While the Front Range had become dominated by suburbs and Volvos and yuppies, Colorado's Western Slope remained a land of ranches and cowboys and big-game hunting. It was rustic, traditional, Old West, like Don Kattner himself.

Kattner stood tall, his face bearded and weathered, his attire comprising beat-up blue jeans, a thick leather belt, denim shirt, bandana around the neck, and hunting cap topping it all. His belly extended horizontally in a pronounced paunch, the result, at age forty-two, of more than two decades of beer consumption. (Asked what makes a good lion hunter, he once replied, "Persistence, patience, and Coors.") Kattner had been brought up in a remote, rural area of Northern California. "In that country," he explains, "when you come out of the womb, it was with a gun in one hand and a knife in your mouth and a fishin' pole in the other." Anything that walked, crawled, swam, flew, or slithered was considered fair game. Kattner spent boyhood weekends and summers in the woods and fields pursuing bobcats, deer, antelope, bears, squirrels, ducks, coyotes, and raccoons, but his favorite hunts were for cougars. "Once it gets into your blood, it's pretty addictive. You get to a point in your life where you can't get enough of it." So, after the California legislature outlawed mountain lion hunting in the early 1970s, Kattner moved to western Colorado, where killing cougars remained a way of life. He became a professional hunting guide and outfitter, a good one. "I'm not being egotistic or anything," he offers, "but I had a hell of a reputation with just about everybody."

Kattner estimated that by 1990 he'd led more than four hundred successful lion hunts, although many were not for the purpose of killing; he spent six field seasons working for the Colorado Division of Wildlife, tranquilizing lions for the agency's cougar study on the Uncompahgre Plateau. But whether the pursuit ended with a cat asleep or dead, the chase remained the same, and the chase is what cougar hunting is all about.

In late January, after he received a call for help from Mark Malan, Kattner packed up his hunting rig, a 1977 Chevy pickup—tan, rusting, mud-splattered, scratched, and dented—and aimed it toward Boulder County. The truck bed held a large plywood kennel that Kattner called his dog box, and inside were the tools of his trade: hounds.

It is theoretically possible to hunt cougars without hounds, but that's like saying it's possible to play poker blindfolded; though you might succeed at either activity eventually, the achievement would result from nothing more than perseverance and luck. A pack of trained lion dogs distinguishes the true cougar hunter from a hunter who might kill a cougar once in his life. Hounds tilt the odds in the hunter's favor.

Many breeds of hound—fox-, coon-, blood-, stag-—can produce good lion dogs, but few individual dogs make the cut. A cougar hound requires smarts, courage, a strong voice, an instinct for chasing animals up trees and keeping them at bay, "a nose as delicate as a French connoisseur and . . . a constitution like a Roman soldier," wrote Frank Hibben, and indestructible paws. (A hound isn't ready to pursue lions "unless you [can] strike a match on its feet," commented one famous hunter.) But these qualities alone are insufficient. Without proper training, a hound set on the trail of a cougar may become distracted by the scent of deer or elk, rabbit or coyote, and veer after the wrong animal. Dogs that chase improper game are termed trash runners, and hunters employ various means to rid their hounds of this behavior. Some houndsmen will put a dog in a barrel, add severed deer parts, and roll the canine and cervine mixture down a mountain. Others will inject a hound with apomorphine, an emetic, then release the animal on a deer or raccoon trail, causing the dog to vomit copiously while smelling the scent of the incorrect game. A more straightforward approach involves punishing a dog mercilessly—for instance, shocking it with a cattle prod, pelting it with birdshot, or beating it unconscious—if it pursues the wrong animal. ("Catch the dog in the act," writes one long-time hunter, "then put a lasso rope around his neck and hang the dog up under a limb until his toes just [touch] the ground and work him over with a quirt, rope, brush, pieces of electrical light wires made into a quirt or a chain used to raise windows up.") Ben Lilly, legendary hunter and mountain man, pushed this technique to its logical extreme. According to author Frank Dobie, "If, after he had trained a dog, it persisted in quitting the trail of a lion or bear for something else—all else being trivial and irrelevant—he would call his dogs around him as witnesses, explain to them very definitely the crime of interfering with the work of good dogs and call upon them as fellow hunters to see justice in the death penalty. He would talk to the guilty one sternly but without anger, and then either beat him to death or shoot him."

No matter the method, the aim is the same: to make hounds associate an unwanted behavior or improper scent with terrific unpleasantness. This type of learning—called "aversive conditioning" by scientists—is similar in concept to Pavlov's famous experiment with ringing bells and salivating dogs, except that it relies on punishment rather than reward, and pain is a more efficient teacher than pleasure.

Don Kattner claimed to employ more humane conditioning techniques than other hunters used, but he did not pamper his dogs. They were not pets but workers, praised for a job well done, summarily fired if they couldn't perform.

The Cat Man and his dogs arrived in the Boulder foothills one week after the death of Mark Malan and Matt Miller's red deer. Kattner's assignment was a tricky one. His job was not merely to kill a lion but to kill a particular lion; he was an assassin, a hit man. Finding the right target and dispatching it would take a combination of skill and luck—skill in tracking and identifying the appropriate cat, luck in finding it on land where he could legally hunt. Much of the foothills region west of Boulder had been carved into small, private lots, where the running of dogs was impractical if not impossible; in such areas, he would need the permission of every landowner whose property he would cross, and such permission was likely not forthcoming in a community filled with animal lovers. If Kattner was fortunate, he would track the cat onto U.S. Forest Service land. Uncle Sam had no qualms about hunting lions.

Kattner examined the crime scene. He walked down to the paddock where the cougar had ambushed the red deer, knelt, and brushed away a week's accumulation of snow to reveal the killer's prints, still visible in the lower, frozen layers. ("The snow in that country was cold enough that where the tracks were made, it made a perfect impression—just like making a plaster of Paris cast of it.") Lips pursed, Kattner blew away the remaining loose flakes to expose the tracks' contours. The pugmarks were huge, clearly those of a large tom.

Lion paws are created equal at birth, but life leaves indelible marks.

Cougars lead a violent existence; they spar over territory and mates, tumble from cliffs, and endure the flailing hoofs and antlers of their prey, resulting in fractured skulls, lost appendages, and—if a tracker gets lucky—injured feet. Wounded paws produce identifiable prints, enabling a hunter to follow the movements of an individual lion over time and terrain. (Among the cats tracked and killed by famed New Mexico cougar hunter Elliott Barker in 1930 were two with idiosyncratic tracks: Old Cripple-Foot, a tom that had lost two toes when extricating itself from a trap, and Old Lady Scar-Heel, a lioness with a lopsided left hind paw.) As Don Kattner examined the tracks of the red-deer killer, he noticed lines across the imprint of the cat's left front heel, as if the paw were scarred. It was a subtle abnormality, but it provided an identifying marker, "like a fingerprint," that would tell him when he was following the right cat.

Kattner's next task was to pattern the cougar, to determine its habitual paths and haunts. He spent mornings and evenings cruising the back roads of Magnolia and Coal Creek Canyon, speedometer hovering around ten miles per hour, driver's side window rolled down, head peering out to scan for fresh lion tracks. When he'd find a set, he'd pull over, check for the telltale scarring, and follow the cat's movements.

According to old-time hunters, mountain lions travel circuits with the regularity and predictability of a city bus. California cougar killer Jay Bruce contended that such routes were "usually in the form of a loop 25 or 30 miles around" that take "four or five days" to complete. (Texas trapper John Hearn found a different pattern; his lions traveled figure-eight circuits about once every ten days.) "As soon as some part of this beat is learned, the hunter has a clue to work by," advised Bruce, who put the technique to good use. On one memorable hunt, he predicted a cougar's travels with such precision that, according to a reliable witness, the cat "arrived at the designated point within an hour of the calculated time."

Modern telemetry studies reveal lion beats to be largely myth—cougar movements are, in reality, far more haphazard than once thought—yet the cats do follow favorite travel ways within their home ranges, and Kattner was able to perceive a pattern in this lion's wanderings. The tracks traced a deformed oval, about six miles long, with Bill Pierce's property at one end and the Overmyers' neighborhood at the other. The cougar walked the path clockwise. From Bill's place, the lion traveled east along County Road 68—a washboard gravel road that descended through a pine and aspen for-

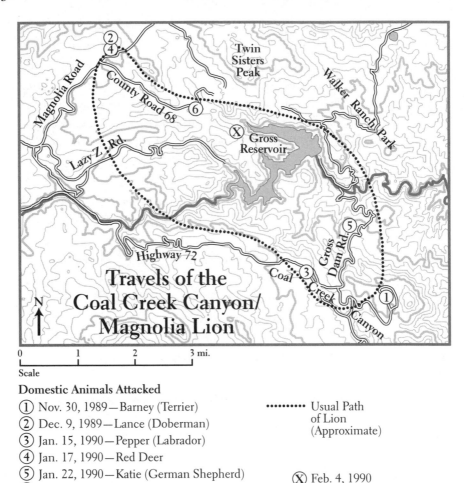

Travels of the Coal Creek Canyon/Magnolia Lion

Scale: 0   1   2   3 mi.

Domestic Animals Attacked

1. Nov. 30, 1989—Barney (Terrier)
2. Dec. 9, 1989—Lance (Doberman)
3. Jan. 15, 1990—Pepper (Labrador)
4. Jan. 17, 1990—Red Deer
5. Jan. 22, 1990—Katie (German Shepherd)
6. Feb. 4, 1990—Sage (Labrador)

•••••••••• Usual Path of Lion (Approximate)

(X) Feb. 4, 1990 Lion Killed

est—and passed a cabin with cedar siding and red-framed windows where, when Kattner drove by, a black Labrador and a Saint Bernard would run up and bark at him. From there, the lion sidled around Gross Reservoir, a man-made lake shaped like a gerrymander among the forested hills, and turned south along Gross Dam Road, past the home where policeman Steve Headley's German shepherd had recently been killed. The cat then entered Coal Creek Canyon in the general vicinity of the pet attacks there. (More than once, Kattner found the tracks leading to a backyard dog kennel. The lion "had one thing in mind," he says.) The cougar then continued to veer right—west along Highway 72, north across Lazy Z Road—to end up back where it began. A full circuit took about a week.

Having deciphered the cat's usual course, Kattner believed he could anticipate its movements. Almost two weeks after his arrival in Boulder County, he predicted that the lion was about to cross Lazy Z Road again. It did. The cougar was now back at the start of the oval, which meant it should head down County Road 68 next. So Kattner planned to focus his efforts there on the following day, a Sunday, February 4.

Morning dawned on a not-so-good-for-lion-hunting day, clear and mild. In open areas, most of the snow had melted—making visual tracking difficult—and the warm sun would quickly vaporize the lion's scent from the ground. Nonetheless, four men and four dogs headed out to patrol County Road 68 in two trucks. Don Kattner was in the lead, with Matt Miller beside him in the cab and the hounds in the dog box in back. Mark Malan and a friend named Alex followed in a 1975, three-quarter-ton, royal-blue flatbed Ford. The men dressed in layers they could peel off: a shirt beneath a sweater under a denim jacket topped off with an insulated vest.

Kattner quickly found a few fresh lion tracks in a small snow patch in the dirt road, but the prints weren't very clear, and there was no way to tell where the cat had gone, so the men continued driving. Several hundred yards farther, they passed the cabin with the two dogs that always greeted Kattner's truck with their barking. Only one dog ran up. *Where the heck is the other dog?* thought Kattner. He pulled over.

A boyish man with long blond hair and bold blue eyes watched the truck approach. The man—who shall here be called Jay Dyer (not his real name)—owned the dogs and the small rustic house with a large stone chimney. Originally built as a summer cabin, the home's only source of heat was a woodstove. Jay, wearing jeans and a gray sweatshirt, stood outside on this morning chopping wood in advance of a family gathering, scheduled for noon, to celebrate his twenty-eighth birthday.

Jay lowered his ax as Kattner pulled over. The grizzled hunter explained he was tracking a mountain lion that had been attacking dogs in the area. "Are you missing any dogs?" Kattner asked.

"No," said Jay. Merlin, his Saint Bernard, was right there. And Sage, his black Lab, frequently ran off to visit the neighbor's house. "She's probably just around here somewhere," Jay added confidently.

So Kattner and his entourage continued on, down four-wheel-drive roads toward Gross Reservoir and around Twin Sisters Peak, a pair of jagged granite spires that towered above the forest. He could find no fresh cougar tracks, no evidence that the cat had continued its clockwise journey.

In the meantime, Jay began to question whether his black Lab was okay. "I got to thinkin', she hasn't been around in a little while," he remembers. "I called my friend Harry up here, and I said, 'Harry, is she up there? Is Sage up there?' He said, 'No.' And I said, 'Oh, *man*. Now I'm getting concerned.'" When Don Kattner drove by again, a few hours later, Jay flagged him down. "Hey, I think we might have a problem here," he said. "Now I'm *not* sure that I'm not missing a dog."

It didn't take long for Kattner to find what he was looking for. He examined the area around Jay's house. Where sun struck soil the ground was bare, but in an area of shadow, on the north side of a woodpile, snow remained. It recorded a brutal story. "What it boiled down to, when I went around the shed there, was lion prints and dog prints and blood—and no dog," says Kattner. "The sumbitch killed the dog." Even without a close examination of the lion tracks, he knew this cat was the one he wanted. "We're going," Kattner told the assembled men. "Let's do it."

From the attack site, the cougar prints and an accompanying drag mark descended a snowy, wooded ravine and entered the Roosevelt National Forest.

Theodore Roosevelt was, it is generally agreed, the greatest conservationist ever to inhabit the White House. During seven and a half years as the nation's chief executive, Roosevelt set aside 230 million acres of federal land (a span equivalent to California, Nevada, and Utah combined) in national parks, monuments, forests, wildlife refuges, and game preserves, and he used his bully pulpit to foster an attitude of stewardship toward America's trees and wildlife, previously perceived as inexhaustible. "The conservation of our natural resources and their proper use constitute the fundamental problem which underlies almost every other problem of our national life," he declared in a speech at Jamestown, Virginia, in 1907.

To Roosevelt, though, protecting nature did not mean closing it to human use. "Conservation means development as much as it does protection," he told Kansas farmers in 1910. "I recognize the right and duty of this generation to develop and use the natural resources of our land; but I do not recognize the right to waste them. . . ." Roosevelt, and the conservation movement he represented, advocated the sustainable harvest of nature's bounty, the husbanding of resources for the future. In this context, the reckless slaughter of wild animals, especially beautiful or useful ones like buffalo, was considered immoral ("Wild beasts and birds are by right not the property merely of the people alive to-day, but the property of the unborn generations, whose belongings we have no right to squander," he famously wrote), yet hunting per se, when regulated and sportsmanlike, was a fine activity.

Actually, it was more than fine. Roosevelt, a lifelong sportsman (at age fourteen, he received a double-barreled, breech-loading shotgun as a Christmas gift from his father) who had willed himself from sickly child to athletic adult through a regimen of vigorous exercise, promoted "manly out-of-door sports, such as mountaineering [and] big-game hunting" to instill courage and self-control, and to stave off effeminacy. Roosevelt advocated hunting as a healthy means for urban, office-bound men to develop and maintain virility.

As Don Kattner prepared to lead his men into a forest named for a gun-toting, cougar-killing president, Matt Miller, young and cocksure, itched to begin the pursuit. "Let's *go*, let's *do* it," he said. "I want to *kill* this thing." Kattner handed him a piece of blue steel in the shape of a Ruger and wrapped in a leather holster. Matt hung the pistol on his right hip. "You're the lead man," Kattner charged. "You protect my dogs." Given that this lion had exhibited unusual bravado around dogs, Kattner feared his hounds might be its next victims. "I will be there," Matt pledged. "He will not touch your dogs."

Meanwhile, the hunting party accreted more people and firepower. Jay Dyer, having lost *his* dog to the lion this very morning and having been invited by Kattner to join the chase, announced to his birthday-party guests, who had by now arrived, "Hey, guys, we're goin' on a cat-huntin'," and grabbed his deer rifle (a Marlin lever-action .30-30, varnished wood and black steel) and his sister's husband, a tall man with a quiet manner and gentle face who will here be named Henry Young. Henry, though an experienced sportsman (pheasants, ducks, elk), was ill prepared for an impromptu cougar hunt and had to borrow his brother-in-law's snow boots and a pump-action .30-06. Also arriving on the scene were Mark Malan's newlywed wife, who had been notified by telephone of the lion's imminent demise, and a neighbor, a fisheries biologist named Don Proebstel, who wore camouflage and packed a revolver. Thus assembled and armed, a throng of eight humans prepared to chase down one lion with the help of four dogs.

Lion hunts are chancy affairs. Even good hounds cannot guarantee success; dogs become lost or injured, cougars escape. Mountain lions are power walkers—"often traveling 25 or 30 miles over rough country in 10 or 12 hours," wrote Jay Bruce—and as the hounds move forward, the cougar may retreat at a faster clip. Tracking can be slow. Lions zigzag and circle, backtrack, and drop from ledges, leaving a trail that is disjointed, confusing, labyrinthine. If the cat's prints are not visible and its direction of travel is therefore unclear—for instance, in an area without snow or soft soil—hounds may run the scent trail in reverse, racing toward where the cougar *was* rather than where it *is*.

Kattner, however, was confident he would catch a lion on this day. He guessed that the cat had not traveled far; with its belly full of Labrador, the cougar was likely resting nearby, digesting, waiting to take another meal from its latest victim. And Kattner had faith in his hounds. He had brought along four of the best in the business: Jack, Jeff, Turkey, and Doc.

The dogs all exhibited similar body types—stout noses, pendulous ears, long torsos—but different coloration. Jack looked like an oversized beagle, with copper ears and a cream body splotched with red and black; he was a Walker, a type of American foxhound created in 1850s Kentucky by a breeder named Walker and a pilfered sire named Tennessee Lead. Turkey and Doc were part Walker and part bluetick, their coonhound heritage exhibiting itself in sooty flecks—"ticking"—that speckled patches of white fur. Jeff, the color of coal and caramel, belonged to a breed known unimaginatively as a black and tan.

Doc, the lead (or "strike") dog, was seven years old, reliable, indefatigable, and battle-scarred. A few years back, after pursuing a lioness into a small cave, the hound had gotten his head torn up so badly that he went into shock and would have died without emergency treatment, including the administration of intravenous fluids in the field. Doc was as good as a lion dog gets. Kattner referred to him as "the Perfessor."

Kattner lowered the tailgate on the pickup and swung open a door to the dog box. Doc crawled out, jumped to the ground, and Kattner led him to the woodpile where the lion had apparently ambushed its recent meal. The hound paced the area, head held low, nose pressed into a carpet of pine needles and kinnikinnick, a glossy, evergreen ground cover (known as bear-berry east of the Mississippi) that grows in sandy soil, which this was, the earth composed of crumbling granite. Doc was silent. A good lion hound won't speak until he gets a strong whiff of a cougar's scent.

While the assembled people smelled only ponderosa pine and wood smoke, Doc—whose nose was as much as a million times more sensitive than a human's—smelled death. He loped downhill, along the bare ground of the south-facing slope and into the snowy ravine where, across a creek, the low-hanging limbs of a blue spruce concealed what remained of Sage, the black Labrador. ("It was ate up pretty good," recalls Kattner.) Doc examined the carcass and the surrounding terrain, trying to determine where the killer had gone. He sniffed the ground, bushes, branches, anything that would retain the fragrance of lion, as a breeze swayed the treetops.

Suddenly, Doc "opened"—began bawling—and dashed eastward through the trees. He ran in classic hound style: "with nose close to the ground," as Jay Bruce described it, "head sweeping from side to side and tail wagging furiously, stopping suddenly as he catches the scent, smelling intensely for a moment to make sure, then throwing up his head and baying loudly as he rushes ahead. . . ." Now that Doc was solidly on the lion's trail, Kattner released the other dogs—Jeff, Jack, and Turkey—and launched Matt Miller behind them with a "You're lead. You *go!*" Matt raced into the woods and found himself mired in knee-deep snow. The young rancher struggled forward as the canine chorus (*ow-ow-ow-ow*) receded into the distance.

The dogs ran half a mile east and veered up a rocky slope on the north side of the ravine. The hill rose several hundred feet above the surrounding countryside and provided a view down to the plains and out to the sky-scrapers of Denver. Here, on a south-facing slope of bare ground and rock, the trailing was difficult and slow. The lion had apparently meandered through this area, leaving a convoluted scent trail. The hounds scrambled over outcroppings of lichen-covered granite and between pines that grew through the cracks, scouring like detectives for a trace of their quarry. New Mexico lion hunter Elliott Barker once described how his hounds conquered such challenging stretches:

The trail is lost. The dogs, who have been trailing together, start circling each on his own to find it again. Their noses work

fast, testing every likely spot for the familiar scent. They work silently and their tails wag slowly as they circle and cut back and forth, hunting anxiously in an ever-widening area for the scent of another track to guide them on.

Then one of the pack gets a faint whiff where the lion has been. He stops still. His body becomes tense. His nose moves ever so slowly over the spot to verify his first impression. His tail begins to wag faster and with more emphasis. If another dog sees him in that posture, he will understand and come to him. When he is sure he has found the trail, he will start forward, giving tongue in a manner and tone of voice that will say as plainly as words, "Here it is. Let's go!" The others will come in a hurry, sometimes stopping to verify for themselves the find, but often accepting the other one's word for it, and plunge forward with him in full cry to pick up the track further on.

The dogs circled among the rocks. Their baying grew louder and fainter, louder and fainter, as heard from below. Matt Miller climbed toward the sound, up the jagged slope. His strength was fading, as was his macho attitude. "I was just dripping, tired," he recalls. Matt stopped to catch his breath. He could barely move his legs.

Meanwhile, Don Kattner walked slowly and deliberately through the snowy ravine below. He was tracing his dogs' tracks while following their progress aurally. Lion dogs communicate with a language of bawls, yips, yelps, cries, howls, bellows, chops, growls, squeals, whistles, and whines that convey with remarkable specificity what the pack sees and smells. In the jargon of lion hunting, hounds don't bark; they "speak" (and hounds that speak inappropriately are "babblers"). Kattner could tell by the pitch, volume, tempo, and urgency of the vocalizations that his hounds were close to the lion. The scent was strong.

Then, in an instant, the barking became staccato and excited. Kattner knew what his dogs were saying: they had jumped their quarry, and it was on the move. He turned to the brothers-in-law, Jay and Henry. "The dogs are on that cat right now," Kattner said. "Get ready, boys."

As Frank Hibben has written, "Lion hounds, with cougar scent in their nostrils, can go faster than galloping horses." And that's what the floppy-eared dogs were doing now—galloping, careening, flying down the rocks.

As they reached the bottom of the ravine, they launched themselves off a twelve-foot ledge, soared across a creek, landed in a snow bank, and scrambled up the forested slope to the south. Kattner didn't see the lion, but it must have been right in front of the hounds.

Matt Miller, still high up the rocky slope that the dogs had just abandoned, dashed downhill at full speed, leaping over rocks and brush, but his progress could not match the hounds'. "I finally got halfway back down the mountain, and I stopped to try to find out where the dogs were, and I look straight across the valley, all the way over to the other mountain, and there are the dogs running up that hill. And I'm like, *Oh, shit.*"

Don Kattner, seeing that Matt could not keep up with the dogs, asked Jay and Henry to take over the lead. "We gotta get on this cat," he said. "I don't want him on the dogs too long." The men, rifles in hand, ran southward and upward, through tangled branches and deep snow, along an east–west trending hill called Winiger Ridge. A throaty, feverish baying permeated the woods before them.

In most contexts, "tree" is a noun, but in cougar hunting the word becomes a transitive verb, and it describes what the dogs had done to the cat. The lion, out of breath (cougars have little lung capacity) and with dogs on its heels, had leapt into the branches of a ponderosa pine where it now rested, panting, glaring at its tormentors through slanted eyes. The dogs surrounded the trunk, necks craned as they jumped and howled at the beast above. Their vocalizations—what hunters call "barking treed"—emanated from deep past and inner wolf, the expression of a million-generation feud, canine versus feline. It was the sound of victory, of enmity, of bloodlust.

Jay and Henry arrived on the scene to find the cougar on its high perch expressing displeasure. "It was pissed off," Jay recalls. "It was lookin' down at the dogs and snarlin', and just raisin' heck." The lion was restless, moving from branch to branch, hissing, and showing fangs. The blackened tip of its tail twitched, and its golden eyes—above a salmon-pink pug nose—darted from dog to dog. This tom was a monster in a brindle coat, with paws as large as a man's hands. The great cat looked like a boxer thrown against the ropes, preparing to lash back as soon as it had the opportunity.

Henry, used to hunting pheasants and other harmless game, was nervous. "I didn't really know *what* to do," he says. "I didn't know if it would come out of the tree after the dogs and us." Jay, awed by the cat's power and stalwart charisma, was worried, too. The original plan had been that whoever first arrived beneath the treed cougar should wait for the others before shooting it, to provide an opportunity for all to admire and photograph the doomed animal. Jay now thought otherwise; he was not about to wait. He turned to Henry: "We'd better take it."

Killing a treed puma is a rather straightforward matter, requiring little more than decent aim and steady hands. ("The shooting of a cougar in a tree is . . . ridiculously easy and anything but a sporting proposition," wrote Arthur Newton Pack, president of the American Nature Association, in 1930.) But a clean shot is critical; should the lion fall wounded among the dogs, the resulting melee can be bloody, producing dead hounds and injured hunters.

Jay and Henry stood back from the lion-bearing ponderosa and chambered bullets with a *chk-chk* of metal against metal. The men positioned themselves on relatively level ground—ten feet apart, Jay on Henry's left—and raised their weapons forty-five degrees, rifle butts against right shoulders and right eyes sighting down barrels. Henry's pulse thumped in his ears. The dogs continued to wail. In a scene that would later be repeated in through-the-looking-glass style, the two humans on the ground readied to extinguish the life of a cougar in a tree. The men aimed for the cat's heart.

Henry and Jay squeezed index fingers with near simultaneity, producing a thunderous boom followed by a puff of smoke. The rifles kicked, but the men didn't feel it; they were conscious only of the lion—collapsing, deflating, now falling, crashing through the branches. Wood splintered with a loud *crack*. The dogs erupted in a frenzy of barks and growls and squeals.

But the lion did not reach the ground. A thick limb halted its downward momentum and seemed to revive the animal. Lazarus-like, the bloody cougar rose; it turned toward the trunk and clawed its way back up the tree with such force that its head snapped branches as it plowed upward.

Jay instinctively cocked his rifle again, ejecting a brass casing from the weapon's side and inserting a new round in the chamber. When the cat neared its previous perch and stopped to rest, Jay fired again. This time, the cougar fell into the waiting pack below. The hounds rushed in and gripped the big cat's skin, tearing at its face and legs and rump, as if seeking revenge for all of their brethren the lion had killed. The cat did not fight back. Its warm body lay limp, its chest scarlet.

Before long, the rest of the gang arrived: the Cat Man, the young ranchers, the rancher's wife, the friend, the neighbor. Congratulations were issued, photographs taken. An examination of the cat's left front paw revealed cuts and scars on the heel, just as Kattner had surmised from the tracks in the snow. Later, back at the ranch—with the red deer safe in their paddock and the vanquished cat's carcass slumped in the bed of the ranchers' truck, its head against a spare tire and its mouth in a grimace—the men celebrated with imported beer: Kiwi Lager, another discovery from Mark Malan's New Zealand honeymoon.

"It would be impossible to wish a better ending to a hunt," wrote Theodore Roosevelt after a similar chase ended the life of another Colorado cougar in 1901. (The vice president–elect's hunt closed on an especially manly note; he finished the cat's life with the thrust of a knife.) Like the Boulder lion, Roosevelt's quarry had destroyed domestic animals, "killing on one occasion a milch cow, on another a steer, and on yet another a big work horse." In 1901 Colorado, killing a stock killer was an unalloyed public good, and Roosevelt's deed was undoubtedly lauded by the community at large.

American mores and the American West, however, had changed considerably in eighty-nine years. The destruction of the dog-eating cat of Coal Creek Canyon would provoke a more complex public reaction.

Teresa Overmyer stopped at Coal Creek Canyon's Kwik Mart convenience store and, adhesive tape in hand, hung a notice in the front window:

MOUNTAIN LION MEETING

FRIDAY, FEB 9, 7:00 PM
CCCIA HALL
COAL CREEK CANYON
Sponsored by Division of Wildlife

The poster, which Rick had designed, featured a photograph of a snarling cougar in the center. Below the great cat, he had written,

The mountain lion continues to kill. Its most recent victims were a German shepherd behind a 6 foot fence and a black

Labrador. See the article in February's Mountain Messenger for details. If the lion incidents are of concern to you, please attend the meeting. Information will be presented on how to protect your family and pets.

The Overmyers and their neighbors, still nervous about the dog-killing lion and unaware that the animal had met its end near Gross Reservoir, continued to urge the Division of Wildlife to address the canyon's cougar problems. The division had offered to convene a community meeting, and Teresa agreed to help organize and publicize it. Wildlife officials saw the gathering as an opportunity to educate residents and soothe their fears, but the Overmyers sought a different outcome; they hoped that a roomful of angry parents would push the state agency to take direct action—to eliminate the rogue lion.

Then, just one day before the community meeting—and four days after the cougar had been quietly killed—news of the cat's demise hit the papers. The timing and slant of coverage could hardly have been more inflammatory.

"Mountain lion's death upsets Division of Wildlife," read a front-page headline in the Boulder *Daily Camera*. Denver's *Rocky Mountain News* proclaimed, "Disposal of cougar's body leaves state with no proof it was wanted dog killer." The Longmont *Times-Call*, the daily paper of Boulder County's second-largest city, topped its story, "Man who killed lion puzzled by fuss." The gist of the articles was this: the game ranchers' cougar hunt had been legally suspect, ethically questionable, and of dubious effectiveness.

The back story read as follows:

On the morning after the successful hunt, rancher Mark Malan drove the dead cougar, chained to the bed of his truck, to the Division of Wildlife's Denver offices and displayed his catch. Per regulation, any lion hunted in Colorado must be presented to the state game agency to certify that the animal was killed legally. After the death of his red deer, Mark had been issued a special hunting license, called a kill permit, that allowed him to shoot the depredating cougar if it returned to his property. Technically, the permit did not authorize him to kill a lion *off* his property, but Mark pled ignorance of this restriction and the license failed to note it—the form had been filled out improperly by a division official—so the agency let the infraction slide. (Mark made no mention of another infraction; namely, the lion had been killed not by him but by Jay Dyer and Henry Young, who possessed no hunting license.) Wildlife officials poured out of the building to admire the large cat in the rancher's truck. They congratulated Mark on a job well done.

After returning to Boulder, Mark drove west into the foothills and parked in a gravel lot beside the Nederland Veterinary Hospital, where he asked "Doc Joe" Evans to perform a postmortem examination on the lion. The veterinarian weighed the animal (it was massive, almost 170 pounds) and placed it on a stainless-steel table beneath a high-intensity light. "We checked its teeth, its claws," Doc Joe recalls. "It was a very healthy cat. *Very* healthy. We checked for any lacerations, abrasions, contusions—anything that would indicate that it in any way had been traumatized that would make it an angry animal." He noticed no abnormalities. Using a scalpel and buck knife, Doc Joe sliced open the cat's abdomen, pulled out its stomach, and looked inside. He found a clump of black hair, apparently from a dog. Mark Malan was relieved; the physical evidence confirmed that the correct lion had been killed.

Then, a couple of days later, the Division of Wildlife telephoned. "They said, 'Where's our cat?'" recalls Matt Miller, Mark's partner. "And we said, 'What do you mean, where's your cat?' They said, 'Where's our cat? We want our cat back.' And then that's when the trouble started."

Had Mark Malan obtained a regular hunting license (costing a mere thirty-two dollars) to kill the cougar, the animal would have been his to keep—to stuff or to skin, as he saw fit—but because it had been hunted with a special kill permit, the body remained the property of the state. (Animals hunted with kill permits are sometimes used for educational purposes.) Mark explained to the division that he had left the lion carcass with veterinarian Joe Evans. Doc Joe claimed to have disposed of the cougar's remains at the Boulder County Humane Society's crematorium. The veterinarian insisted there was no carcass left to return. But wildlife authorities doubted the story; the Humane Society had no record of a cougar's being cremated. Division officials suspected that Mark or Doc Joe was keeping the lion illegally as a trophy, and they weren't going to stand for it.

The division had a history of bad blood with Joe Evans, flowing from a bizarre episode the preceding summer. At that time, Doc Joe was raising a mule deer fawn that some boys had found, just hours old, apparently abandoned by the side of the road. The veterinarian took the orphaned creature into his home, bottle-fed it five times daily, and named it Sweetheart, at his daughter's suggestion. After the local paper ran a touching feature about the compassionate animal doctor and his baby deer, two Division of Wildlife officers arrived at the Evans house unannounced, accused Doc Joe of illegal possession of wildlife, and forcibly removed Sweetheart. ("Kidnapped" was the word Mrs. Evans used.) Doc Joe, in turn, accused the division of "Gestapo-type" tactics. Sweetheart, too tame for release back to the wild, was eventually given to a South Dakota zoo.

Wildlife officials had misgivings about Mark Malan for related reasons; he, like Doc Joe, had defied the natural order by domesticating wild animals. To the division, game farming—which transformed noble, free-roaming creatures into little more than antlered cattle—was a morally repugnant, vile enterprise. In early 1990, the agency was pushing to outlaw red-deer ranching in Colorado, and would do so before year's end, arguing that the exotic animals posed a genetic threat to native ungulates, with which they might interbreed. The resulting tense political climate made Mark Malan a perceived enemy.

So, when the Division of Wildlife failed to receive its dead cougar, it did not issue Mark a warning or quietly fine him, as it might have done. Instead, the agency took its case to the media. Wildlife biologist Kathi Green did the talking. "[Mark Malan] understood very clearly that the lion was the property of the state," Kathi told reporters. Because the cougar had not been returned, she added there was "no way of knowing if this is the lion that was causing any of the problems." She chastised Mark for conveniently ignoring the stipulation (which, she insisted, he knew) that his kill permit be used only on his property. "That led to him hunting all over creation," she said. "You're not supposed to just go out looking for lions. You're not supposed to treat predators like vermin that ought to be exterminated just because they exist." Kathi concluded the diatribe: "We are discussing filing charges—theft of wildlife—with the Boulder County district attorney." (Indeed, Mark Malan was eventually fined five hundred dollars.)

Mark was furious. Not only had the lion killed his livestock; not only had he spent several weeks and substantial sums (Don Kattner's services cost $1,200) to track down the cat; but now he was being slandered as an irresponsible, crazed vigilante. "The whole God-damned community owed me a huge thank you," he complained years later, still bitter. "We've alleviated a giant problem, and yet I'm the bad guy." Mark believed that state wildlife officials were crucifying him because he had made them look foolish. After all, the division had told concerned residents repeatedly that it couldn't—or wouldn't—hunt down the problem lion, and now a private citizen had shown the agency up. "I just did something they should have done," he told one reporter. "It was only a matter of time before that lion attacked a small child," he said to another. In a television interview on Denver's Channel 4, Mark commented insightfully, "Monday I was a hero. Today I'm a villain."

The vilification of Mark Malan, a small thing in and of itself, would trigger much larger forces—public anger, the reinforcement of stereotypes—with grave consequences. In the near term, the spreading news of Malan's kill would alter the dynamics of the community gathering scheduled for the following night and noted on Michael Sanders's desk calendar: "7:00 Mtn Lion Meeting @ Coal Creek Comm. Hall."

11

CULTURE— HUMAN AND ANIMAL

An apocryphal story is told of the Boulder Valley's discovery by its early white settlers. In autumn 1858, a small prospecting party led by Missourian Thomas Aikins paused at Fort Saint Vrain, an abandoned trading post along the South Platte River. Aikins recalled in later years,

> I took my fieldglass, and from the walls of the old fort could look over the country. I told the boys that the Boulder mountains showed the best for gold diggings—gold was what we wanted. I could see that the Boulder valley was the most beautiful of all the valleys—could distinguish bands of game and Indian ponies near the foothills.

This Edenic view prompted the pioneers to ford the river and to head to the mouth of Boulder Canyon, where they pitched tents, found gold in the mountains, and established the Boulder City Town Company.

In its small details, Boulder's creation myth defies logic; one cannot see Boulder Valley from the site of Fort Saint Vrain—intervening hills obscure the view. In broad outline, though, the story checks out. Arriving at the base of the Flatirons, Thomas Aikins and his party did find gold, game, and Indian ponies. Indeed, they found Indians: Southern Arapahos, equestrian nomads of the Great Plains, a handsome tribe whose culture, existence, and fate were inextricably linked to the bison that once blackened the prairie in thunderous herds. (The Arapahos ate buffalo meat, wore buffalo robes, slept in buffalo-hide tipis, spun buffalo sinew into thread and bowstrings, fashioned spoons from buffalo horns, carved buffalo bone into knives and arrowheads, stuffed pillows with buffalo hair, carried water in buffalo-bladder canteens, and burned buffalo dung for heat.) The Indian band's leader, Chief Left Hand, approached the squatters, who had camped in territory promised to his tribe and the allied Cheyennes under the Fort Laramie Treaty of 1851.

"Go away," Left Hand reportedly told Boulder's forefathers. (The chief spoke fluent English, having been tutored as a child by his sister's husband, a white trader.) "You come to get our gold, eat our grass, burn our timber, and kill and drive off our game."

The newcomers, of course, did not go away. Rather, they were joined by a rising tide of European Americans, enticed by further gold strikes (such as George Jackson's at Idaho Springs), that soon inundated Indian lands all along the Front Range. Realizing the inevitability of the white invasion, Left Hand chose a path of peace. He befriended Jackson and other gold seekers, and he tried repeatedly to ease the growing tension between natives and new arrivals. In 1861, after a performance of *The Lady of Lyons* at Denver's Apollo Hall, Left Hand addressed the crowd in what the *Rocky Mountain News* called "a handsome speech." "He wished his white brethren would stop talking about fighting with his people," the newspaper reported, "because his people had no enmity against them whatever—but looked on them as brethren—that, as they came here hunting for gold, they would hunt after the gold, and let the Indians alone. . . ."

The white men still did not leave the natives alone. Colorado's settlers corrupted the Indians with liquor, exterminated their bison, raped their women, goaded them to make war, and slaughtered those seeking peace— including Left Hand, mortally wounded at the infamous Sand Creek Massacre in 1864. The white soldiers at Sand Creek, many hailing from Boulder, gunned down entire Arapaho and Cheyenne families and then collected scalps and other gruesome battlefield trophies; "men had cut out the private parts of females and stretched them over the saddle bows, and wore them over their hats while riding in the ranks," recalled an eyewitness to the butchery.

Despite such atrocities, the story of the West's settlement was long presented as a heroic affair, a tale of hardy pioneers and high-sitting cowboys.
Theodore Roosevelt spoke for a grateful nation when he praised Colorado's
residents—*white* residents—in a 1901 address:

> **No other task has been so important as the conquest and set-
> tlement of the West. . . . It is a record of men who greatly dared
> and greatly did; a record of wanderings wider and more dan-
> gerous than those of the Vikings; a record of endless feats of
> arms, of victory after victory in the ceaseless strife waged
> against wild man and wild nature. The winning of the West
> was the great epic feat in the history of our race.**

By the late 1960s, many Americans were rethinking this traditional,
mythic view. Through the lenses of multiculturalism, feminism, and environmentalism, and with the reemergence of a Native American consciousness, the conquest of the West now looked like a story of greedy, racist,
corrupt white males engaged in genocide and earthly plunder. Manifest
Destiny, in hindsight, was simply capitalism run amok. "[Profit motive]
was the passion at the core of the Western adventure," wrote CU historian
Patricia Limerick in her 1987 book *The Legacy of Conquest*, a watershed tome
that helped launch what academics called the New Western History. She
and like-minded colleagues chastised their forebears, the *old* western his-
torians, for writing "nationalistic history, celebrating the winners and
downgrading or ignoring the losers." Limerick added, "Defending the
integrity of the profession, one can only hope that one's ethnocentric pre-
decessors can be credibly and rapidly disowned."

The disowning of old ideas was also evident outside the ivory tower, in
Boulder and other western cities that attracted newcomers sporting progressive ideas. Author Michael Johnson labeled these people "New Westers." "You can make a game out of categorizing the differences between Old
and New Westers," Johnson has written. "Old Westers eat meat, mostly
beef. New Westers tend to avoid red meat; some are vegetarians. Old Westers are lusty conservatives. New Westers are neopuritan liberals. . . . Old
Westers believe the West was *won*. New Westers are concerned with how
it was *lost*—or is being lost or will be."

The moon rose full above a Rocky Mountain evening, cool and breezy. To the Boulder Valley's early inhabitants, the Southern Arapahos—who did not name the days or parcel time into hours and minutes—this lunar cycle was known as "split moon" or "failure-to-make-successful-hunt moon." To the white New Westers packed inside the Coal Creek Canyon Improvement Association hall, the moon shone irrelevant. Paper calendars indicated the date—Friday, the ninth of February—and digital watches the time: 7:00 P.M.

Michael Sanders stood toward the back of the hall's main room, a generic, rectangular space paneled in dark wood and illuminated by fluorescent fixtures. He looked across a sea of flannel- and jean-clad bodies. The turnout for the Division of Wildlife's mountain lion meeting was impressive. The crowd, some two hundred strong, filled every available chair, neatly arranged in parallel rows on the hardwood floor, forcing latecomers to stand against the walls, perch on windowsills, or squeeze into a small kitchen in back. Children fidgeted on parents' laps. A few cowboy hats poked above the crowd.

Michael had come to the meeting not to speak but to observe. Since much of Coal Creek Canyon lay just outside Boulder County (and therefore beyond his jurisdiction), and since the Division of Wildlife had convened this gathering, Michael had no official role, yet he felt a stake in the meeting's outcome. A year and a half into their collaboration on the Boulder Lion Search, Michael Sanders and Jim Halfpenny had recently computerized their database of cougar sightings, now exceeding 150. Michael had spent the preceding weekend entering information from the handwritten Observation Report Forms into an IBM computer at Jim's office. For each incident, Michael keyed in the date, location, time of day, and a quick, often cryptic summary of what had occurred: "lion using school sandbox for bathroom, observed in town"; "attack dog then layed on rock, woke owner who threw wood, no fear from cat finally walked away"; "at house heard dog woman came 25 ft eyed lion lion stood ground looked at her moved away slowly est much gt 75lb." Having reviewed the entirety of the reports, Michael felt more strongly than ever that the behavior of Boulder's lions was building toward a dangerous climax, and he hoped this meeting would produce solutions.

All the principal players were here. The Overmyers, publicizers of the meeting, sat prominently in the front row—long-legged Rick with his left foot propped on his right knee, Teresa with arms neatly folded across her waist. Other residents whose dogs had encountered the lion dotted the audience: Bill Pierce, owner of Lance, the Doberman; Mary Miller, still mourning Katie, her German shepherd; John and Barbara Bennett, whose black Lab, Pepper, lay in the cold ground just a few hundred yards from the hall. Game ranchers Mark Malan and Matt Miller, notorious after their recent lion hunt, hid in the crowd incognito. ("We weren't sure if we were going to be cheered or if we were going to be stoned when we walked into that meeting," says Matt. "We kept our mouth shut.") A stuffed cougar, mounted in mid-stride, its mouth in a snarl, watched from atop a table in the corner. Its artificial eyes stared impassively.

The bulk of the meeting's attendees were unrecognized by the Overmyers and wildlife authorities. Given the widespread news coverage of recent events—of both the cougar's rampage and Mark Malan's—the evening's gathering had attracted an audience from a large catchment area, from well beyond the neighborhoods immediately affected. Officials from the Division of Wildlife assumed that this unknown majority had also come out of concern for the safety of pets and children, and they opened the meeting as planned, with prepared remarks meant to educate and calm nervous parents.

Wildlife biologist Kathi Green, who had criticized Mark Malan in the preceding day's newspapers, stood at the front of the room, a Division of Wildlife patch affixed to the right shoulder of her gray sweater. A woman of old western stock, the great granddaughter of Wyoming homesteaders, Kathi was friendly with a no-nonsense edge. She gave a primer on cougars, laid out the facts. "There are probably between fifteen hundred and three thousand lions in the state of Colorado," Kathi said, pronouncing the name of the state (collar-*ad*-o) like a native. "We don't have good data on how many mountain lions there are in the Coal Creek Canyon area," she added, "but based on home ranges of lions and habitat types here, we estimate there could be thirty or more" in the foothills and canyons west of Boulder. Kathi rubbed her hands nervously as she spoke. Those seated in the back of the room stretched their necks and tilted their heads to see through the crowd.

Boulder's district wildlife manager, Kristi Coughlon, followed with tips for living in lion country. "Do not encourage deer into your yard," she urged. "Do not encourage wildlife." Kristi advised residents to remove thick vegetation around their homes to eliminate potential hiding places for lions, and she counseled parents not to let their children play outside alone. Cougars "will avoid confrontations as long as you don't surprise them," she reassured, and suggested, "Wear a bell. Make a lot of noise when you, as adults and children, come and go at those hours where the mountain lions are going to be active." (Although recommended for hikers in grizzly country, bell wearing and noisemaking have not been shown to avert lion attacks.)

"If you do encounter a lion, do not panic," Kristi continued. Talk calmly to the cat, she advised, and back away slowly. If the cougar acts menacing, "try anything that is available to you at the time. A water hose might be a great idea." And if the lion attacks, "curl up in a fetal position and protect your head and neck with your arms." (This last bit of advice is now known to be precisely wrong; playing dead with a cougar can quickly lead to *being* dead. The division later changed its recommendation to "If a lion attacks you, FIGHT BACK!")

While acknowledging the possibility of a lion attack in the Boulder area, Kristi stressed the improbability of such an incident. "There are many things that you and your children do that are as much a risk to their lives," she said. "All of you should be able to live with that small amount of risk. There is more of a chance of being struck by lightning than of your child being attacked by a lion when there is an adult present." Kathi Green added, "You do things in everyday life that are much more risky than being attacked by a mountain lion."

It quickly became apparent, however, that Kristi and Kathi had misread the crowd. Many in the audience did not fear for human safety; their concern was the well-being of the *lions*. Mark Malan's controversial hunt, portrayed by the Division of Wildlife as the reckless act of an outlaw rancher, smacked of the Old West, a place where white males waged ceaseless war "against wild man and wild nature," as Theodore Roosevelt had put it. Surely, modern Boulder was more enlightened, more compassionate, more evolved than that.

A sizable portion of the crowd shared the sensibility of a woman standing toward the back of the room, preparing to talk. As she would later explain of her presence at the meeting, "I wanted to make sure there was somebody there to speak on behalf of the lions." She had come to defend the cougars' rights.

In Boulder, in 1990, it was not unusual for people to speak about the rights of wild animals, or of trees and mountains, for that matter. Yet, in the broad sweep of Western thought, the conferring of rights to the natural world was a revolutionary, modern concept, in the words of a prominent environmental scholar, "one of the most extraordinary developments in recent intellectual history."

The early conservationists, such as Roosevelt, did not think in terms of nature's rights. To them, the protection of game and forests was a pragmatic business, an act of enlightened self-interest; careful control of hunting and logging produced, in the long run, more meat and wood for human beings. Even national parks were created, ultimately, not for the benefit of trees and animals but to provide recreation for people. Conservation was utilitarian, economically justified, human centered.

In the 1960s and 1970s, environmentalism shifted onto a new philosophical foundation with a push from Aldo Leopold, who helped change America's mind about predators. In *A Sand County Almanac*, Leopold urged a new paradigm for man's place in nature, "from conqueror of the land-community to plain member and citizen of it." He preached humility and respect in man's dealing with wild animals, plants, water, and soil. Leopold proposed a "land ethic":

> **Quit thinking about decent land-use as solely an economic problem. Examine each question in terms of what is ethically and esthetically right. . . . A thing is right when it tends to preserve the integrity, stability, and beauty of the biotic community. It is wrong when it tends otherwise.**

Modern environmentalists turned Leopold's ethic into action. Activists lobbied Congress to pass unprecedented environmental laws, such as the Endangered Species Act of 1973, which granted nonhuman organisms a near-absolute right to exist regardless of the economic costs. Radical environmental groups, such as Greenpeace ("Humankind is not the center of life on the planet," read an early statement of the group's philosophy) and Earth First! ("No Compromise in Defense of Mother Earth"), faced down enemies directly, staging sit-ins in ancient trees and blocking harpoons with their bodies.

This new environmentalism challenged religion, too. Some activists traced Western society's callous attitude toward nature to the Bible, specifically God's injunction to humankind: "Be fruitful and multiply, and fill the earth and subdue it; and have dominion over the fish of the sea and over the birds of the air and over every living thing that moves upon the earth." Ecologically aware Christians and Jews turned eastward in search of more earth-friendly faiths: Taoism, Jainism, Hinduism, Buddhism. And, ironically, many Americans embraced religious beliefs that their government had once tried to expunge, those held by the continent's original inhabitants.

A renaissance of interest in Native American spirituality, combined with a mélange of mystical beliefs termed New Age, swept much of the nation in the 1980s. White suburbanites erected backyard sweat lodges, chanted and drummed, attended powwows, staged sun dances, and undertook weekend vision quests. Some real Indians resented the newfound interest in their traditions, charging cultural theft. (Native American anger culminated in a 1993 "Declaration of War" issued by a coalition of tribes against "non-Indian 'wannabes,' hucksters, cultists, commercial profiteers and self-styled 'New Age shamans' and their followers . . . exploiting, abusing and misrepresenting [our] sacred traditions and spiritual practices. . . .") Still, many non-Indians who embraced Native American religion did so with pure motives: to cleanse the spirit, to seek life's direction, to live in harmony with Mother Earth.

The lions' self-appointed spokesperson at the Coal Creek Canyon meeting—a blond, square-jawed woman named Christie Ann Miller—was just such a convert. Though raised Lutheran, Christie Ann felt drawn to Lakota spirituality. ("One of the things that I have really learned and am trying to live is *mitakuye oyasin*—'we are all connected.' *All* life is sacred, and not just life of a crustacean or a mammal, but rocks have a life force. The dirt does. Wind does. It's all sacred.") Christie Ann had moved from Florida to Colorado in the 1970s to climb mountains, reacquaint herself with silence, and live "closer to the edge"—which she now did, with husband and daughter, in a passive-solar, modified saltbox of a house in the forested upper reaches of the canyon.

Christie Ann had perceived a negative attitude toward cougars among many Coal Creek Canyon neighbors. So, at the meeting, she argued the other side. "It's a privilege to share this habitat with mountain lions," she announced from the back of the room. "We need to learn to live with them. They were here first."

The remark struck a chord. Gary Emerson, a self-described "fanatical environmentalist" (he had been a charter member of Earth First!) who lived in the foothills south of the canyon, was pleased to hear a pro-cougar comment. "We moved up there *for* the wildlife," he explained later, "and that certainly includes the lions." Judy Lehmkuhl, a canyon resident and passionate adherent to Aldo Leopold's land ethic, also sought coexistence with the cougars and attributed recent problems to human carelessness: "What I blame is the people that don't have enough sense to bring their dogs and their dog food in at night—city people that moved up here, bring the city mores with them, and then say, 'Oh, go shoot the lions, because I want my city life in the country.'"

Other cougar defenders soon spoke up. "It concerns me that a lot of residents are in an attack mode," a woman said, prompting applause. A man in the crowd implored, "If you love your pet and you're worried about mountain lions, bring them inside." Another resident added, "You moved in on top of [the lions]. They've adapted to you. Now let's just try to adapt to living with them." The audience clapped again.

The meeting's protectionist direction stunned Rick and Teresa Overmyer. They and other worried parents and pet owners had hoped this gathering would persuade the Division of Wildlife to take stronger action against pet-killing cougars, but just the opposite was happening. The pro-lion contingent grilled wildlife officials: Why did the Division of Wildlife allow Mark Malan to chase and kill a lion—quite possibly a *harmless* lion, according to the agency's published comments—off his land? "I am the one to blame for that," biologist Kathi Green responded. "I didn't specify that permit only gave the man permission [to kill] the lion if it were on his own property. I'm fairly certain I won't be issuing any more kill permits in this area again." The division was now pledging to do *less* in the future, and yet, for all anyone knew (given the confusion about Mark Malan's hunt), the dog-eating lion remained at large.

Mary Miller, having lost her German shepherd to the cougar, was so livid she was almost trembling. "I think this cat should be killed," said Mary, her blond hair pulled back in a ponytail, her wool sweater adorned with gentle images of a steaming pie and maroon house cat. Mary challenged the lion lovers, "How would you feel in my situation?"

"It's the risk you took when you moved to the mountains," someone replied.

The Overmyers, sitting three chairs from Mary, felt the crowd didn't understand their position. "We don't want *all* lions killed," they said. "Just this one. Something needs to be done about just this one." But the distinction appeared to make no difference.

Someone near the back of the room stood up, pointed toward Rick and Teresa, and said, "If you don't like it, leave the canyon."

The Coal Creek Canyon Improvement Association hall, a place where neighbors often congregated for pancake breakfasts and square dances, now witnessed the community coming apart. "They were hollering at each other," recalls the Division of Wildlife's Kristi Coughlon. "We kinda lost control."

Kristi's colleague Tom Howard—the division's wildlife manager for the district south of Coal Creek Canyon—watched the meeting unravel from his post in the corner. "It was hot," he recalls. "I mean, there were umpteen different opinions and preferences. It was emotional. There was no one consensus in the audience." Yet the dominant opinion soon became clear.

Someone called for a show-of-hands vote. As the *Mountain Messenger* later reported, "over half of those present were strongly opposed to killing the Lions, and the majority opposed killing any lion that walks across a family's property."

By the time the meeting disbanded and chairs were cleared, this is where things stood: the Division of Wildlife, chastened by the community for its handling of the Mark Malan case, hardened its policy of leaving lions alone. Cougars loitering among homes and eating pets would not be shot. They would not be tranquilized and relocated. They would not be fitted with radio collars so that their movements could be tracked.

Michael Sanders recalls being furious. While he sympathized with the residents' pro-lion comments ("Yes, they *were* here first," he says. "You *do* have to learn to live with them"), he adamantly disagreed with the division's hands-off policy. "Every once in a while, there may be a lion that has become so habituated to eating dogs instead of its natural foodstuffs," he argues, "you have to take things in your own hands. It's kind of like moving into downtown Chicago, and you get ripped off. You moved into the burglar's territory, but he still ripped you off." Michael believed that, just as urban police don't let criminals run rampant, the Division of Wildlife needed to take responsibility for troublesome cats.

Yet the agency "did not accept accountability for this thing at all," Michael contends. "They should have been *much* more proactive. But they did nothing. They did nothing at all. Period."

It is a reasonable question to ask, and one that has often been posed: Why, given the cougar's awesome strength and superior hunting ability, does it so rarely prey on human beings?

A 1903 book on American wildlife proposed a reasonable answer:

> When the white man came the wild beasts of the wilderness found that they had a . . . dangerous enemy to face. The guns of the early settlers were not very handy or reliable weapons, but when they did go off they were capable of scattering half a handful of slugs in the most painful manner; and from that time to this there has hardly been an opportunity for the slyest cougar to attack man, woman or child without bringing down sudden and awful retribution on his head.
>
> Even now almost every farmhouse in the country has a rifle or shot-gun behind the door.
>
> I believe that if lions and tigers had been indigenous to North America, they would long ago have learned to leave man unmolested.

American pioneers, in other words, subjected the cats to a crude form of aversive conditioning. In the same way cougar hunters train their hounds to ignore deer by brutalizing dogs that chase the "wrong" quarry, settlers taught mountain lions to avoid people by punishing cats that exhibited the moxie to perceive humans as food. This Pavlovian state of affairs actually began *before* Europeans arrived in the New World. Native Americans, too—many tribes in many places—killed cougars (and, undoubtedly, injured many more) with regularity.

Boulder's early inhabitants, the Arapahos, hunted lions for hides and glory, as reported in an 1874 issue of the sportsmen's magazine *Forest and Stream*:

> A young officer of the Eighteenth United States Infantry, while stationed at Fort Reno [Wyoming], one day saw an Arrapahoe brave promenading with a lion robe thrown gracefully about his shoulders. Being blessed with a fair portion of this world's

goods, and desiring to send his friends a sample of the fauna of the country in which he then dwelt, he tried to purchase the article. But . . . [n]othing could induce the Indian to part with his treasure. He was a brave, and a chief of braves, for he had killed the beast single handed, without help from mortal man, and as he strutted about the admiring eyes of all the maidens of his tribe followed his steps, and the old men of his nation spoke well of him, and gave him a seat in their council, for though not old in years, nor a chief by birth, was he not the acknowledged leader of the young men of his tribe, and had he not met and slain, with his single hand, the monarch of the forest, the dreaded lion of the mountains? No, no; money could not buy that trophy. The "Lion Killer of the Arrapahoes" could not part with his credentials. . . .

Among the Arapahos—as well as Cheyennes, Nez Perces, Mandans, Navajos, and Pueblo cultures of the Southwest—lion hide proved a popular material for making quivers; cougars "were believed to possess spiritual power, and the use of their skins tended to impart some of this power to the user of the quiver," wrote famed anthropologist and conservationist George Bird Grinnell. The Pimas of Arizona, Coast Salish of British Columbia, and tribes of the Southeast killed lions for meat. (Cougar flesh "is very white, and remarkably like veal in taste," remarked Charles Darwin, who enjoyed a meal of puma while exploring South America on the *HMS Beagle*.) Apaches killed lions for meat *and* quivers—"Consequently, no opportunity to shoot a cougar is overlooked by the hunters," wrote a longtime ethnologist of the tribe.

Cochití men killed pumas to gain admittance to the prestigious Warriors Society. (A prospective member could, alternatively, kill and scalp a Navajo.) Blackfeet and Lakotas made saddlecloths of cougar hides. Osages used the skins for ceremonial costumes. Senecas harvested lion claws for amulets.

Native Americans killed cougars to *use* the animals, not to eradicate them as European Americans attempted later. Yet, ironically, ancient Indians may have come closer to exterminating the species than twentieth-century lion hunters ever did.

A team of cat-obsessed scientists at the National Cancer Institute recently announced a startling discovery: mountain lions apparently went extinct in North America some twelve thousand years ago. The researchers, who specialize in feline genetics, probed the DNA of 315 pumas from throughout their historic range—ocean to ocean, Canada to Argentina—and concluded that North America's modern lions descend from a small band of South American cats that wandered north and repopulated the decougared continent toward the end of the Ice Age. If true, this means North America's original cougars died off in the mass extinction that also saw the disappearance of mammoths and mastodons, camels and llamas, and a fantastic bestiary of other creatures—beavers the size of bears, sloths as large as elephants—that once roamed the continent, a mass extinction that many scientists blame on humans. (A leading theory holds that when people first migrated from Siberia to the Americas, New World animals were naïve to the dangers of the scrawny, spear-wielding, bipedal newcomers and quickly fell victim to an unrelenting frenzy of hunting, or "blitzkrieg" as some call it.) Paleoindians, therefore, may have achieved what Ben Lilly, Jay Bruce, and Uncle Jim Owens could not—the eradication of the cougar from all of North America.

Whatever the truth of events from twelve millennia ago, this much is clear: the people of modern Boulder, in their attempt to re-create a mythic past—a time when man and beast lived in harmony, before the corrupting influence of white invaders—had actually created something new. They had declared a unilateral cease-fire in the long struggle with cougars. They had withdrawn the aversive conditioning.

In the weeks following the contentious meeting, tempers rapidly subsided in Coal Creek Canyon. Mark Malan, though vilified by some, had made life easier for all. It soon became clear that he and his entourage had, in fact, slain the troublesome cat. Neighborhood dogs ceased to be killed, pugmarks no longer appeared in yards, the Overmyers' phone stopped ringing. The menace was gone. But similar problems now emerged in canyons to the north.

Culture is not the exclusive domain of humankind. Animals, too, develop local traditions that evolve and spread like a fad or fashion. In 1921, residents of Swaythling, Southampton, England, noticed titmice (small, chickadee-like birds) perching on their doorstep milk bottles and prying off the lids to drink. This annoying habit, uncommon at first, spread inexorably across the British Isles as birds learned the trick from their neighbors (or invented it themselves); within a few decades, titmice throughout England and in parts of Scotland, Wales, and Ireland had begun pilfering milk with cunning and bravado. "There are even several reports of parties of tits following the milkman's cart down the street and removing the tops from bottles in the cart whilst the milkman is delivering milk to the houses," scientists reported in 1949. Milk-bottle opening had become a British avian cultural phenomenon.

Feline cultures also exist. A cat's prey preferences are not hard-wired; they are learned, and eating habits can therefore spread through a population, parent to offspring. In one ghoulishly fascinating experiment, scientists trained female house cats (by inserting stainless-steel electrodes into their brains) to eat a food they would otherwise reject—sliced banana. The banana eaters' kittens were then allowed to watch their mothers at mealtime. Through mere observation and mimicry, the young cats developed a similar fondness for the yellow fruit, a fondness that proved so strong and persistent that, after separating from their mothers, the kittens continued to eat banana even when offered more-typical feline food—meat pellets. Such food preferences, passed from one generation to the next, can develop into a local culture. African lions exhibit marked differences in their choice of prey from region to region; some prides specialize in hunting buffalo, others wildebeest, others man. (British big-game hunter George Rushby, who in the 1940s exterminated a leonine gang in Tanzania responsible for perhaps fifteen hundred human deaths, saw "no doubt that most of these lions were born and brought up to man-eating.")

In Boulder, preying on dogs had become the cougar culture, and it was spreading like milk-drinking titmice. One week after the community meeting in Coal Creek Canyon, Michael Sanders found a troubling note posted at a county trailhead a couple of miles west of Boulder, well north of the recent troubles around Coal Creek and Magnolia. The handwritten sign, directed to hikers of the Anne U. White Trail, had been scrawled in apparent haste:

SUNDAY
2/18/90

HIKE THIS TRAIL AT
YOUR OWN RISK —
SMALL DOG WAS
ATTACKED AND EATEN
BY MOUNTAIN LION
NEAR MID-TO-END

OF THE TRAIL. MTN LION
CAME WITH-IN 10 FEET
OF THE HIKER.

Mark Malan may have eliminated one dog-eating cat, but the tradition had apparently been passed on.

With the arrival of spring, lions stalked and killed dogs at an accelerating rate in the foothills west and northwest of town. On the night of March 23, Beverly Goldthwaite waded through fog-shrouded snow below her Lefthand Canyon home to check on her goats (Nubians, raised for the show circuit); as she entered the barn, a cougar snatched one of her herding dogs, a kelpie named Winona, who issued a canine scream and then fell silent as the lion carried its living meal into the dark brush. ("I've been afraid of very few things in my life, but I was terrified," says Goldthwaite.) Three weeks later, a pair of spaniels—Buddy, of the cocker variety, and Jeremy, a Brittany—experienced a feline near-miss; Fourmile Canyon resident Peter Moore summoned the dogs from an early-morning outdoor romp when a lioness and cub suddenly appeared in the yard just vacated by the pets. (Moore mumbled, "Holy shit," as the cats stared through the window at the dogs, now inside.) Around the same time, farther up the canyon, Sydney Hope's Australian shepherd, Blue, inexplicably vanished. Two more neighborhood dogs disappeared in early May, this time explicably; Bob and Valerie Hodgetts found the carcass of their husky, Tasha, with bite marks on her neck and her belly cut open ten feet from a lion-killed deer, and Joseph Aentara discovered the remains of his Afghan–golden retriever mix, Oshy, by a small creek. ("What was left was his head, his face, his paws, and his spinal cord," says Joseph.) Meanwhile, a few miles south, in the Sugarloaf neighborhood, Doug Kremer awoke at four in the morning to a lion attacking his basset hound, Bernice, in a backyard pen; Kremer shot at the cougar, whereupon the cat dropped the dog. Bernice survived, after $421 in veterinary bills, but Kremer's bullet had apparently missed. A search in daylight revealed no blood trail or injured cougar, and a short time later the family next door rescued its chow puppy, Pooper, from a middle-of-the-night encounter with a lion, probably the same one.

As dogs fell victim, or nearly so, in successive subdivisions, the dynamics of Coal Creek Canyon were replicated. Despite the nervousness of parents and pet owners, most residents sought peaceful coexistence with the lions. And the Division of Wildlife held additional community meetings, where it dispensed advice and reassurance while reaffirming its policy not to kill, remove, or otherwise harass cougars without clear evidence of danger to human beings.

The division's Kathi Green explained the thinking behind her agency's stance. "Lion attacks on people are very, *very* rare," she told National Public Radio reporter Howard Berkes in March. "They've definitely happened, but they're *really* rare, and I don't think of it as the level of risk that is anything to get too worried about. But I do think that people who live and work in the mountains should know how to behave around wild animals and what to expect. That's the reason why we're taking the approach that we're taking. We're trying to get people educated so that everyone knows that lions are there, first of all, and—second of all—knows what to expect and how to protect their pets, and what to do around their homes, and that kind of stuff. Because removing the lions from an area like that is an impossible task. You would basically have to return to the kind of philosophy that existed in the West when the West was first settled, that all predators are bad and all predators should be killed. And that is an approach and an attitude that I don't think has public acceptance, and I also don't think it's biologically responsible."

Kathi's logic was based, however, on a false dichotomy. Other management options existed besides either exterminating all cougars or completely leaving them be. In fact, in rural parts of Colorado, the division took a targeted approach to cougar control; it routinely shot (or allowed to be shot) cats that ate livestock. By law, the division was financially liable for domestic animals harmed by cougars, and therefore the agency sought to eliminate stock killers before they cost the state too much money. The division could have taken a similar approach to Boulder's dog-killing lions, but it had little economic incentive to do so; a black Labrador is far less pricey than a Black Angus, and few pet owners seek reimbursement for a cougar-slain dog, anyway. The agency also faced a political *dis*incentive, namely the ire that any hunting would provoke among Boulder's environmentalists.

Michael Sanders perceived another crack in the division's logic. Agency personnel kept stressing the rarity of mountain lion attacks; as Kathi Green pointed out, "The history of mountain lions and people in the West clearly shows that lions attacking people is not the normal mode of operation for lions." But such statements were based on past experience. Cougar behavior appeared to be changing; history might be irrelevant in modern-day Boulder. In Africa and Asia, a big cat habitually preying on pets or livestock is considered an ominous sign and a cause for action. When predators eat domestic animals, they "educate themselves on the sights, sounds, and activity patterns of humans," and are then more likely to switch to people as prey, according to scientists who have studied the matter. An example from Hong Kong: a tiger "began by killing pigs in a village, then chased deer through the village streets, and finally grew just bold enough or hungry enough to circle round an old woman cutting grass a mile from another village. . . ." Michael Sanders feared that, in Boulder, dogs could be the "gateway drug" that turned cougars on to humans.

Frustrated, Michael vented his concerns to the *Denver Post*. "We have an urbanized mountain lion here, one accustomed to people—not to the extent that deer are habituated, but it wouldn't surprise me to find a fresh paw print in my driveway, wouldn't surprise me at all," he told reporter Claire Martin, who included the comments in a lengthy feature on the recent cougar troubles. "We know a lot about mountain lions, biologically. We know their home range size. . . . We know when they have cubs. But we don't know how many mountain lions there really are in Colorado. There's been no census of Front Range mountain lions. . . . We don't know anything about how cats react when they're in urbanized areas.

"And from Coal Creek Canyon to north Boulder County, you have development—Gold Hill, Springdale, Jamestown, Boulder Heights and others expanding everywhere—that's constantly decreasing lion habitat. Wherever you build a house, you decrease the habitat of an animal that needs to range, and you increase the chance of a human-lion encounter. I can't count how often people have told me that we're living on borrowed time. That it's only a matter of time until it's a child instead of a dog or a cat.

"Mountain lions have been known to attack children in other states. Where do we go and what do we do if a child is attacked here? How do we adapt our approach to lions then? We shouldn't have question marks in our heads about what's going on. We should know why animals behave the way they do, and it's the Colorado Division of Wildlife's responsibility to collect information on these Front Range cats, to know what they're doing at 3 A.M., at 10 A.M. and in the afternoon.

"And right now," Michael asserted, "the division is not addressing those things."

Part Three

PLAGUE

12

THE LONG SUMMER

Isabella Lucy Bird, portly English spinster and prolific travel writer of the Victorian age, journeyed to Colorado in 1873 seeking healthful air and adventure. Fresh off a trip to Hawaii, where she penned what would become the well-received *Six Months in the Sandwich Islands* (as the British then called the archipelago), Isabella spent a Rocky Mountain autumn riding horseback along the Front Range—visiting mining camps, braving blizzards, driving cattle, and flirting with a rugged, hard-drinking, one-eyed desperado named Mountain Jim. Plucky and opinionated, Isabella shared her impressions of frontier Colorado in the classic *A Lady's Life in the Rocky Mountains*. Her words often ran caustic. "Boulder is a hideous collection of frame houses on the burning plain," she wrote of the young settlement, virtually treeless in its early years. Denver she disdained as "the great braggart city." Isabella reserved her praise for the mountain scenery and for Mountain Jim. ("He has large grey-blue eyes, deeply set, with well-marked eyebrows, a handsome aquiline nose, and a very handsome mouth," she noted, apparently so blinded by Jim's beauty that she forgot momentarily that his eyes were not plural.) As for mountain *lions*, Isabella parroted the hatred common in her day, complaining of the cougars' "hideous nocturnal caterwaulings" and labeling the creatures "bloodthirsty as well as cowardly."

Five years later, after a dreary tour of Japan, Isabella Bird once again ventured to a land of big cats—the Malay Peninsula—where, between elephant rides and jungle tramps, she ate stewed tiger ("I . . . found it in flavour much like the meat of an ancient and overworked draught ox") and obtained tiger teeth and claws as souvenirs. "The Malays have many queer notions about tigers, and usually only speak of them in whispers," she wrote in an account of her Southeast Asian journey, *The Golden Chersonese and the Way Thither.* "[T]hey think that certain souls of human beings who have departed this life have taken up their abode in these beasts, and in some places, for this reason, they will not kill a tiger unless he commits some specially bad aggression. They also believe that some men are tigers by night and men by day!"

Such lycanthropic beliefs run deep among native tribes of Malaysia and Indonesia. (Lycanthropy, the magical ability of humans to take the form of ferocious animals, is best known in its European incarnation: the werewolf.) According to myths of the Malay Peninsula, Sumatra, and Java, were*tigers* lived in the forest, in remote villages where they maintained "a regular form of government" and inhabited houses "made out of human bones and thatched with the long hair of women who had been eaten." These tiger-men prowled the forests as animals and then changed into human form to infiltrate towns. "They can be distinguished only by the absence of the vertical groove in the upper lip between nose and mouth," according to a report written in the 1870s. "They will go to a house and ask for a place for the night, and when everyone is fast asleep they will, in their tiger shape, attack the sleepers and devour the hearts of the people."

It is little surprise that such frightful tales would emerge from the jungles of Malaysia and Indonesia. In the nineteenth and early twentieth centuries, the area's inhabitants suffered periodic, intense outbreaks of tiger attacks on humans. These tiger plagues, as they were known, prompted residents to keep nightly vigils and to fortify homes against the marauding beasts, but such measures often failed, forcing in some instances the abandonment of entire villages. Environmental historian Peter Boomgaard, who has studied the bloody relationship between tigers and people in the Malay world, attributes the plagues to a combination of human and natural factors. Although the sudden onset of man-eating may sometimes have been triggered by drought or disease that wiped out the tigers' usual prey, Boomgaard contends that the underlying conditions were artificially created. Specifically, as people cleared the jungle for cultivation (sugarcane, coffee, rubber, tobacco), they increased the forest edge, the ideal habitat for wild boar and deer. As these prey animals moved toward villages and prospered there, the tigers followed:

> The "birth" of man-eaters can perhaps be demonstrated most convincingly in the case of Banten [Province in West Java]. Up to 1881, man-eating occurred regularly, but in small numbers, probably due to the fact that "culture" and "nature" were rather neatly separated, with the tigers in the southern wastelands and the people in the northern districts. Then, however, European entrepreneurs started to acquire long leases for large tracts of "jungle" in the southern area, with all the land reclamation and hunting such an acquisition entailed. All of a sudden Banten was hit by a series of tiger plagues, starting in 1882 and lasting until 1888. . . . The frontier thus was created by humans, who were responsible for the creation of typical tiger areas and the multiplication of the tiger. Humans had themselves conjured up the (evil) spirit they lived in constant fear of and whom they tried to kill at the same frontier that had brought him into being.

Boulder in the 1980s, like Java a century earlier, had experienced a coming together of culture and nature—as people cleared forest for homes, planted gardens in the city, and thereby enticed deer among the dwellings. Of course, mountain lions are not nearly as deadly as tigers, and that was fortunate for Boulder, because by early June of 1990, events had reached a critical point. The city had entered a cougar plague.

A sip of water, and Lynda Walters departed on her afternoon jog. She exited the front door, turned left, and ran—into the trees and away from her textbooks and the stresses of studying. With two years of medical school behind her and board exams ten days ahead, Lynda had come to her parents' home in the Boulder foothills to cram in solitude. After a day of mind-numbing concentration, she allowed herself one indulgence, one reward: a five-o'clock run. It was a soul-cleansing ritual, a tranquil interlude in a busy life.

Lynda jogged through late-afternoon sun and ponderosa shade. The blond twenty-eight-year-old had long found solace in nature and athletics. Several years back, in what seemed another life, Lynda had ranked as one of the nation's top cross-country skiers. A three-time all-American while an undergraduate at CU, Lynda became a member of the U.S. ski team and raced against the world's best in Canada, Austria, Switzerland, Italy, Norway, Sweden, Finland. With her sights set on the 1988 Winter Games in Calgary and a place on the U.S. Olympic team all but assured, Lynda's aspirations died, suddenly and painfully, in a career-ending tumble on hard ice during a training run in New Hampshire, a crash so severe that doctors feared she might never walk again. Months of physical therapy and acupuncture restored Lynda's body to a semblance of its old self (and suggested a new goal, a career in medicine). She would never again ski competitively, but she still enjoyed her runs in the hills.

Clad in running clothes and sneakers, Lynda jogged west along Sunshine Canyon Drive—a road that, contrary to its name, did not follow a canyon but traced a high ridge, providing a view from foothills to plains. To Lynda's right, the terrain dropped into an undeveloped, forested gorge that met the county's Anne U. White Trail. To her left lay Fourmile and Boulder Canyons, and above them the communities of Magnolia and Sugarloaf. Lynda knew this landscape well, had grown up a tomboy in these mountains, had traipsed the drainages and mining roads with siblings and friends. Back then, in the 1960s and 1970s, no one spoke of lions.

Now Lynda was jogging through what had quickly become lion territory, a land of cat-mangled dogs, and she knew it. Lynda had followed the controversy over Mark Malan's cougar hunt in February. She had sided with his critics. ("Oh, great," she told her mother at the time. "It's like the old view of Indians—the only good Indian is a dead Indian. People are just gonna start shooting lions.") In April, she had read the *Denver Post* article featuring Michael Sanders's warning that attacks on dogs could presage the mauling of a human. (She dismissed any suggestion of risk to her personal safety; Lynda's encounters with wild animals had always been benign.) Also in April, Lynda's parents had seen a lion, their first, at ten past seven on a Monday morning while motoring down Sunshine Canyon Drive; the cat loped in front of their pickup truck near the intersection with Poorman Road while they cried, "Hey! Isn't that *neat?*" (Lynda's father, Bill, reported the sighting to Jim Halfpenny and Michael Sanders, who recorded the

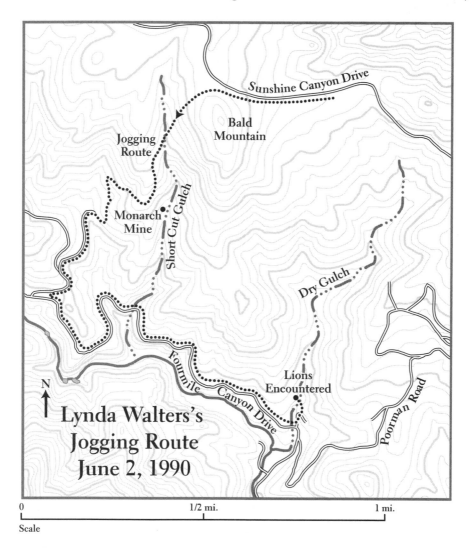

Lynda Walters's
Jogging Route
June 2, 1990

observation in their Lion Search database as incident number 315.) Lynda envied her parents. "I wish *I* could see one," she had said.

After jogging for a quarter mile, Lynda neared the base of Bald Mountain, a small, mostly treeless summit within a Boulder County park. She passed a tumbledown corral and loading chute, rusting and splintered, a relic from the days when the land was ranched. The property had since been returned to nature; deer replaced cows in the high meadow. Lynda contoured around Bald Mountain and veered southward, away from the road, down a gentle slope with a view of the high Rockies beyond. This was her regular shortcut—called, appropriately, Short Cut Gulch—and constituted the western leg of her counterclockwise jogging loop. Lynda's calves brushed through mountain muhly, a native grass, mixed with cheatgrass, a Eurasian weed; the stalks bowed deeply, their tops heavy with seed. Penstemon, cinquefoil, phlox, and asters added color to the carpet of green. Wild herbs added aroma. (Celestial Seasonings founder Mo Siegel, in his early days, harvested wild oregano, parsley, and raspberry leaves not far from this area of the Boulder foothills.)

Lynda followed an old mining road that had since grown over, its former path evident only by a ribbon of artificial flatness in the hilly topography. She soon connected up with a private gravel road that descended in sharp switchbacks past mountain residences, including the glass-walled home where, a year and a half earlier, Sondra Donovan had watched a lion haul off a freshly killed deer on a crystalline winter's morning. Lynda passed within a hundred yards of the Monarch Mine, the "Hilton of mountain lion dens" that Michael and Jim had discovered to be the cat's temporary lair.

As Lynda approached the asphalt of Fourmile Canyon Drive, she turned left again, continuing her loop toward home. She stayed off the blacktop but followed the sinuous road, paralleling the shoulder along a path through the pines. Shadows lengthened as the sun sank toward the western mountains. Lynda concentrated on her breathing.

She soon arrived at a row of mailboxes where Poorman Road split off from Fourmile Canyon and rose into a rural subdivision. This intersection marked the final turn in her jog, the point where she began the ascent back to her parents' house. Lynda once again veered from the pavement and angled into the woods, climbing a small rise and then descending into a ravine known, misleadingly at this time of year, as Dry Gulch. A tiny creek flowed in the bottom. The trickle supported a minor oasis, a riot of willow and grasses and wildflowers in a landscape otherwise dominated by prickly pear and yucca.

Lynda ran toward the creek, down a loose slope of gravel and pine needles. A jagged cliff of lichen-encrusted granite emerged from the earth to her right. As she was about to step into the lush vegetation at the bottom of the gulch, Lynda saw what she'd been hoping to see.

A lion stood on the opposite side of the creek, not fifteen feet away. Lynda stopped. *Cool!* she said to herself, astonished by the cat's size and proximity.

The lithe beast stared back, golden eyes and erect ears aimed at the woman. Lynda did not particularly like cats (she had grown up with dogs), and the lion's gaze unnerved her. She felt disturbingly like a mouse before a house cat. The lion tensed its body and flicked its tail. It crouched, belly against ground.

In Lynda's past encounters with wildlife (coyotes, bears), the animals had always fled when they'd seen her, but this creature displayed no fear. Lynda shouted "Hyaaa!" and threw her arms skyward to assume a formidable air. The lion did not budge. Lynda extended her right hand toward the rocky slope behind her, fetched a fist-sized chunk of granite, and hurled it at the cougar's feet. The lion hissed and crept closer.

As Lynda stood, perplexed by the cat's recalcitrance, her peripheral vision detected movement ninety degrees to the right. She turned and saw, on the low granite cliff that defined the edge of Dry Gulch, a second cougar, crouched. It circled slowly behind her. Panic descended.

Lynda attempted an escape. She dove for the embankment behind her and scrambled upslope, animal-like, on all fours. She threw a second rock at the lion by the creek, this time striking its shoulder; the jolt interrupted the cat's advance, but the other lion now pursued. Lynda continued her fast retreat, tossing cobbles and branches behind her to dissuade the cats from following. She reached a ponderosa at the top of the slope and, without conscious thought, began to climb. She moved instinctively.

Lynda raised herself into the tree more than a human's height off the ground, her bare legs—flesh in color and substance—evident against russet bark and olive needles. She clutched overhead limbs, squatted on her left leg, and momentarily rested her right foot on a lower branch. While in this position, hunched in the pine's sharp embrace, Lynda felt a sudden pain in her right calf. She looked down.

One of the lions had followed her into the tree. Its whiskered face stared up, an arm's length away, as it hugged the trunk with one front paw and gripped the branch beside Lynda's right foot with the other. Lynda immediately saw what had caused the pain. Three claw marks traced parallel lines down her leg and dripped crimson toward her white sock. *This is it*, Lynda thought. *I'm going to die.*

Nearly twenty years earlier, in 1971, a woman in Southern California was savagely beaten and raped despite having a black belt in karate. A friend, martial arts instructor Matt Thomas, recognized a fundamental flaw in self-defense programs at the time; they taught women how to spar in the classroom, not how to fight in the street. From that realization, Thomas developed a new type of training he called Model Mugging, in which female students practiced fending off a male assailant (wearing a helmet and fifty pounds of protective gear) by jabbing his eyes, kneeing his groin, stomping his feet. The training emphasized the strength in a woman's legs and, by forcing students to practice the techniques over and over, eroded their inhibitions and seared the lessons into muscle memory. Lynda Walters had taken such a course a few years back. Now, faced with an attacker of an unanticipated sort, she modified her training to fit the circumstances. She raised her left leg and stomped on the lion's head. The cat tumbled to the ground.

Lynda scanned the terrain for the other lion but couldn't find it. This heightened her anxiety; she feared that the invisible cat would leap out of nowhere and alight on her back. Lynda began climbing again, hoping that altitude would confer safety. She pulled herself up through a maze of branches and needles, which grew thicker the higher she went. She contorted her body and squeezed through the tangle. When she was halfway to the top, the tree shook as if struck by a sudden wind. The second lion had now jumped onto the trunk and was creeping upward. Lynda scrambled higher and faster while the cat climbed with slow precision, picking its way through the limbs, its eyes focused on the woman above.

Nearing the end of the line, the top of the tree, Lynda changed tactics. She snapped a dead limb from the trunk and broke off its smaller branches, fashioning a primitive spear, then thrust the weapon downward with both hands as if harpooning the cat. "Fuck you!" she screamed as she jabbed her tormentor. The cat hissed and batted the stick with its paws. "Fuck you!" she yelled again. The lion backed down.

With both cats now at the base of the tree, and with time to think, Lynda's terror intensified. From her perch twenty-five feet up a ponderosa pine on the edge of a fifty-foot cliff, with Dry Gulch in evening shadow, Lynda watched one lion recline while the other paced, occasionally nuzzling its partner. She guessed the cats were waiting for nightfall, at which time they would climb the tree and devour her. Actually, she was sure this was their plan. The cats eyed her from below. The more restless of the pair sauntered back to her tree and crouched as if preparing to leap into the branches. Lynda banged her stick against the trunk and screamed until the animal backed away and returned to its partner. The cats were patient. They were in no rush.

Lynda could hear civilization—cars snaking through Fourmile Canyon, children playing in a nearby subdivision, a dog barking. People were outside enjoying a Saturday evening on the cusp of summer. The preceding weekend, the city had launched its season of festivities with the twelfth running of the Bolder Boulder and the third annual Boulder Creek Rubber Duck Race. (The Memorial Day weekend celebrations had also included a motley People's Parade that featured a ten-foot Earth balloon meant to promote environmental awareness; "The balloon tipped over several times," reported the *Daily Camera*, "hitting a marcher dressed as Mother Earth.") As Lynda contemplated her death and clutched her tree, Boulderites inner-tubed on the creek. They walked the Pearl Street Mall. They picnicked at Chautauqua Park in advance of a Shawn Colvin concert.

Treetop Lynda felt utterly alone. Her screams ("Help! Somebody help me!") echoed in Dry Gulch. The lions paced. The sun descended. Nobody came.

Swallows flitted in silhouette against the evening sky; the fork-tailed birds folded their wings, darted forward, then abruptly changed direction as they chased insects above the forest canopy. In the forest floor, ant lions—pincer-headed larvae of the insect family *Myrmeleontidae*—hid beneath self-constructed conical pits in the sandy soil and waited for their formic prey to fall in and be eaten. Lynda had become an intimate participant in nature's food chain, and despite her position in the tree, she was not at the top. A mere four months earlier and six miles away, a lion in a ponderosa had stared down at two armed men preparing to end its life. Now Lynda was the treed quarry, the lions the hunters.

Lynda imagined her death, painful and prolonged, her body shredded by claws and teeth. Her medical school board exams, the source of so much stress a mere hour ago, seemed distant, trivial. Lynda studied the cats. One loomed slightly larger than the other, but both appeared full-grown; neither exhibited the spots of kittenhood. The lions' relationship was unclear. The cats may have been mates, normally solitary adults that had partnered temporarily to procreate. They may have been adolescent siblings traveling together, as some do, in advance of striking out on their own. Perhaps the pair comprised a lioness and her almost grown cub.

Whatever their relationship, the cougars' background was more certain.

The lions had likely resided in the Boulder area for much, if not all, of their lives. Like Boulder, they existed in the penumbra between civilization and nature, neither wild nor tame, their behavior modified by interactions with people and people's things. The animals were, in a sense, part cat and part human—the cougar equivalent of Sumatra's dreaded weretigers.

Fortunately for Lynda, these cougars had not lost their taste for game meat. A gentle rustling from across Dry Gulch caught the lions' attention. They snapped their heads toward the opposite hill where a deer picked its way through the forest. In an instant, the cats vanished from the base of the ponderosa as they silently pursued new prey.

Lynda hesitated momentarily, then took her chances. She scrambled down the trunk and fled upslope, still clutching her spear, not daring to look back.

While Lynda Walters evaded feline consumption, Michael Sanders vacationed in Mexico. He, too, was engaged in a game of hunter and hunted, although he was playing on the opposite team and for less serious stakes. Michael was enjoying the peculiarly modern sport of catch-and-release fishing, hooking marlins off the coast of Baja then liberating them back into the Pacific's warm belly.

Michael returned to Boulder to find a changed, electrified atmosphere. Though Lynda Walters had survived her encounter, and though her injuries proved minor, the lions had crossed an invisible line. Killing dogs was one thing, stalking humans quite another. Even liberal Boulder had reached its limit. News of Lynda's ordeal prompted frantic phone calls to county commissioners and state officials. The politics of lions had shifted.

Turmoil struck the Division of Wildlife. "[Boulder residents] are up in arms about the mountain lion situation," noted an internal memo, which reported that "the Governor [is] also receiving calls" and cautioned that matters were "on the verge of exploding in our faces." "We damn well better get on top of this," division director Perry Olson told his troops. One of his underlings, Jerry Apker—an eight-year agency veteran who had recently been charged with overseeing Front Range wildlife management from Boulder to Idaho Springs—agreed that urban lion issues had not received adequate attention. "Well, *this* will finally get us off our asses," Jerry told his wife, in private.

In public, the division maintained its veneer of calm and control. Boulder District Wildlife Manager Kristi Coughlon minimized the gravity of Lynda Walters's experience. "This I would not consider in any way an attack," Kristi told the *Rocky Mountain News*. "This was an encounter. If those lions had wanted to attack her, they had ample opportunity to do so." (Wildlife officials made similar comments to other local papers.) The point was not entirely without merit—if the lions had sought to eat Lynda, they should have struck with their teeth, not swatted her with a paw—but the statements smacked of dissembling. By any commonsense definition, Lynda had been attacked; a lion had pursued her and drawn blood.

"What a piece of government-ese and denial" was Jim Halfpenny's reaction to the division's spin control. As he saw it, what had happened to Lynda Walters "was verification of what we'd been warning people about." Boulder's lions really *were* habituating to humans and growing more dangerous, a fact that seemed plain enough to journalists at the *Daily Camera*. "The bizarre incident may foretell a new era in the uneasy coexistence of human and beast in this area," the paper editorialized the week after Lynda's frightening experience. "The urban deer that charm some people and enrage others have become more and more fearless over the years, and so may the mountain lions that feed on them." Even the Division of Wildlife could no longer deny the change in lion behavior. "I think the lions are becoming bolder," Kristi Coughlon acknowledged to a reporter. "[B]ut we don't know how to stop it. There's never been an 'urban cougar' study and we don't know what to expect from lions that are habituated and lose their fear of humans."

Michael Sanders saw a political opening. With public concern at an all-time high and the division admitting ignorance, he pressed again for a radio-collar study of urban lions. This time, instead of going directly to the state, he lobbied Boulder County's commissioners. "We need to look at adaptability of these cats and how they're adapting to urbanization," Michael testified at a July hearing. He spoke passionately from the podium, arms waving, his words amplified by a microphone and filtered through his Tennessee upbringing. The commissioners hardly needed convincing; a quick, unanimous vote resulted in a polite, but urgent, letter to the state: "As you are aware, there is growing public concern in Boulder County over the increase in encounters between mountain lions and humans. . . . Therefore, the Boulder County Board of Commissioners is requesting that the Division of Wildlife initiate a comprehensive study of the mountain lion population along the front range where urbanization is likely to give rise to conflicts between humans and mountain lions."

The plan backfired. Boulder County's request, intended as an olive branch—an offer to work together—was perceived by the division as an exercise in blame shifting, an attempt by the community to shirk responsibility for its own mess. "Boulder had pretty much created their problem, with the vast amount of open space they had and the fact that it made managing the numbers of deer so problematic that we couldn't do a thing with it," recalls former division director Olson. "All the hunting was cut off; the deer numbers went up through the roof. Boulder County's general attitude was, 'Screw management. We don't care about that. We'll just protect everything.' And the same people that are preaching that kind of bullshit are sitting around and whining, then, when the consequences don't turn out exactly like they wanted them to." Some division officials balked at the idea of spending the agency's funds, collected from hunting licenses, to help a community that prohibited hunting. Others held a personal grudge against Michael Sanders; they resented his criticism of the agency in the *Denver Post* and were in no mood to bow to his public pressure. "The Division shares your concern about the growing problem of lion-human interactions," the agency wrote in its official reply to Boulder County, "but we do not plan to initiate another lion study in the near future." Michael sat slack-jawed when he read the response.

Given political realities, the division could not do *nothing*, however. The agency announced plans for a meeting the following spring—a follow-up to the 1988 mountain lion workshop in Arizona—where it would gather cougar experts from across North America to discuss the surge in human-lion interactions and to brainstorm solutions. (Jim Halfpenny saw this as a cop-out, a stalling tactic intended to delay any decisions on how to manage urban lions.) And the division boosted its public relations; it sent brochures ("The Facts About Mountain Lions") and reassuring letters to thousands of foothills homes. "At present there is little risk to your safety," wildlife officials insisted in the mass mailing, and then added—to placate concerned parents—that if a lion ever *did* become a "significant threat" (a term left undefined), the division would endeavor to "remove such threat," presumably by killing the animal. "We believe that you should be able to enjoy your home and community with a sense of security," the agency vowed.

Meanwhile, as local politicians jousted with state officials, as humans bickered over who caused the lion problem and how to solve it, the cats continued to take liberties, going places and interacting with people in unprecedented ways.

Five weeks post–Lynda Walters, late one night in early July, a lion prowled the parking lot of Boulder Community Hospital, a four-story edifice of blond brick on busy North Broadway downtown, and jumped into an enclosed courtyard. In daylight, nurses and orderlies lunched on the patio at umbrella-shaded metal tables; now, in darkness, the furniture sat empty, except for one man—Bob Bachant, third-shift computer operator—slumped in a plastic chair beside an upright ashtray. With an unfiltered Camel perched on his lips, Bob was savoring the mix of nicotine and hot smoke when his eyes detected a shadowy figure sauntering across the concrete a table-width away. *What a beautiful dog*, he thought. Then he saw the creature's enormous tail. Bob jumped to his feet and thrust a chair at the cat, lion-tamer style. The cougar bared its teeth and hissed. Bob yanked open the door to the cafeteria and retreated inside while the lion hurdled an eight-foot wall toward Broadway. Two large cubs followed.

The following weekend—Saturday, July 14, 6:00 A.M.—Peter Ramig awoke to a growl outside his bedroom in Pine Brook Hills, a picturesque subdivision of modern homes on the first high ridge west of north Boulder. Peter ran downstairs, video camera in hand, to film two large lions on the adjacent grass- and yucca-covered hillside. As he stepped onto his redwood deck, he narrated into the recorder, "Okay, now I'm outside, and they've spotted me." The cats, not fifty human paces away, stiffened their tails and raised their ears. They locked their eyes on Peter—lanky and middle-aged, clad only in undershorts—who suddenly realized his vulnerability and trembled in their glare. The frightening moment passed when the cats resumed their forward motion. One lion walked uphill and out of sight while the other strolled beneath a maple just off the deck, reclined, and calmly observed Peter, soon joined by his eleven-year-old daughter and two neighbors. The cat remained for half an hour, yawning and preening, watching the gaggle of humans with interest and ease, as if taking in a movie.

Another cougar loitered in similar fashion outside Richard Partridge's home on the southern slope of Boulder Canyon, uphill from Happy Times and below Magnolia, toward the end of July. The cat, a ninety-pound, six-foot male, had hung around for almost twenty-four hours—perched on the picnic table, lounging in the grass, sitting by the garden—when, at eight-fifteen on a Wednesday evening, four-year-old Ryan needed to visit the out-house. (The Partridge home, though just fifteen minutes from downtown Boulder, had no running water and was disconnected from public utilities; the dwelling, a log cabin on an old mining claim in dense forest, seemed to exist back in time.) The outhouse, of the sort one might find at a con-struction site, fashioned from pistachio-green plastic, stood about forty feet from the front door, at the edge of the trees. Richard believed that the lion had now left—an hour earlier, he had pelted the animal with stones to scare it off—but he took no chances; he tucked his revolver in the waist of his Levi's and escorted his son to the toilet. As the pair neared the outhouse, young Ryan, freckled and ponytailed, said, "There he is." The cougar peered from behind a boulder twelve feet ahead. Slowly and deliberately, the tall man and his skinny son reversed direction, Ryan clutching his father's back pocket. Each step backward prompted the lion to step for-ward, until the large cat emerged from hiding and appeared ready to jump. Richard, a self-described lover of nature and its creatures, saw no alterna-tive; he raised his arm, squeezed his finger, and propelled a bullet through the lion's teeth and into its brain, knocking the cat backward and causing it to tumble downhill. Walking over to the twitching cougar, Richard shot twice more and then sat beside the beast, placed his hand on its warm body, and sobbed. (Wildlife officials did not press charges against Richard Partridge; they deemed the killing justified.)

Michael Sanders followed the events of July with trepidation and frus-tration. Having repeatedly warned the public, and having butted heads with the Division of Wildlife too many times, he saw little more he could do about the growing clash between people and cougars. Soon the spread-ing plague grew personal. It landed on his street.

As midnight approached on August 23, a warm Thursday evening, University Hill—Boulder's student-filled neighborhood near the CU campus—was frenetic. The start of the fall semester was less than a week away, and along Thirteenth Street, the heart of the Hill, young people in T-shirts and shorts spilled out of bars and pizza parlors. Old friends greeted one another. Couples embraced. On front porches and rear patios, students gathered in drunken clumps for impromptu parties. The bass from com-peting stereo systems thumped in the late-summer air.

Six blocks away, in a slightly quieter area, Michael Sanders lay asleep in his low-ceilinged basement apartment decorated with wildlife photographs and framed animal scat. The phone rang. Michael lifted the receiver and listened to a voice in the dark. "There is a mountain lion sighted in your neighborhood," said the caller, a dispatcher from Boulder's emergency communications center who knew of Michael's obsession with cougars. The lion had been reported amid the revelry on Thirteenth Street; someone had spotted the cat in the shadows, watching people. *I hope nobody's down*, thought Michael as he hung up the phone and quickly dressed to go outside, throwing canvas shorts over his boxers and slipping on a pair of Tevas. Michael feared that his nightmare scenario was about to be realized, that a lion would jump an inebriated human. (The concern was reasonable; African lions and leopards have been known to target drunks as easy prey.)

The police were similarly worried. Patrol Sergeant Jim Hughes, afraid that some intoxicated student would "get the idea to go pet the kitty," ordered half a dozen officers to the Hill to find the cat and to prevent it from tangling with people. The lion had been reported near the Flatirons Theatre, at the corner of Thirteenth and College, shortly after the last screening of the *The Exorcist III*. (A serial killer, apparently resurrected after his execution years earlier, stalks the streets of Georgetown, mutilating his victims by decapitating them, draining their blood, and removing their vital organs. George C. Scott stars.) Officer Dave Allen—tall and muscular, with taut cheeks that folded back in pleats when he smiled—crept behind the movie theater to an alley lined by dumpsters and parked cars. A lone streetlight cast long shadows. The pavement, coated with broken glass, sparkled.

Officer Allen had been skeptical of the reported lion sighting, had thought the animal would turn out to be a golden retriever, but as he scanned the alley he saw a large, long-tailed cat emerge from shadow, lope across pavement, and sink back into darkness. The lion was ambling toward College Townhouses, a three-story brick apartment complex surrounding a pool and concrete patio. Officer Allen could hear parties in the courtyard. He and a partner ran to the pool and yelled to the assembled students, "Stay in your apartments. We've got a mountain lion loose." The partygoers, apparently more interested in beer than a wild carnivore, calmly complied.

Other officers, in black-and-white cruisers and on foot, attempted to follow the cat as best they could, glimpsing it as it crossed streets and alleys. The lion walked from Thirteenth to Twelfth, Twelfth to Eleventh, Eleventh to Tenth, past fraternities and a youth hostel. Meanwhile, Michael Sanders headed down Tenth Street, past onlookers drawn by the flashing lights and the squawk of emergency radios. Up ahead, the lion crossed Tenth and snuck behind a two-story Tudor Revival on the west side of the street, but Michael could go no farther to investigate; police had cordoned off the block. Frustrated, he stood and watched from a distance, angered not so much by his inability to enter the scene as by the whole chain of events that had led a lion to prowl University Hill on a crowded night.

The police cautiously followed the lion into the backyard, where an unkempt lawn bordered a concrete driveway. Rotting fruit from three apple trees covered the ground. The air smelled of cider. Officers found the cougar in a Chinese elm in the northwest corner of the lot, beside a dark, unpaved alley. It lounged on a horizontal limb about ten feet up, eyes shining in the glare of flashlights, its fat, droopy, pendulous tail swinging. The police had hoped the cat would walk back to the foothills on its own, but now that the animal had treed itself, they changed plans. They decided to remove the lion with force.

Presently, a red-haired man arrived who resembled Robert Redford in *Out of Africa*, donning the attire of a big-game hunter: heavy boots, forest green shorts, gray shirt with epaulets. He carried a long-barreled weapon, a meter-long blowpipe stuck on the end of a turquoise-and-orange plastic, CO_2-powered pistol, a dart gun.

Clay Leeper, animal control officer, frequently received calls from the police to tranquilize wayward and injured wildlife, deer mostly. He had never sedated a lion, and he wasn't sure how much drug to use. Too little, and the cougar might wake up prematurely, a dangerous situation. Too much, and he could kill the cat. Yet Clay had little time to ponder. With the police anxious that the cougar might escape at any moment, he immediately prepared his darts.

Assembling tranquilizer darts is a complex task requiring speed, precision, and care, because an accidental needle stick can land one in the hospital. (Clay once received an inadvertent canine distemper shot in the thigh.) Sitting in the sliding door of his van, Clay opened a black tackle box and removed a five-inch syringe made of white, translucent plastic. This syringe, the body of the dart, contained two chambers back-to-back. Clay carefully filled the front chamber with three cc's of tranquilizer (a mixture of two powerful anesthetics), then attached a stainless-steel needle that, instead of having one hole in its tip, had two in its sides. He slipped a tiny silicone sleeve over the needle to block the holes and keep the tranquilizer from leaking out, then filled the syringe's rear chamber with pressurized air. If all went as planned, when the dart hit the lion, the needle would penetrate its hide, the silicone sleeve would slide up the needle and expose the holes, and the pressurized rear chamber would force the drugs from the front chamber into the lion's body. Clay completed the dart by attaching a tailpiece made of bright red yarn that would help propel the dart from his gun and stabilize it in flight. Then he prepared a second dart, just in case. ("I figured I'd miss one," he says.)

With darts ready, Clay entered the backyard and approached the Chinese elm while two cops flanked him for protection. Glen McCarthy, tall and hefty, stood to the right with a .45-caliber Smith & Wesson revolver trained on the cat; Officer Dave Allen stood to the left, a twelve-gauge Remington shotgun in his hands. The three men advanced in unison. The cat observed calmly.

About thirty feet from the lion, the trio halted. Clay sat among the rotten apples and planted his feet flat on the ground, knees raised to brace his shot. He held the gun to his right eye and aimed for the lion's upper thigh, a large mass of muscle that would quickly absorb the drugs. Cassiopeia hung above the cat, a twinkling W in the sky.

As Clay pulled the trigger, the burst of CO_2 sounded a muffled *thup*. The cat jerked and scrambled a few feet higher in the tree. The needle had struck, but Clay wasn't sure whether the drug had been delivered; sometimes a dart will depressurize before injecting its dose of tranquilizer. He quickly removed the blowpipe from the pistol, loaded the second dart, reassembled the gun, aimed, and fired again. The cat flinched. Growing woozy and losing its grip, it leapt from the tree and vanished into the dark alley.

On the ground, the cat was high. One of the tranquilizers flowing through its bloodstream—ketamine, a veterinary anesthetic—is a hallucinogen, with psychedelic effects so vivid that it has gained an ardent following among human drug users who routinely burglarize animal hospitals to steal supplies. Ketamine goes by various street names: K, Vitamin K,

Special K, Cat Valium. Injected, snorted, or smoked, it produces an intense high that users call K-land or, in its ultimate incarnation, the K-hole.

As the mountain lion staggered down the alley past a broken-down Porsche, then headed west between two houses, it was wandering through K-land, a fantastic world of disorientation and color. Ketamine disrupts impulses between the body and brain. Pain dulls. Coordinated movement proves difficult. ("My legs turn to rubber," comments one ketamine user. "It's as if I'm walking across the room in a pair of platform shoes made of marshmallows.") Time slows, and spatial relations warp. A sapling may seem a towering redwood, a few steps a marathon. Self-identity dissolves; a user might believe himself a robot, a chair, a flowing liquid, a rhythm. Some imagine themselves characters in a TV sitcom.

The lion, mind-altered, stumbled across Lincoln Place, a shady street of bungalows lined by maples, locusts, and ashes. It crawled up a driveway, past a discarded Coca-Cola can and beside a blue-gray Toyota Land Cruiser. It lurched forward a few more steps, toward a chain-link fence by a stucco garage. Then it fell into the K-hole, collapsing into a misshapen heap: flat on its stomach, hind legs spread-eagle, upper body twisted leftward, front legs outstretched. Its right cheek rested on concrete, a cigarette butt in front of its nose.

As the police approached, the cat lay motionless, its drug-induced sleep soothed by chirping crickets blended with the sound of distant parties, the music of man and nature intertwined, a modern Boulder lullaby.

"Everything was done perfectly," Michael Sanders commented later, when he learned the complete story of the cougar's capture and subsequent release. Though he had not been involved (and had, in fact, returned to bed before the incident was over), he was heartened by the episode's resolution.

Clay Leeper, after hauling away the sedated cat in his van, transferred his sleeping captive to the Division of Wildlife in a middle-of-the-night hand-off. Tom Howard, district wildlife manager for the area just south of Boulder, took custody, first examining the lion (it was a female, seventy-five pounds, about two years old, apparently healthy), then affixing to its ear a purple plastic tag with the number ten printed in black numerals. Placing the lion in a pet carrier secured by bungee cord to the bed of his pickup, Tom transported the lion fifteen miles south of Boulder to a restricted gravel road that provided access to a uranium mine. He unlocked the gate and drove into a dark, desolate canyon, where he hefted the groggy cat from its cage and deposited it near a creek. Tom remained for some time, observing the cat ("baby-sitting," as he put it), ensuring that it awoke in good health. When, around 4:00 A.M., the cougar looked up and snarled, Tom said to himself, *Alright. She's gonna be okay. I'm out of here.* Just a few hours after roaming downtown, the cat was back in the mountains, on its own.

"I believe that's the proper way of dealing with animals like that," said Michael Sanders. "They found the cat, they tranquilized it, they took health conditions of it, they ear-tagged it, they took it far away, and they let it go." He hoped the unpleasant experience of being chased, drugged, and moved would provide a dose of aversive conditioning, dissuading the cat from mingling with people again. And if the cougar were to resume its troublesome behavior—a definite possibility, since translocated animals often return to the scene of the crime—its ear tag would identify the cat as a repeat offender, one requiring further, perhaps lethal, control. Michael lamented, "It's kind of a shame we didn't do that with the Coal Creek Canyon lion" or the Boulder area's other dog-eating, people-stalking cougars.

By the end of summer, Boulder's cougar problems gradually and mysteriously eased. Through the fall of 1990, though the occasional lion was still glimpsed in a driveway, the occasional puppy attacked, the occasional farm animal eaten (in September a llama, in November a goat), interactions between humans and cats seemed less frequent, less threatening. It was as if Boulder's troublemaking lions—some of them, at least—had moved on. They had.

At around two years of age, male cougars (and some females) depart their childhood homes to establish adult territories in which to live and breed. These dispersing lions, termed "transients," become nomads, searching the land for open range and challenging older, established lions for territory. Boulder's new generation of urban lions, those born in summer 1988, had reached this stage of life by autumn 1990. The two-year-old cat tranquilized on University Hill and released in the foothills with a purple tag on its ear was identified several months later in Manitou Springs, eighty miles south of Boulder.

Dispersing cougars may travel tremendous distances, more than three hundred miles in extreme cases, but the cats generally remain much closer to their birth homes, often as near as twenty miles, which is the distance—along a straight line, as a cougar would walk it—between Boulder and Idaho Springs.

13

FINAL RUN

Pen in hand, Scott Lancaster inscribed another entry in his book of life. **Hrs. sleeping:** *4–5.* **Weight:** *124.* **Pulse/Waking:** 55. **Rising:** *62.* **Diff.:** *7.* In the autumn of 1990, at age eighteen, this was how Scott measured his days—with numbers that described his bodily functions and words that summarized his physical activity. "Worked on technique," he wrote below the day's vital statistics in his spiral-bound *Cyclist's Training Diary.* "Lost a lot of aerobic fitness from strength and power training on bike. Will regain later in season with new program."

The enthusiastic child who had raced his last Red Zinger Mini Classic in Boulder in July 1988 was now a young man, a senior at Clear Creek High School in Idaho Springs, bespectacled and athletically lean. (At New Shanghai, the Chinese restaurant where Scott earned money as a busboy, coworkers called him Slim.) Scott sat at his desk, beside his waterbed, in his dark, cavelike room, surrounded by bicycles and related paraphernalia—inner tubes, chains, wrenches, wheels, cycling books, medals. The room resembled a bicycle shop. It smelled of grease.

Scott had given his life to cycling; his goal was to become a professional racer. Scott's parents had recently bought their son a world-class road bike, custom-made by accomplished Colorado cyclist and frame builder Rich Gängl. (Scott had been fitted for the bicycle as if for a suit. Among the measurements taken: inseam, arm length, shoulder width, height.) The lightweight steel frame, bicolored per Scott's request, gleamed mariner blue at the joints grading to pearl in between. The lugs, metal sleeves that held the tubes together, were adorned with the insignia of Gängl Custom Cycles—small cut-out hearts.

Several months earlier, in July, Scott had ridden his Gängl in one of Colorado's most grueling competitions, a race that ascended the highest paved road in the United States. Starting by the high school in Idaho Springs at an elevation of 7,540 feet, Scott and more than four hundred other riders climbed almost 7,000 feet higher to the top of Mount Evans. The route, twenty-eight miles of blacktop, traversed conifer forests, skirted the lips of granite cliffs, and emerged onto alpine tundra where the riders encountered fierce winds, snow, scant oxygen, and hoofed spectators. (Mountain goats, a seemingly natural sight among the rocky crags of Mount Evans, were actually non-native to Colorado; they had been artificially introduced by the Division of Wildlife.) Olympic gold medalist Alexi Grewal took the top prize, reaching the summit in a record time of one hour forty-six minutes twenty-nine seconds. Scott's time, more than two hours twenty-four minutes, placed him sixteenth out of twenty-five competitors in his age group. Not bad, but not nearly good enough. Scott needed more power, acceleration, endurance. He enlisted the help of a professional, a coach for the U.S. cycling team, who started him on a strenuous training regimen and encouraged him to track his progress in a diary.

Hrs. sleeping: *4–5*. **Weight:** *123*. **Pulse/Waking:** *53*. **Rising:** *61*. **Diff:** *8*. "Need to strengthen my <u>legs, real weak</u>."

In the fall of 1990, Scott trained constantly—before school, after school, during school. He took long rides in the mountains, practiced short sprints to the point of exhaustion, lifted weights, jogged.

Hrs. sleeping: *4–5*. **Weight:** *123*. **Pulse/Waking:** *53*. **Rising:** *59*. **Diff.:** *6*. "Felt good running. . . . Might have to quit ski team in order to get in biking schedule."

Scott grew stronger, more disciplined. He improved. At Colorado's cyclocross championships in November, he placed an impressive second in his division. He became obsessed.

Hrs. sleeping: *3–4*. **Weight:** *123*. **Pulse/Waking:** *56*. **Rising:** *57*. **Diff.:** *1*. "Need to keep in my mind that <u>I'm a Biker</u>. That's all that I am. I'm a Biker. Need to keep my mind set on Worlds next season."

Given the Lancaster household's intense focus on cycling during summer and fall of 1990, Scott and his family did not take note of Boulder's cougar problems, and there was little reason why they should have. Events in Boulder seemed of little relevance. Lines of politics, class, and commerce separated the high-tech, liberal college town from small, blue-collar Idaho Springs.

The diminutive city of Idaho Springs, population 1,834 per the 1990 census, inhabited a picturesque crease in the Rocky Mountain foothills thirty miles west of Denver. Filled with Victorian homes, flanked by forested slopes, and straddling the whitewater of Clear Creek, the town traced the canyon bottom and assumed a peculiar shape—lanky, snakelike. "Three miles long and three blocks wide" was how locals described their elongate hamlet.

Although the mining of precious metals had long ceased to be a major part of the economy, Idaho Springs continued to embrace its glittering past. The monument to prospector and lion killer George Jackson, which commemorated "the first discovery of gold in the Rocky Mountains," sat in front of the high school, just south of downtown, where students hailed their mascot, Gus the Golddigger, a pick-wielding miner clicking his heels while displaying a fistful of nuggets. (The town's past also embraced its present; the abandoned shafts and tunnels that honeycombed the land occasionally swallowed whatever lay above—a horse, playground equipment, a sixteen-year-old boy.)

Idaho Springs now survived on the economic coattails of the huge Henderson molybdenum mine nearby and on tourist revenue. In winter, skiers drove past on Interstate 70 toward Vail and Aspen, stopping just long enough for a hamburger or slice of pizza and a tank of gas. In summer, families visited town for mine tours and to bathe at the Indian Springs Resort, where hot water bubbled out of the earth into a swimming pool beside an old gazebo. Not much happened in Idaho Springs on a typical day, even less on an average night.

In the early morning hours of January 11, 1991, a Friday, the air was cold, the sky dark and moonless, the town quiet. Officer Darren White was patrolling the east end of Idaho Springs in a blue Jeep Cherokee with a rack of emergency lights on top and the word *POLICE* displayed on the side in white, reflective letters. Young and newly hired, on the force just two months, White had been saddled with the graveyard shift, an assignment often as dull as death. On this particular morning, however, at three-thirty, a cryptic call crackled over the police radio; someone had reported a "large, roaming creature" on the seven hundred block of Colorado Boulevard. White was dubious, thinking this might be a practical joke. Relations were strained between the new officer and others on the force, and he suspected a cop in an animal outfit was awaiting his arrival. "I'll be en route," he responded into the radio, then swung his Jeep west on Colorado Boulevard, the town's main thoroughfare.

The two-lane strip of asphalt made a slight S-curve as it ran east–west, mimicking the shape of Clear Creek Canyon. White drove past the Texaco station and A&W, the Safeway and 7-Eleven. Off to the right, on the hill north of town, an assemblage of red corrugated-steel buildings climbed the slope. This was the Argo Mill, which once processed ore transported through the Argo Tunnel, a marvel of late-nineteenth-century engineering. Stretching 22,000 feet under the mountains, the tunnel had housed a sub-terranean railroad that shuttled men, explosives, and tools to gold mines and hauled rock back out. The passageway also drained water that would otherwise have accumulated, a valuable service that turned fatal in 1943 when a powder blast released a flood from an untapped mine; the ensuing torrent gushed through the tunnel and across Colorado Boulevard for six hours. Searchers eventually recovered the drowned bodies of four mineworkers encased in mud. Abandoned since the disaster, the Argo Tun-nel was now a federal Superfund site that continued to leak toxic cadmium and lead, poisoning the once pure waters of Clear Creek.

Continuing west, Officer White drove by the Idaho Springs firehouse, a low building of cinder block and wood shingle, at the corner of Twenti-eth Avenue. At Seventeenth, he passed the turnoff for the "Oh My God" Road, the winding route up Virginia Canyon with hairpin turns and steep drop-offs that cars occasionally plunged down. Two blocks farther, Vince Hennigan's funeral home occupied a corner on the left; the stout brick structure—originally an attorney's house—sported stained glass above a heavy front door, and a wooden sign on the lawn that declared, in black let-ters on a white background, **TOMFORD MORTUARY**. (Hennigan had taken over the business in 1986 but kept the sign up out of respect for Mr. Tomford, who had owned the funeral parlor for a quarter century and still lived in town.)

Around Thirteenth Avenue, White entered the most elegant section of

Colorado Boulevard, bordered by grand homes, the residences of mine owners, bankers, and merchants in the 1880s and 1890s. The houses exhibited a hodgepodge of styles: Italianate, with tall windows and bracketed cornices; Gothic Revival, displaying steeply pitched, gabled roofs; Queen Anne, with wraparound porches and decorative trim, all gingerbread and finery. Beyond Eighth Avenue, the houses grew modest, more tightly packed, less ornate. This, the western end of town, had long been a poorer district, had in fact been the original cemetery. Although the burial ground moved across Clear Creek in 1874, graves had been inadvertently left behind, only to be discovered decades later by residents digging beneath yards and streets. City workers, while replacing a water line, once exhumed the corpse of a man in a leather jacket. "When they attempted to move the body," writes a historian of Idaho Springs, "everything in the grave, except the leg bones, turned to dust."

Arriving at Seventh and Colorado, where a vacant lot overlooked a trailer court and Interstate 70, Officer White spied the "large, roaming creature." It was clearly not a cop in a costume, and it was not currently roaming. The creature, a burly cougar, sat hunched over a fresh deer carcass on the side of the road, fifteen yards away. The cat was feasting. It briefly looked up, a chunk of flesh hanging from its teeth, then lowered its head and resumed its meal.

Officer White sat wide-eyed. Though he had grown up hunting with his father on Colorado's Western Slope, he had never seen a cougar up close, and as an urban cop, albeit in a small city, he never expected to see one on the job. *There's no way I'm getting out*, he told himself. Instead, he rolled down the window with his left hand and grabbed his Glock nine-millimeter semiautomatic pistol with his right. The gun had a night sight at the end of the barrel, a tiny vial of tritium that glowed a faint firefly green. White held the firearm out the window, centered the radioactive dot on the cat's head ("I got a good bead on this cougar," he recalls), and squeezed the trigger with his index finger, pulling with about two pounds of force. The gun was set to fire at six pounds.

Then White reconsidered. "It occurred to me, I had no legal reason to shoot this cat," he says. "I was a little startled, and I was concerned that it was in a populated area, but then—okay—so what? You don't have a hunting license. The cat hasn't done anything to you. The cat's not directly threatening property or life. There's no reason for you to shoot this cat."

Besides, unlike Boulder, Idaho Springs had had no recent history of lions endangering people. White holstered his weapon. "If I had any moment in my life to take back," White would remark later, "I would have emptied the clip on that nine-millimeter."

A couple of honks on the horn prompted the cougar to move along. The cat slowly picked itself up and trotted eastbound on Colorado Boulevard. White executed a quick U-turn and followed for about fifty yards. The cat dashed between houses and was gone.

Officer White could still feel an adrenaline rush as he drove to the Derby Restaurant, the town's only twenty-four-hour eating establishment, where he met the usual collection of state troopers and sheriff's deputies for coffee in the middle of the night. They sat around a large table with a faux wood top while White told his story, and they all laughed as he wrote up the incident report with unpolicemanlike flair and humor.

Under "Type of Incident," White scribbled, "Mountain lion at large." In the narrative portion of the report, he wrote that he found the cougar "having breakfast" on Colorado Boulevard. "The R/O [responding officer] did not contact the cougar outside his car! After blowing the horn several times, the cougar abandoned his meal and left town."

The Idaho Springs Police Department did not contact the Colorado Division of Wildlife about the lion in town. Authorities did not notify the public. No one was particularly worried.

The following day, before dawn, a groggy Clear Creek ski team assembled in the high school parking lot beside the monument to George Jackson. The Golddiggers were off to compete at a cross-country meet seventy miles southwest in Fairplay, Colorado. (Another mountain town with auriferous origins, Fairplay had been founded by disgruntled prospectors ejected—unjustly, they believed—from nearby mining camps; they named the new settlement as a rebuke to their rude neighbors.) Some fifteen boys and girls, swathed in flannel and wool and down, loaded skis and poles in the luggage compartment of a school bus, then piled into its brown vinyl seats. Driver Lee Campbell steered the vehicle left on Chicago Creek Road and onto the highway. As the bus struggled up Interstate 70 toward the high mountains, the students promptly fell asleep.

Ski coach Conradt Fredell anticipated a disappointing day. Clear Creek High School's team, severely underfunded compared with those from wealthy resort areas such as Vail and Breckenridge, often ranked at the bottom of its league in cross-country skiing. Coach Fredell encouraged his team to "try not to be last," but even that meager goal seemed ambitious on this day; the Golddiggers' star Nordic skier, senior Scott Lancaster, would not be racing. Scott, maniacal about bicycling, had let his grades slide to the point where he was temporarily ineligible to compete in team sports. He was failing two courses, math and government, but he didn't seem to mind. Although he focused intently on cycling (or perhaps because he did so), he took little else seriously. Admired for his wit and individuality, Scott was idiosyncratic in his life and attire. In winter, he was prone to show up at school in shorts and old sandals patched with duct tape. (One bone-chilling day, English teacher Mike Dallas confronted Scott about his odd choice of clothing. "What the hell are you doing?" Mr. Dallas asked. "I've declared a manly day," Scott explained. "The human spirit has got to persevere. The weather out here sucks, and everybody is huddling down from the winter. I'm not going to let winter interfere.") Apparently unashamed that he could not race, Scott accompanied his teammates to the ski meet to cheer them on.

The Golddiggers arrived at the Fairplay Nordic Ski Center—a small, privately owned recreation area nestled in a high valley—around nine. Mr. Campbell pulled the bus off the shoulder, and the team tumbled out into a blue winter's morning. As the racers waxed skis and limbered up, Coach Fredell handed Scott a video camera and gave him an assignment: record the meet. Scott did, and the resulting film, with its scattershot images, jerky camera work, and abrupt edits, plays like a memory, a stream-of-consciousness recollection of an American adolescence.

SCOTT LANCASTER *stands before the camera. He wears a Lycra Nordic ski suit (black with red sleeves), a blue hat with a pompon hanging from a tassel, and his signature mischievous smile. Beside him is classmate* JAMES VALDEZ, *with dark brown hair, and brown eyes hidden behind mirrored sunglasses. ZZ Top blares in the background. ("It must have been the way that she kissed me, made me weak as a lamb.")* SCOTT *slaps* JAMES *on the back with his right hand.*

SCOTT: This is my pal James. We're just here to watch the team. (JAMES *and* SCOTT *were close, like brothers. They had met at age eight while playing midget football. During senior year, they shared lockers and clothes and an addiction to Dr. Pepper.)*

JAMES: No food. We're hungry.

SCOTT: I'm not racing, [not] because I'm ineligible. I'm not racing because—I don't *want* to. (SCOTT *plants his hands on his hips, sticks his elbows out, and mocks the camera.*)

(*Change of scene. Skiers take warm-up runs on snowy trails through a forest of aspens and evergreens. The camera pans to* ERIC SIMONICH, *boys' team captain. He has high cheekbones and a dimpled chin and is wearing a navy ski jacket over a T-shirt displaying a picture of Albert Einstein.*)

SCOTT: Eric!

ERIC: (*Walking toward the camera*) Is the mike on?

SCOTT: How's it goin', man?

ERIC: I think I've got something in my nose. (ERIC *inserts the tip of a ski pole in his right nostril. He and* SCOTT *and others on the boys' team were known jokesters who occasionally engaged in mischievous pranks. Several years earlier, while playing with lighters and nondairy creamer—a powder that becomes explosive when poured over a flame—they and their friends ignited a hillside of dried grass and clematis vines behind the high school. The fast-spreading blaze burned uncomfortably close to tanks of propane. As punishment, the perpetrators were forced to wash trucks at the firehouse on Colorado Boulevard.*)

(*The girls' race is about to begin. Female skiers wearing white bibs with large black numerals stand at the starting line.*)

SCOTT: There's Melissa at the start. She's gettin' ready. She's psyched. Let's go, Melissa. Woo! Here we come, Olympics. All right! (*One by one, at fifteen-second intervals, the skiers take to the course and climb a broad trail.*) Look at that excellent technique, in those tight tights. (*Despite* SCOTT*'s encouragement, many of the Clear Creek skiers exhibit poor technique. They appear to be walking on skis, while competitors from other teams speed past, each step a perfect stride.*)

(*A succession of images follows: the boys' race, a snowball fight, students buying candy at a concession stand. Then the Golddiggers pile back on the bus, where they snack on Doritos and orange wedges while awaiting their departure.*)

SCOTT: (*Talking to the girls*) I'm not videotaping anybody. It's not even on. I'm just playing with, playing with the zoom. (*But he is filming, clandestinely videotaping female body parts—knees, thighs, buttocks.* SCOTT *laughs.*) I can't wait to watch this.

Despite the Clear Creek ski team's lackadaisical attitude, the Golddiggers performed better than Coach Fredell had expected at the cross-country meet on Saturday, January 12, 1991. The boys' team placed eighth and the girls' seventh out of ten schools competing, although no one would know the results for several days.

Monday, January 14, 9:40 A.M. Scott Lancaster's first class—after homeroom, which he rarely attended—was health, an awkward subject for postpubescent teens. Mrs. Donahue, a tall woman who also taught phys-ed, led discussions on sexually transmitted diseases, substance abuse, drunk driving. The room added to the sense of discomfort. The class met in the second-floor "fishbowl," so named because internal windows ringed the walls, offering views into a hallway and adjacent rooms, providing constant distractions. The poorly designed space, with carpeting the color of Dijon mustard, was small, stuffy, trapezoidal. Clear Creek High School, a 1960s-modern structure, was laid out on a hexagonal floor plan; right angles were scarce. Scott, in blue Levi's and a white T-shirt, slumped at a desk by the blackboard and doodled.

10:29. Math. Scott's classmates represented a cross-section of the New West, the sons and daughters of miners mixed with children from professional families that lived in the wealthier, eastern reaches of the county, nearer to Denver. Scott came from one of these outer suburbs, a wooded neighborhood of A-frames and ranches and log homes. His father, a mechanical engineer, worked in the aerospace industry. Despite this pedigree, Scott showed little interest in math. He often read cycling magazines in class.

11:16. Scott was scheduled to attend English with Mike Dallas, but he ditched it. He ran into Eric Simonich, ski team captain, and asked to borrow a music cassette by the Police. Scott associated the song "Every Little Thing She Does Is Magic" with his girlfriend, Heather Tilley—small, tough, fearless on the ski slopes, an attractive tomboy with flame blue eyes. "I'm so in love with her," Scott said. "I've gotta listen to this song." Eric handed the tape to Scott, who took it to James Valdez's car, a silver Audi Fox, model year 1978, which James left unlocked with the keys in the ignition. Scott sat and listened to his song for Heather.

12:03. Lunch. Scott and friends usually spent their half-hour meal period at the 7-Eleven on Colorado Boulevard, playing video games and munching microwavable burritos. On this day, Scott ate pepperoni pizza.

12:37. Back at the high school, fifth-hour classes began, but Scott had a free period that he devoted to physical training. In consultation with his cycling coach, Scott had devised a daily run that circled the high school in hilly terrain, providing a good workout. He entered the boys' locker room, stripped out of his T-shirt and jeans (exposing green boxer shorts with figures of Santa Claus), and opened locker 61, which he shared with James Valdez. Scott proceeded to dress in James's gym clothes: faded blue cutoff sweatpants, a black hooded sweatshirt (with the Clear Creek ski team logo on the back and a handwritten label—"James"—on the front), purple-and-green ski gloves. Scott opened Eric Simonich's locker and removed a pair of running shoes.

Dressed in borrowed threads, Scott emerged into a brilliant winter's afternoon. Turning right in the high school's asphalt parking lot, he jogged down the driveway and onto Chicago Creek Road heading south, toward Mount Evans, the route he had bicycled to the summit in July. A chain-link fence surrounded the high school track up the hill on the right, and Chicago Creek burbled along the road to the left. Scott followed the dirt shoulder past the Seventh Day Adventist church, a small building of stone and brown wood with a tall white spire, followed by a collection of ranch-style homes. Business teacher Candice Michael, returning to the high school after her daily stress-reducing stroll, saw Scott run past. The two waved at each other.

A thousand feet from the high school, Scott veered right onto Spring Gulch Road, a maintained dirt street that sloped gently upward through a narrow gully. A small stream flowed by on the left, lined by aspens and evergreens. Scott cut up the slope on the right, turning back toward the high school. There was no defined trail, but this was a route he and his friends frequently jogged for ski team practice. In the rocky terrain, clumps of bluegrass and fescue grew between mountain mahogany bushes.

As Scott topped the ridge, he ran between junipers and ponderosa pines and beneath high-tension power lines strung between colossal metal towers. From this tall hill, he could see the high school parking lot just a few hundred yards away, the Victorian homes of downtown Idaho Springs in the distance, and the town cemetery, where the victims of the Argo flood were buried, across Chicago Creek. He could hear the hum of tractor trailers on the interstate, as trucks headed toward Denver and Salt Lake City.

After jogging above the running track, Scott descended to the back of the school. Mike Dallas was teaching his fifth-hour English class in room 270, with a large bank of windows looking out at the hill, the very area that

Scott and his friends had set on fire several years before. As Scott ran past, he knew he had an audience. He flailed his arms and ran on wobbly legs, as if he had no control over his body. Scott's schoolmates laughed and anticipated the next humorous jog-by. Scott usually ran several laps, each lasting approximately fifteen minutes.

Scott continued northbound, to the back of the U.S. Forest Service ranger station. An American flag flew out front. He cut through the parking lot to Chicago Creek Road, turned right, passed the high school, and began his second circuit: by the running track and church, right on Spring Gulch Road, beneath the power lines, up the rocky slope, and out on the ridge that stood tall and steep, like an Aztec temple, above the city of gold.

Dr. David Livingstone, Scottish missionary and African explorer, the man famously greeted by journalist Henry Morton Stanley in Zanzibar in 1871, was, at age thirty, mauled by a large cat. In February 1844, while helping African villagers hunt a pride of cattle-killing lions, Livingstone—armed with a double-barreled weapon and dressed in a tartan jacket—spied one of the beasts at thirty yards. He fired at the animal, wounding the cat and prompting it to attack. The lion grabbed Livingstone by the shoulder and, before succumbing to its injuries, shook him violently. The Scotsman later recalled:

> The shock produced a stupor similar to that which seems to be felt by a mouse after the first shake of the cat. It caused a sort of dreaminess, in which there was no sense of pain nor feeling of terror, though quite conscious of all that was happening. It was like what patients partially under the influence of chloroform describe, who see all the operation, but feel not the knife. This singular condition was not the result of any mental process. The shake annihilated fear, and allowed no sense of horror in looking round at the beast. This peculiar state is probably produced in all animals killed by the carnivora; and if so, is a merciful provision by our benevolent Creator for lessening the pain of death.

Automobile crash survivors, disaster victims, and soldiers in battle often describe similar sensations. Trauma can trigger an altered state of con-

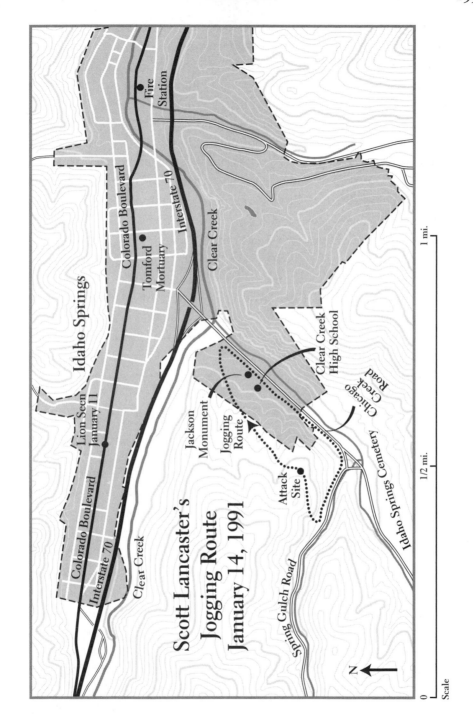

Scott Lancaster's
Jogging Route
January 14, 1991

Idaho Springs

Fire
Station

Colorado Boulevard

Interstate 70

Clear Creek

Tomford
Mortuary

Clear Creek
High School

Chicago
Creek
Road

Lion Seen
January 11

Colorado Boulevard

Interstate 70

Clear Creek

Jackson
Monument

Jogging
Route

Attack
Site

Idaho Springs Cemetery

Spring Gulch Road

N

Scale

0   1/2 mi.   1 mi.

sciousness, a momentary split between the self that observes the event and the self that experiences it, a phenomenon psychiatrists call *peritraumatic dissociation*. In this state, the individual may feel as if he had left his body and were watching the traumatic event from a distance, calmly and dispassionately.

During trauma, time slows, mental processes accelerate, and pain dulls while other senses are often heightened. Some victims of wild-animal attacks describe an acute awareness of sounds: the scraping of teeth against bone, the *pop-pop-pop* of claws puncturing skin. Many survivors of trauma also report the experience of *panoramic memory*, a flashing of one's life before one's eyes. Such were the recollections of a man who, when crashing his motorcycle at age sixteen, believed himself about to die:

> **I started seeing good and bad things in my life. They were scenes that flashed rapidly before my eyes like lantern slides shown in rapid succession. They started when I was about two years old. A funny thing. I remembered dumping a bowl of cereal upside down on my head. I remembered being spanked when I brought home a bad report card. I remembered high points like the first time I kissed a girl, the first time I got drunk and other things like that. With each one I had the feeling like I had then. It was like living them over again.**

Survivors of trauma often compare the experience to a drug-induced high—which, in fact, it is. Stress causes the brain to release a flood of hormones, including morphine-like endorphins, that help energize the body and focus the mind at a moment of crisis. These self-manufactured pharmaceuticals probably evolved to aid survival in dangerous situations. By erasing fear, they enable the victim to think rationally in the face of unimaginable horror; by easing pain, they allow one to concentrate on self-defense rather than on one's wounds. They may also, as a fortunate by-product, ease death.

During the fifth hour of classes at Clear Creek High School, while his friends were studying a few hundred yards away, Scott Lancaster was thrown to the ground. His glasses flew and his blood poured, and the rapid loss of pressure in his arteries caused his heart to race in a desperate attempt to send oxygen to his brain. Scott's body struggled, but his mind was likely elsewhere, watching with detachment, distance. For a brief eternity, as he faded from consciousness beneath a cougar's amber gaze, Scott's universe became time and sound and memory.

When a person turns up missing—especially a rebellious teen performing poorly in school—law enforcement is likely to suspect a runaway, a reasonable starting assumption. So, after Scott failed to come home Monday evening, after his mother frantically called the parents of James Valdez and Eric Simonich, hoping to find her son, after she reported Scott's inexplicable absence to the authorities, the Clear Creek County Sheriff's Office quickly imagined the following scenario: frustrated by his poor grades and angry at being ineligible to compete on the ski team, Scott had skipped town. Evidence bolstering this theory included the fact that on Monday afternoon Scott had missed government, a class he was failing and in which a final exam was scheduled for Tuesday. Scott had also neglected to meet friends Monday afternoon for a planned study session in advance of the test. On Tuesday morning, sheriff's deputies cornered Scott's friends in the halls of Clear Creek High School and plied them to fess up. "Why don't you tell us where he is?" a deputy badgered Eric Simonich. "Why don't you just tell us he left town?" Eric's entreaties of ignorance—as far as he knew, Scott had *not* run away—brought only further grilling and harassment. ("It really made me angry," says Eric, who recalls being "about ready to go punch the cop.") English teacher Mike Dallas intervened on the students' behalf. "You are wrong," he told the deputies. "I know what you're thinking—that these kids are lying to protect him. But you're wrong. You don't know Scott." Scott had no reason to run away. He didn't care about academics or participating in ski meets; all that mattered to him was biking. Scott's mother told the police the same story. "No way" was Gail Lancaster's response to the theory that her son had left town voluntarily. "He would never leave his bike." Scott's Gängl, his custom cycle with the cut-out hearts, was sitting at home.

The last time anyone could remember seeing Scott was during his run behind the school on Monday. The more Scott's friends talked, the more certain they were that he had never returned. The students in Mike Dallas's fifth-hour class couldn't remember Scott jogging past the window a second time, as he usually did, and when James Valdez opened their shared locker, he discovered his gym clothes missing and Scott's street clothes in their place. James, Eric, Heather, and other schoolmates conducted impromptu searches of the hill behind the school. "Hey, Scott!" they shouted as they climbed the rocky slope. "Scott!" They heard no reply.

By late morning, getting nowhere with the runaway theory, the sheriff's department summoned trained searchers to comb the area where Scott had been jogging. Alpine Rescue Team, an organization of volunteers expert at finding lost hikers and skiers in the Colorado backcountry, established a base of operations on the side of Chicago Creek Road near the Seventh Day Adventist church. Standing around a chartreuse rescue vehicle, searchers in parkas and wool hats swigged hot soup while planning strategy.

Locating lost souls, whether in the wilds or on the edge of town, requires careful coordination and efficient execution. Those who organized the search for Scott Lancaster began by imposing order on the chaotic landscape. On a topographic map, they sketched Scott's regular jogging route—indicating where he was last known to be—and then carved the surrounding hills and drainages into an irregular grid, defining thirty-two zones bounded by roads and ridgelines and gullies. Each section, about twenty to fifty acres in size, was assigned a number. The search process was itself divided into phases, with more meticulous methods employed at each successive stage. The idea was to start with the fastest search techniques in the areas where Scott was most likely to be discovered, maximizing the odds of finding him in a timely manner. If those methods failed, Alpine Rescue Team would then revisit the same ground with slower, more painstaking techniques while also widening the search area.

Among the first to be sent into the field were canines. Three search dogs, after sniffing Scott's leather moccasins as scent articles, worked the hillside behind the high school (search areas 1 and 2) and detected Scott's essence, pheromones and other organic compounds exuded by his body, in abundance. A bloodhound named Reliant tracked the scent to the U. S. Forest Service parking lot, fueling speculation that Scott had met someone, hopped into a car, and departed town. Meanwhile, small groups of human searchers, termed "hasty teams," checked along roads, trails, and creeks, shouting Scott's name while looking for clues. They found nothing of note.

In the afternoon, the operation entered phase two. Searchers organized themselves into a loose column, spaced about seventy-five feet between them, and swept across the terrain en masse, marching through the brush and trees while looking for a piece of clothing or a footprint that might hint at Scott's whereabouts. Again, no one could find evidence that Scott was anywhere near the high school, let alone in Idaho Springs. As dusk descended, Alpine Rescue Team's leaders suspected they were engaged in a "bastard search," a futile attempt to locate someone who wasn't there. For safety reasons, they suspended operations until morning.

Tuesday night found Scott's friends and family baffled. Gail Lancaster imagined that her son had been hit by a car and was lying by a roadside. Larry Lancaster thought Scott had been kidnapped. Mike Dallas feared that Scott had dropped down a mineshaft. James Valdez was unable to conjure any rational explanation: "I had it in my head that he'd been abducted by aliens."

The search resumed Wednesday at first light. Alpine Rescue Team moved its base of operations to the firehouse on Colorado Boulevard. Out among the fire engines, trained searchers, Vibram soled and Gore-Tex clad, crowded around tables of coffee and donuts, waiting to be sent into the field. Reporters now gathered outside, and helicopters from Denver television stations hovered overhead. Scott's family and schoolmates huddled at the fire station, awaiting news. Eric Simonich couldn't believe the level of activity generated by his missing friend. *This isn't Idaho Springs*, he thought. *Nothing happens here. Nothing happens in our daily lives except for Dr. Pepper and video games*. Eager to participate in the search, Eric added his name in black felt tip to a sign-up sheet of townspeople volunteering their help.

Alpine Rescue Team generally avoided using untrained searchers in its operations. Inexperienced individuals, however well intentioned, can muddle things; they get lost, injure themselves, and ultimately can impede attempts at finding a missing person. For this operation, however, situated on the edge of town and in relatively easy terrain, the rules were bent. Brendan Dallas, Scott's old biking buddy, helped search the hillside between the cemetery and the Indian Springs Resort. Ski coach Conradt Fredell combed the ravines of Virginia Canyon off the "Oh My God" Road. Eric Simonich and James Valdez joined a team on the northern slope of Spring Gulch, part of Scott's jogging route. Across the gully, to the south, Heather Tilley, Scott's girlfriend, and schoolmate Abby Heller climbed a ridge with a senior member of Alpine Rescue, John Peleaux, a slender, baritone mountaineer dressed in pile pants and a Patagonia windbreaker. He had invited the girls to join him on a high lookout to scan the terrain from a distance using binoculars that hung from his neck on a brown leather strap.

The search had now entered its third and most painstaking phase. The leaders of Alpine Rescue Team had all but concluded that Scott was not on the hillside behind the high school, but before terminating operations there they had to ensure that no clue had been overlooked. That meant conducting a line search.

A line search is a standard technique employed by rescue teams. A group of searchers, usually half a dozen or more, begins by arranging itself along one border of the area to be inspected. The team members stand tightly spaced, about twenty feet apart, but they may be much closer; the rule is that adjacent individuals must be able to see everything between them. A searcher at one end of the line holds a compass and walks slowly forward, maintaining a constant bearing, while the others march forward in parallel. As they progress, they scan the landscape, gazing up in trees, checking beneath fallen logs, peering behind boulders. When the team reaches the opposite end of the search area, it shifts as a unit to the left or right, turns around, and heads in the opposite direction. The idea is to sweep back and forth the way one might mow a lawn—in overlapping strips, until the entire area is covered.

Line searches are tedious, especially when you're convinced you're not going to find anything. Such was the mind-set of Steve Shelafo, the twenty-eight-year-old emergency medical technician, outdoor enthusiast, and eight-year veteran of Alpine Rescue who was designated a team leader for the final search of zone 2, the area just southwest of the high school. *We're not here to find something,* Steve remembers thinking. *We're here to prove he's not here.* Futile or not, the search had to be thorough. Thin-faced and mustachioed, in a gray fleece jacket and bright orange gaiters, Steve assembled his men in the sun-warmed snow at the northwest corner of the zone. From there, the phalanx trudged eastward, down the rocky slope, beneath the high-tension power lines, between widely spaced ponderosas and low-growing brush. The search progressed routinely, turning up nothing out of the ordinary, just some deer—skeletonized carcasses as well as live animals stotting into the distance. Steve Shelafo's team reached the eastern extent of its assigned area, shifted south, and had just started its sweep westward when a couple of searchers gestured toward a large juniper and shouted, "Steve, we found him."

"*What?*" Steve responded, dumbfounded.

"He's over here," they answered.

Steve approached, and the closer he came, the more astonished he grew. At first glance, from a distance, the body appeared as if sleeping, as if anesthetized for surgery. The corpse, frozen and snow dusted, lay supine with its head on a pillow of pine needles. The pose was disarmingly relaxed: the right arm rested comfortably on the ground, the left arm was bent at the elbow with the hand placed gently on the abdomen, the legs were extended, and the feet tilted slightly outward. The sneakered feet, the bare legs, the gloved hands that emerged from the sleeves of a sweatshirt appeared intact, normal, but the young man's chest was not intact, far from it. A cavernous hole gaped in the upper torso, and the insides had been removed. The left lung was missing. So was the heart. More frightening still, the murderer had peeled off his victim's face—nose, lips, cheeks, forehead—and left a grinning skull that stared at the sky with eyeless sockets. "Man, someone did somethin' bad to this guy," Steve said with astonishment.

Steve got on the radio. "Secure all Alpine Rescue Team radios for a transmission," he said. This was a signal to his colleagues and the police that a sensitive message was about to be relayed. In other words, *Don't let Scott's family or friends or the media hear what I'm about to say.*

"We have a code four," Steve said, indicating that a body had been found. Then: "Oh, God, this is not good."

"Is there any hope for resuscitation?" someone asked.

"Negative," Steve answered.

High on the opposite hill, standing in a clearing about twenty yards from a steel tower supporting the high-tension power lines, Heather Tilley and Abby Heller screamed, "Oh, my God," when they heard the exchange on the radio, then collapsed in a tearful embrace on a large log. John Peleaux, who had met the girls only minutes before, tried to comfort them. He began sobbing, too.

Eric Simonich and James Valdez, perhaps a hundred yards from where the body was found, heard "code four" on the radio and watched uncomprehendingly as the other searchers on their team leaned in to their walkie-talkies with the volume down low. A man eventually approached to explain the situation. "We have found a body," he said. "We believe it is Scott. I'm not going to tell you to turn around and go back to the fire station. I can't tell you that. You can come up and see what's going on. But I advise you not to. These are memories that can haunt you for life." Eric turned to James and said, "No. We're going. He's our buddy, he's right up there."

Meanwhile, Steve Shelafo, standing by the body, was back on the radio summoning help: "We want Sheriff Cahill up here."

Clear Creek County Sheriff Bob Cahill was at the firehouse, sitting in a small, linoleum-floored lounge with two members of the Lancaster family—Scott's father, Larry, and Scott's brother Todd, an air force pilot who had flown up from Texas that morning and arrived in military dress. The sheriff, a boyish forty-two-year-old with nicotine-stained fingers, wore civilian clothes: blue jeans and cowboy boots, a staple of his wardrobe since age eleven. When he heard the call from the other room, he excused himself quietly, grabbed two colleagues—Idaho Springs Police Chief Stu Nay and a deputy, Don Krueger—and quickly headed to the scene. The men parked by the Seventh Day Adventist church and started marching uphill. Deputy Krueger, in the lead, cut an imposing figure—six feet two, 220 pounds, with a large brown mustache, sideburns, and dark sunglasses; though off duty, he carried a nine-millimeter Smith & Wesson semiautomatic pistol in a brown leather holster on his right hip. Chief Nay, sporting a mustache above a mouth that seemed in a perpetual scowl, was the only one in uniform, a golden badge adorning the left breast of his blue shirt.

As the law enforcement trio ascended, Steve Shelafo instructed his team to examine the corpse and surrounding area for clues while being careful not to disturb anything. Someone noticed streaks of blood in the lower layer of snow, beneath a dusting from the night before, as if the body had been dragged to its current location. Steve spied what looked like moss and dirt covering the legs and lower abdomen. Then, still bewildered by the weird, horrific scene, Steve heard team member Shane Becker say, in a voice calm but insistent, "Hey. Right behind you." Steve, fearing that a crazed murderer lurked in the trees, thought, *There's some whacko behind me. There's some bizarre dude behind me.* Steve turned and saw a cougar.

The lion, some fifteen feet away, sat on its haunches in a small grove of junipers. The cat's ears stood up and alert, and the fur on its face appeared matted, as if wet, perhaps with blood. The beast watched the men intently. Steve tried to remain calm, but this was a complication for which he was unprepared. "Everybody stand still!" he shouted to the group of searchers behind him. Suddenly the lion came to attention, as if preparing to spring, which prompted Steve to contradict his first order. "Get the hell out of the way!" he hollered while backing off from the lion and swinging his arms to herd his troops into a huddle.

Steve got on the radio again. "Mission base," he said, trying to sound unruffled and professional, "we have a mountain lion on the scene." He thought, *This is exactly what we don't need, a mountain lion in the middle of a homicide investigation*. At that point, the lion and Scott's death were two separate issues. No one had yet linked them.

The hill was quickly filling with people. Other search teams, some with horses and dogs, converged on the scene. Eric Simonich and James Valdez arrived nearby, stunned by the sight of the lion and their friend's mutilated body. Sheriff Cahill was halfway up the slope when he heard the radio transmission about the lion. Fearing that the cougar posed a threat to the gathering crowd, he assigned Deputy Krueger and Police Chief Nay to find the cat and to kill it. The mountain lion, meanwhile, apparently feeling itself boxed in, took off toward the southwest, loping through junipers and over a rise, where it vanished from view.

In pursuit of the missing cat, Deputy Krueger skirted the ridge to the left, toward Spring Gulch Road, while Police Chief Nay, heading straight up the hill, radioed for backup. "Call 201," he said. "Have him respond with a sniper rifle to help us deal with this cat." "201" referred to Patrol Sergeant Dave Wohlers, a trained SWAT sniper who looked like a Marine, with a crew cut and a swagger in his walk. Wohlers grabbed his bolt-action rifle, jumped in his cruiser, and sped to Spring Gulch Road, where he scrambled up the rocky slope toward Scott's body, using his left hand to balance against the hill and his right to carry the weapon.

Meanwhile, Heather Tilley and Abby Heller, on the opposite hill, were watching the scene unfold across Spring Gulch. Beside them, John Peleaux peered through his binoculars and could see the lion, which—rather than fleeing the area now swarming with dozens of people—started to circle back toward Scott's body. As the cat did so, it neared Deputy Krueger, though Krueger couldn't see the animal for the vegetation. Peleaux called over the radio. "The cat's above you," he said, then continued to guide the deputy in a blind hunt. "He's on that rock outcropping. Now he's going to your right."

Deputy Krueger soon spied the cat's whiskered face staring from behind the branches at the base of a juniper some thirty feet away. "I've got him," Krueger radioed, then slowly reached toward his right hip and unsnapped the holster, removing his pistol. It contained seventeen rounds in the magazine and one in the chamber. The bullets were hollow-point, especially lethal because they mushroom upon impact.

Krueger held the weapon out straight, clutched in his right hand and braced by his left. A black dog, a stray that had been bounding across the hillside all morning, suddenly ran into view and toward the lion. The cougar registered no concern. Krueger aimed at the cat's head. The gunshot echoed down Spring Gulch.

The cougar flipped over backwards and down a small ledge. Krueger was sure he'd made a direct hit. He hadn't. John Peleaux, watching through binoculars, saw the lion rise to its feet. "Uh, he's up and running," Peleaux called on the radio.

At about this time, Sergeant Wohlers was nearing the top of the ridge with his rifle. He saw the mountain lion rushing toward him, apparently unhurt. The cat veered south, down toward Spring Gulch Road. As it vaulted through the grass and brush, its long, black-tipped tail stuck straight in the air.

Within seconds, the cat had reached the road and was heading up the other side, toward Heather Tilley, Abby Heller, and John Peleaux. Peleaux quickly scanned the terrain for an escape. His eyes fixed on the nearby electrical tower. He told the girls to run for the pylon and prepare to climb.

As the lion continued uphill, Sergeant Wohlers positioned himself across Spring Gulch. He sat back against the slope, his rear end on the ground, his knees pulled up toward his chest. He cradled the rifle in his right hand and rested the butt against his left shoulder with his left eye peering through the scope. He could see the lion, magnified by a factor of six, about two hundred yards away. He waited for the cat to pause and look back, providing an opportunity for a clean shot. He didn't want to wound the lion; he feared that might enrage the cat and make it even more of a threat. The cougar kept moving, soon to be hidden by trees. Wohlers pulled the trigger. The bullet struck the ground by the lion's hind feet. The cat turned slightly but continued running.

Abby and Heather arrived at the tower. They stepped up on the concrete base, grabbed the cold metal lattice, and frantically looked for footholds.

Dave Wohlers reached over the rifle with his left hand and yanked the steel bolt handle up and back. The spent shell casing went flying. He thrust the bolt forward and down, locking the next round in the chamber. He fired again. This time, the bullet struck the cat behind its shoulders, in the rib cage. The lion slumped against the hill. The snow bloomed red.

With the lion dead, Sheriff Cahill and his law enforcement colleagues regrouped at the death scene to begin their investigation. Deputy Krueger pulled Scott's frozen body up by the left arm while Chief Nay—who also served as the county's deputy coroner—looked at the undersides of Scott's thighs. In the hours after a person dies, blood settles due to gravity, pooling in lower areas and producing a maroon skin discoloration called *livor mortis* or *lividity*; forensic pathologists check for the condition to help determine time of death and whether a body had been moved postmortem. If Scott had died in the face-up position in which he was found, his body should have exhibited lividity along the backside. Nay found none. In other words, Scott had likely been killed, and had lost much of his blood, prior to his placement beneath the juniper.

Sheriff Cahill paced the surrounding area and noticed an object glinting in the sun. He approached and found a pair of gold-colored, metal-frame glasses in the snow beneath a crushed buckthorn bush, its branches splayed and its thick stems broken. About ten feet downhill a large pool of blood soaked the ground, and from there a long drag mark led to Scott's body. Pieces of the puzzle began to fall into place.

The sheriff got on the radio. He summoned the Division of Wildlife.

14

THE INVESTIGATION

District Wildlife Manager Tom Howard was working out of his home, a shag-carpeted, 1970s split-level in the Apple Meadows subdivision south of Boulder. Five months since transporting a woozy lion from University Hill back to the mountain wilds, Tom was dealing with more routine calls: the alleged poisoning of a fox, the case of a wildlife-chasing dog. His scanner squawked on the kitchen table.

Tom's boss, Jerry Apker, called over the radio. "Have you got something going, 'cause I really need ya," he said. "Can you meet me at I-70 at the Morrison exit?" By the tone of Jerry's voice, Tom knew something big was up, something Jerry didn't want to divulge over the airwaves.

Tom said sure, he'd be there in fifteen minutes.

A moment later, Jerry radioed again. "Oh, by the way," he added, "do you have a bunch of big plastic bags? *Big* plastic bags?" Tom grabbed some plastic liners for fifty-five-gallon drums, threw them in his tan Chevy pickup, and drove toward the mysterious rendezvous. Slender and cleft-chinned, his hair neatly trimmed, garbed in his official-issue green Levi's and gray shirt with patches on the shoulders, Tom was always fastidiously groomed and meticulous in his work. The thirty-nine-year-old Virginia native had proven reliable and detail oriented, a good choice for a tough assignment.

Heading west from Denver, the Morrison interchange was the first turnoff after Interstate 70 began its ascent from the plains to the mountains. The exit sat on a hogback, a sharp ridge of sedimentary rock, where a road cut exposed colorful strata of limestone, sandstone, and mudstone, the fossiliferous rocks chronicling forty-five million years of birth and death, creation and extinction. Tom arrived at a parking lot on the north side of the interstate and found Jerry Apker waiting in his Division of Wildlife truck. It was almost noon. Tom pulled up so that his driver's window faced Jerry's. "Have you heard yet?" Jerry asked.

Tom hadn't. "Heard what?"

"An eighteen-year-old man—looks like he got killed by a mountain lion at Idaho Springs."

Tom was stunned. Sure, he had investigated cougars killing dogs and llamas, had attended the meeting in Coal Creek Canyon, had known of the growing boldness of Front Range lions and the growing concern by the public, yet he never expected a fatal attack, certainly not an adult as the victim.

The two wildlife officers caravanned to Idaho Springs and parked by the fire station on Colorado Boulevard. As they walked toward the building, a reporter spied their uniforms and approached, but the men revealed nothing. "We aren't saying anything about somebody being killed by a lion until we're pretty damn sure that that's in fact what has happened," Jerry had instructed Tom.

Despite all appearances that a cougar had slain a healthy, full-grown man, other scenarios could conceivably have explained the bloody scene behind the high school. Perhaps Scott had been murdered, or had died of heart failure, and the lion then stumbled on his body and began to eat; cougars do, rarely, scavenge. And even if a lion had killed Scott, there might have been contributing factors. Perhaps Scott had hurt himself or had fallen ill prior to the attack, prompting the lion to view him as a wounded animal. Perhaps the cat had been desperate, sick. (*Was he starving? Was he diseased? Was he injured?* Tom wondered.) Perhaps the cougar had worked with an accomplice, like the duo that stalked Lynda Walters, a possibility that raised a disturbing question: Might a second man-eating cougar remain at large?

Jerry and Tom entered the firehouse and climbed to a second-floor meeting hall furnished with a billiard table and decorated with bowling trophies and an American flag. The room, used for the fire department's annual chili supper and community gatherings, bustled with sheriff's deputies and members of Alpine Rescue Team. The two wildlife officers sought out the men who had found the body.

"Who was involved in actually first removing snow and seeing if it was Scott?" Tom asked. A mustachioed gentleman stepped forward. "And your name is what?" Tom inquired.

"Steve Shelafo."

"Were you present when the snow was first removed from the corpse?"

"No one ever removed snow from it," Steve said. The light dusting of flurries had melted in the sun.

"What I'm getting at is," Tom continued, probing for clues, "once you could see the corpse free of snow, was there any debris on top of it at all?"

"Yes," Steve said. "I saw some moss and things over parts of his legs. It was up around the groin area and towards the abdominal region where the cavity was open that there was dirt and some moss scruffed up on the body. It was at that point, when I was close to the body, that the cat was noticed by Shane here."

Tom turned to Shane Becker. "Can you tell us what the cat was doin'?"

"It was just sitting on its haunches, looking at us," said Shane.

"He was just kind of posed, just eyeballing us real good," Steve added. "When I looked at him, I was like, *Yeah, wrong place.*"

"Did it ever snarl or anything?" Tom wanted to know.

"No," Shane said. "He wasn't worried at all."

"I felt like he was guarding," Steve appended.

"Guarding the body?" someone asked.

"Just sitting there guarding the area," said Steve. "I don't know. Just guarding. Period."

Steve Shelafo and fellow Alpine Rescue Team members escorted the wildlife officers to Spring Gulch Road and up the rocky hillside to show them the death scene. By this time, Scott's body and the lion carcass had been removed—transported to Vince Hennigan's funeral home, the old Tomford Mortuary—but the site remained otherwise unaltered. Jerry sketched the scene: the crushed buckthorn bush, the blood-soaked ground, the drag marks that led to the sepulchral juniper. "It was obvious that there

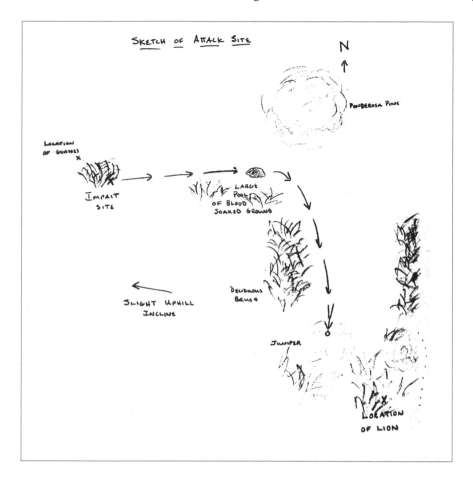

SKETCH OF ATTACK SITE

N

PONDEROSA PINE

LOCATION OF GLASSES
X

IMPACT SITE

LARGE POOL OF BLOOD SOAKED GROUND

SLIGHT UPHILL INCLINE

DECIDUOUS BRUSH

JUNIPER

X LOCATION OF LION

had been a struggle," recalls Tom. The shrubbery "was just trashed. It was like bodies had caved in on it, rolled around on it, struggling and breaking off the stems." The physical evidence painted a consistent picture: Scott had been ambushed, there had been a brief struggle, and then the lion hid Scott's body and began to feed. "It was pretty hard to find any evidence contrary to the fact that a lion was responsible."

Tom Howard then drove to the mortuary. The funeral home's main floor, used for wakes and memorial services, evoked stability and permanence with its Victorian decor: a birch-mantled fireplace beneath a beveled mirror, a carved oak banister up the central staircase, floral upholstery, pocket doors. Tom entered the garage, which presented a very different scene, spare and cold. A naked bulb dangled, illuminating cinder-block walls and the dead body of a mountain lion splayed on a red tarpaulin on the concrete floor. Tom stooped to examine the beast, which displayed a bullet wound in its left midsection, burgundy staining the tawny fur. Rigor mortis held the lion's jaws shut, but Tom was able to check the cat's dentition by pulling back the lips, revealing inch-long canines that curved and tapered to a sharp point. The cougar, an adult male, probably two to three years old, measured four feet from nose to rump and weighed about a hundred pounds. Tom noticed that the animal was missing two toes from its right hind foot, but the wound was old, long since healed. "That injury alone certainly would not have, in my opinion, caused the lion to be desperate enough to jump on an adult human," Tom concluded. Overall, the cat appeared to have been healthy.

The police ushered Tom into the basement morgue, a tiny chamber that the funeral home workers affectionately called "the dungeon." The room sported a giant sink, stainless-steel walls, and a low ceiling that could induce claustrophobia. Scott's body, nude save for running shoes (medical examiners had removed James Valdez's shredded gym clothes), lay on a central table. Tom Howard reeled at the sight. It appeared to him as if someone had taken a commercial-grade can opener, cut a 360-degree hole in Scott's chest, and removed his insides. The open cavity and absent organs looked familiar, like any lion-killed deer or elk, but this carcass was hauntingly different; it was human, and faceless. *Good God*, thought Tom. *I hope they never let the family members see this*. Tom noticed puncture wounds—bite marks—on Scott's left hand and forearm. The skin was bruised, a sign that Scott had been alive—his heart was pumping—when he was bitten. In other words, Scott had tried to defend himself. "He was fighting for his life," Tom reckoned.

Tom returned to his truck and retrieved one of the large bags he had brought from home. He eased the plastic over the lion's head, stuffed the animal inside, hefted it into his pickup, and commenced an hour-and-a-half drive to Fort Collins, where he was to deliver the dead lion for a thorough postmortem exam at Colorado State University. As he headed north and the sun fell behind the Front Range, Tom couldn't shake the image of Scott's body from his mind. He was convinced that a firestorm of protest was soon to rage. *Once the word gets out*, he concluded, *there's going to be a tremendous pressure to annihilate every lion in the state.*

After transporting the dead cougar to the university and starting toward home, Tom switched on the FM radio in his truck. "Tonight the battle has been joined," President Bush told the nation in an address from the Oval Office. At 5:00 P.M. local time, 3:00 A.M. in Iraq, U.S. and allied forces had begun to pummel Baghdad with bombs and Tomahawk missiles. The Gulf War had begun.

Scott Lancaster's death would have been top news if not for Operation Desert Storm. Late on that Wednesday, January 16, Denver TV stations reported the shocking discovery of Scott's body and the unsettling likelihood that a cougar had been his murderer, but saturation coverage of the fighting in the Middle East soon preempted all else. The *Denver Post* that arrived at Gail and Larry Lancaster's home the following morning screamed atop the front page, "IT'S WAR." News of their son's death was relegated to page 4B.

While events in the Middle East transfixed America, Scott's presumptive killer lay on a wheeled, stainless-steel table at Colorado State University's Veterinary Diagnostic Laboratory, the final destination for many deceased animals throughout the Front Range. Carcasses routinely arrived at the facility from ranchers, pet owners, the Denver Zoo—anyone seeking to determine how an animal had died and what its health had been in life. The lab's necropsy room, at the back end of CSU's sprawling veterinary teaching hospital, was stark, industrial, whitewashed. A hook hung from the ceiling to hoist large-animal remains in and out of an adjacent meat locker. The concrete floor sloped to a long, rectangular drain that captured a steady flow of bodily fluids. The air held the pungent aroma of fresh meat tinged with formaldehyde and the stench of an outhouse. A typical day might find a horse dismembered in the middle of the room—its entrails, ribs, and spine in a pile—while lab workers at nearby tables dissected the flayed bodies of dogs, deer, and sheep beneath high-intensity lights.

On Thursday morning, January 17, responsibility for examining the mountain cat from Idaho Springs fell to Bob Glock, D.V.M., Ph.D., veterinary pathologist and the lab's director. Of middle age and German ancestry, Glock looked the part of an Amish butcher—a thick gray beard framing his pink, un-mustachioed face; cotton coveralls, rubber boots, and latex gloves clothing his body; a freshly sharpened, eight-inch boning knife in his right hand. Glock approached the lion and began to probe for more than skin-deep answers to the enigma of Scott's death.

With the cat sprawled on its left side, Glock raised its right legs and sliced deep and hard along the inside of the joints, leaving small flaps of skin and muscle attached. This allowed him to fold the legs up and back at an unnaturally severe angle, giving the lion the appearance of a circus contortionist and providing easy access to its belly and chest, which he began to incise. Glock slid the sharp blade up along the lion's underside, genitalia to neck. The skin parted along a straight line as if unzipped. He inserted fingers and peeled back the hide, revealing the deep plum of the cat's interior and a thin but healthy layer of subcutaneous fat beneath the sand-colored fur.

Grabbing a set of giant pruning shears, Glock placed the blades straddling the cat's sternum and then the ribs; he thrust the long handles together to split the bones, one by one, each cut producing a loud *crack*. He sliced through the diaphragm and lifted the triangular flap of bones and muscle up and back, exposing the internal organs.

With the cougar's chest now open, Glock continued cutting up to the cat's jaw and removed its tongue, trachea, esophagus, and lungs in one piece. The left lung showed evidence of bleeding, apparently due to the bullet wound, but the cat's respiratory system looked otherwise healthy. The spleen, the liver, and the kidneys (which, when freed from their covering of fat, looked strikingly—though not surprisingly—like oversized kidney beans) came out next. Cutting a series of parallel slices partway through the organs, Glock fanned each back accordion-style to examine the tissue inside. The hue and consistency were perfectly normal; no discoloration, no abscesses, no lesions, no parasites. Glock removed the cat's heart and halved it, revealing a complex of holes and connections like a purple spider's web of tissue. Again: healthy.

Running his knife along the cougar's neck, Glock found where the skull met the first vertebra. He sliced through muscle and ligament and slipped his blade in the gap to sever the lion's head, which an assistant neatly carved open with a Stryker saw, cutting a window in the skull to extract the brain. Glock sent one hemisphere to the virology lab for a fluorescent antibody test, which could reveal the presence of rabies by eliciting an apple-green glow from infected tissue. He placed the brain's other half in formaldehyde to be preserved, sliced, and examined under the microscope. (A while later, the rabies test would come back negative and the histopathology exam would similarly detect nothing abnormal—"no tumors, no infarcts, no strokes, no viruses, no bacteria," says Glock.)

In any necropsy, it is routine to open the animal's digestive tract to determine what the creature had been eating. In this case, that task was particularly sensitive and important, and it was the unenviable responsibility of Division of Wildlife biologist Kathi Green, who had come to observe and assist. Kathi, who had long stressed in public meetings and media interviews the great unlikelihood of a fatal lion attack, was now confronted with gruesome evidence that the improbable had occurred. As Bob Glock opened the stomach and intestines and removed their contents, Kathi rinsed the mass of material in a colander. Sorting through with gloved hands, she found pine needles. She found tapeworms, not uncommon in a cougar's gut. And she found what she had hoped she would not. Clumps of sandy hair. A strip of blue cloth. Fragments of rib. A piece of aorta. As the mother of young girls, Kathi flashed on the pain Scott's parents must have been feeling. She empathized with them as she sorted Scott's pieces into sterile polyethylene bags, rolled down the tops, and secured them with wire closures.

Kathi Green had hoped that the day's exercise would provide some answers for the Lancasters, a reason why this lion had killed their son. But there was no good explanation. "There wasn't anything obviously wrong with the lion," says Kathi. "Everything looked normal. I mean, he was lean, but he wasn't starving. He was not skinny. There was no sign it had any illness of any kind."

After the necropsy, Kathi drove her Division of Wildlife pickup truck back to Denver and headed west to Golden, where she stopped at the Jefferson County Coroner's Office to make a delivery. She entered the front door and surrendered the baggies of material from the cat's stomach, to be matched with the missing parts of Scott's body, as well as a cardboard box, inside of which, wrapped in blood-soaked paper towels, lay the lion's head.

Dr. Wilbur Richie, Jefferson County coroner, had been expecting the cat's head. The gray-haired dentist, with a thick mustache and a penchant for bolo ties and motorcycles, poured water into a large, war-surplus pot, placed it on the stove, and added a dash of Biz detergent. Unwrapping the package from Kathi Green, he dropped in the brainless skull for an overnight simmer.

Richie, a nationally known forensic odontologist, was frequently called upon to apply his dental know-how to criminal and accident investigations. By comparing dental records to a deceased's teeth, he could identify bodies that were otherwise unrecognizable (decomposed, mangled, charred). In the case of Scott Lancaster, Richie had been asked to examine the *lion*'s dentition, and that's where the head in the pot of sudsy boiling water came in. By the time he returned to work the next morning, the skin and tissue had separated from the cat's skull and jaws. He extracted the clean bones from the goopy water and fished around for teeth, which he reattached with Krazy Glue.

Scott's corpse, which had been transported to Richie's Jefferson County morgue for the examination, lay thawing in his cooler, an old meat locker—purchased second hand from an Albertson's supermarket—that maintained a constant temperature of forty degrees. Richie carried the cat's skull to Scott's left thigh, which displayed a distinct bite mark. He placed the feline jaws against human skin. The teeth coincided with the impressions. "I could match up to those bites perfectly," Richie recalls. Punctures ringing Scott's chest cavity and on his neck also matched the cat's canines in size and spacing. The bite-mark analysis suggested a clear conclusion: the lion that consumed Scott was the same one that attacked him. There was no second killer cat.

The final phase of the death investigation comprised a thorough examination of Scott's body, to be performed by Dr. Ben Galloway, a large and jowly forensic pathologist who consulted for many Colorado counties. Galloway gowned up and entered Jefferson County's autopsy room, which—with its stainless-steel table beneath a bright light—could easily have been mistaken for an operating room, if not for the patient laid out for inspection, who was clearly not alive.

"This is the unembalmed, well developed, well nourished, extensively traumatized body of a white male appearing consistent with the stated age of eighteen," Galloway dictated into a handheld tape recorder. "The major portion of the head is skeletonized." Scanning the naked corpse, Galloway moved his deep-set eyes downward, past the chin. "A large portion of the tissues of the upper neck are absent," he noted. "Numerous horizontal antemortem incised wounds are present, totaling five in number."

Continuing his narrative in cold detail, Galloway noted the obviously absent chest and peered at the wounds surrounding the hole, judging them postmortem—a result of feeding, not killing. He found antemortem injuries (cuts and punctures that had bled) on Scott's upper back, inflicted by teeth and claws. He observed the defensive wounds on Scott's left hand and wrist, seen earlier by Tom Howard. And he found scratches covering Scott's legs, perhaps acquired in a struggle atop the splayed branches of a bush.

Galloway probed Scott's interior, cutting with surgical instruments and observing as he went. He found no sign of disease in what remained of the spleen, liver, gallbladder, pancreas, and kidneys. Dipping a test tube into the open chest cavity, Galloway collected blood, and then he sampled urine from the bladder. These fluids would reveal whether Scott had been chemically impaired at the time of the attack. He had not; both the blood alcohol test and the urine drug screen proved negative. X-rays detected no bullets in Scott's head, chest, or abdomen.

"The autopsy revealed no evidence of any contributory factors which may have caused the assault to occur," Galloway wrote in his final report. The fatal injury appeared to have been the gash on Scott's neck. The cat's teeth had punctured the right internal carotid artery, which supplies oxygenated blood to the brain and eyes, and severed the right internal jugular vein, which returns blood from the head to the heart. Scott had exsanguinated; he had bled to death. "I don't think he lived very long, bless his heart," says Galloway. "Luckily, it all happened so fast."

Exactly what happened behind Clear Creek High School at approximately 1:00 P.M. on January 14, 1991, became a matter for speculation and debate. Some suggested that Scott might have bent to tie a sneaker, making him look like easy prey to a hiding lion. Others conjectured that Scott had spooked a deer that the lion had been stalking, prompting the cat to shift its attention to the two-legged creature running past. Tom Howard of the Division of Wildlife guessed that Scott might have spied the lion in the bushes, panicked, and done what he shouldn't—turned his back and run—triggering the cat's predatory instincts.

Tom's boss, Jerry Apker, reached a different conclusion. "I don't believe Scott ever saw the lion," says Jerry. "He was probably focused on the track in front of him to make sure that he wasn't stepping on a rock wrong and turning an ankle. He was a mountain runner, so he had to be fairly conscious of where he was going to be placing his feet. So he's running along, and I think that the next thing that he knew was, *boom*, he got hit from behind and knocked down to the ground." The wounds to Scott's upper back, quite possibly caused by the cat's initial strike, supported this scenario.

The injuries to Scott's left hand prompted yet another reconstruction from Idaho Springs Police Chief Stu Nay. He proposed that the lion had attacked from the front, and Scott had glimpsed the animal as it leapt toward him. "He put his hand out defensively," says Nay. "He got bit. The weight carried Scott uphill into the bushes. They probably wrestled around a little bit down to where the pool of blood was. And I would imagine that's where the cat got ahold of his throat."

Despite disagreements over the mechanics of the attack, by Friday, January 18, enough details were clear for the Division of Wildlife to issue a press release confirming that, for "the first time on record," a cougar had killed a human in Colorado. "This is a terrible tragedy, and our hearts go out to Scott's family and friends," commented division director Perry Olson. "It is unfortunate that nature can be so harsh at times."

The news, carried by local papers, reverberated throughout the Front Range. Upon learning of Scott's death, Ponce Gebhardt recalled the Division of Wildlife's dismissive attitude about lions when one had loitered in her Boulder yard. "*Yes*," she said to herself. "They *are* dangerous." The Overmyers, who had feared for the safety of their young daughters when the dog-killing lion had stalked their Coal Creek Canyon neighborhood, were shocked by Scott's age. "This was almost a full-grown man," Teresa remarked with astonishment. Lynda Walters's reaction was more personal. Reading a description of Scott's body, she pictured herself in his place, a fate she had narrowly escaped. Four words rose into consciousness: *I was really lucky*.

Michael Sanders, though he had long predicted a fatal mauling, found the reality of it strange and the circumstances surprising. Rather than an inebriated college student, the victim had been a fit high school athlete. "You just didn't think it was gonna happen to a kid like that," he says. Intrigued and saddened, Michael made a pilgrimage to the bloodstained hillside in Idaho Springs. He viewed the crushed buckthorn bush where Sheriff Cahill had found Scott's glasses. ("It looked like the lion had hit Scott so hard that the force of both their weights had uprooted this bush.") He found cougar tracks in the snow and followed them along the ridge. Although Michael couldn't say for sure, he suspected that the prints were those of the cougar as it hunted Scott. "The lion looks as if it followed a very long distance and then decided to make the attack," he concluded. "It wasn't a spontaneous thing."

Friday night, Michael met Jim Halfpenny at their usual watering hole, the old Peggy's Hi-Lo, now operating under the name Boulder City Limits. A band called Savannah Boogie played on the bar's small stage while the men discussed lions, politics, and mortality. Although the provenance of the Idaho Springs cat was unknown, Michael couldn't shake the feeling that "this could have been a lion that was in Boulder two days ago." In fact, the lion might have been one represented by the red and orange dots on the wall map in his office, a cat seen lingering in Boulder's driveways and eating dogs, perhaps half of the duo that had treed Lynda Walters. "If we had all been doing our homework," says Michael, "if we had at least been proactive enough to set traps and try to at least get some tags on these lions," the cougar's progression of dangerous behavior might have been detected while intervention was possible. Of course, that's exactly what Jim and Michael had long requested from the Division of Wildlife—permission to radio-collar the cats and to track them—and it is what they had been repeatedly denied. Michael was furious at the agency and angry with himself. *If we had been better at selling our program, we might have—could have—saved his life*, Michael thought.

Jim, less emotional and more fatalistic than his scientific partner, suspected that the tragedy would have occurred anyway, but the death did leave him feeling vindicated. After years of being labeled an alarmist, Jim had been proven horribly right. The question—for Boulder, for the Division of Wildlife, for Jim and Michael—was what to do now.

At this point, Michael made one important decision—to wrap up the Boulder Lion Search. The way he saw it, he and Jim had taken the study as far as it could go. "Everything that could happen had now happened," says Michael. "All the way from pets being killed to people being stalked to killing a kid. The whole gamut. And at that point, I felt that our research was done." The time had come to present the findings, to tell the story of Boulder's lions.

15

EXEGESIS

A somber crowd filled long, metal bleachers and rows of chairs arranged on a rubberized floor. The ceiling, high above, sprouted immense mushroom-shaped fixtures that illuminated basketball hoops and championship banners. A table near the door displayed mementos of Scott Lancaster's brief life: his bicycle helmet, his glasses, a photograph of the eighteen-year-old, grinning and mud splattered, after a cyclocross race. On a far wall, a painted image of Gus the Golddigger clicked his heels in incongruous merriment as Scott's classmates struggled to eulogize their friend.

"He taught me so much about everything," James Valdez told the audience, packed inside Clear Creek High School's gymnasium. "Scott, my friend, I'll miss you greatly," added Eric Simonich. Students, teachers, local residents, fellow cyclists and skiers, members of Alpine Rescue Team—some six hundred people had come, on the Sunday after Scott's death, to bow their heads at his memorial service. Brett Lancaster, speaking for the family, recalled his younger brother's love of nature and read a passage from his diary. "I have it all together when I'm in the woods," Scott had written. "The mountains are my home. . . . The mountains draw me out." During a pause in the service, a guitar ensemble sang and strummed a John Denver classic. (*He was born in the summer of his twenty-seventh year, coming home to a place he'd never been before.*) "Rocky Mountain High" reverberated in the vast confines of the gym.

Near the front of the audience, trying not to attract attention but finding it hard to blend in, sat a contingent from the Colorado Division of Wildlife: Kathi Green, Tom Howard, Jerry Apker, and several colleagues donning dress uniforms and cowboy boots, and wearing black armbands as a sign of mourning. They had come to express, by their presence, their agency's sorrow. "We would be really soulless people if we hadn't attended the funeral," says Kathi. Showing up had not been easy for the wildlife officials. "Everybody's going to be looking at us and wanting to blame us for this," Jerry Apker had feared. Indeed, sitting among Scott's family and friends, Tom Howard imagined himself harshly judged. "We could feel eyes on us like we're responsible, we're supposed to keep charge of these lions," he says. "It was awkward."

"Scott has died and is no longer with us in this life poets have called this valley of tears, this vale of woe," preached the Reverend J. Patrick Jordan of the United Church of Idaho Springs, the Lancasters' pastor, in concluding remarks. "Death is an ending of one thing but with a starting of something else. . . . May [Scott's] very short life continue to be an example for us all." The crowd adjourned to the school's commons area for a buffet dinner provided by the Booster Club. The beverage selection disappointed Scott's friends. *What the heck? This is Scott's memorial service—no Dr. Pepper*, thought Eric Simonich. *Who planned this one?*

Several days later, in a private ceremony, the Lancaster family buried Scott's ashes at the Idaho Springs cemetery, in plain view of the hillside where he had died, beneath a black granite tombstone carved with images of him as a bike racer and a skier. Returning in the evening to visit her son, Scott's mother caught her breath. She glimpsed, in the dark, a ghostly form: a large, long-tailed creature running among the graves.

The Division of Wildlife braced itself for a backlash—against the agency, and against lions in general. It never came. Despite Tom Howard's feeling of condemnatory eyes upon him, many who attended Scott's memorial service appreciated the presence of the wildlife officials. The people of Idaho Springs did not blame the agency for the fatal attack, and Coloradans did not rise up against cougars, did not call for a resumption of the historic campaign of extermination. Rather than exacerbating conflict and anger,

Scott Lancaster's death catalyzed positive change. The tragedy provoked soul-searching, cooperation, expiation.

In February—while, in the Middle East, U.S. and allied forces ejected Iraqi soldiers from Kuwait (an attempt, as President Bush put it, to forge "a new world order" in the aftermath of the Cold War)—Colorado's wildlife officials sought to establish a new order of their own, to find new strategies for coping with an increasingly peopled and re-predatored landscape. Division manager Jerry Apker, who suffered tremendous remorse over Scott's death ("I should probably go talk to a counselor," he says. "I'm not responsible for the actions of that lion, but I sure *felt* a lot of guilt over it"), called for a sit-down with representatives of the city and county of Boulder to heal old wounds and to hash out collaborative strategies for wildlife management.

Boulder, which had long frustrated the Division of Wildlife with its hands-off stance toward urban deer, adopted a more active approach to lions. In early February, when a cougar was seen lingering on a trail near Chautauqua, city park rangers blasted the cat with an air horn and shot bullets toward its feet to scare it away, thus beginning what would become a regular program of aversive conditioning to counteract the lions' habituation to humans. (In later years, Boulder would haze the cats with rubber bullets, M-80s, and beanbags fired by shotgun.) The city instituted a policy of posting warning signs on trails where recent lion activity had been noted, advising hikers to leash dogs and proceed with caution. And when homeowners reported lion-cached deer in their yards, city workers removed the carcasses to dissuade the cats from returning for a meal.

The Division of Wildlife, meanwhile, took a harder line against dog-snatching cougars; a week and a half after Scott's death, police in Colorado Springs, with the approval of the state wildlife agency, shot and killed a 151-pound lion as it tried to abscond from a porch with a cocker spaniel. Over the coming months, in a series of meetings, the agency devised an "action plan" for dealing with suburban lions. The document formalized definitions—for instance, an attack is "when a human is bodily injured or killed by contact with a mountain lion," a description that now included Lynda Walters's encounter—and delineated a policy for handling problem cougars. Under the new rules, any lion frequenting a city or town would be captured and relocated, and any lion deemed a substantial threat to public safety would be killed. To prevent problems from developing, the division vastly increased its public education, distributing thousands of "Living with Wildlife" brochures and visiting schools to teach residents how to avoid dangerous confrontations.

Many homeowners took their role seriously. The Overmyers and neighbors in Coal Creek Canyon constructed new dog pens with fenced tops that were impervious to cougars. And when Boulder resident Peter Ramig, who had videotaped two lions off his deck in the summer of 1990, later found lions *on* his deck, he loaded his twelve-gauge shotgun with rubber buckshot, provided by the Division of Wildlife for just this purpose, and gave one of the cats a painful pelting in the rump. "After that, I never saw one on my deck," he says. The combined efforts of government agencies and the public helped keep Boulder's lions in check. Although problems did not cease, they stopped escalating.

Despite the newfound caution and pragmatism in its dealings with cougars, Boulder did not relinquish its compassion for the creatures. Little more than a week after Scott Lancaster's death, and just over three years since a lion family had visited Happy Times and triggered a lengthy search for an injured cat, a man who raised geese and chickens at a Boulder Canyon home shot and killed a poultry-stealing lioness, leaving four young cubs motherless. A new search ensued; concerned residents and the Division of Wildlife, with help from Jim Halfpenny and Michael Sanders, tromped hillsides seeking the orphans, three of which were eventually captured. (The fourth, struck and killed by a car, was necropsied at Colorado State University and found to contain dog in its stomach, evidence of the unnatural foodstuffs its mother had been providing.) The rescued kittens were raised in captivity on a diet of road-killed deer and elk, provided in such a way that the young lions would not associate humans with food, and were eventually set free in southern Colorado, far from the homes and pets of Boulder County. Human intervention arguably had given the cats a better chance at a wild existence.

The lack of vengefulness against cougars, the backlash that never came, perplexed the Division of Wildlife. "That has been a mystery to me for forever," says Jerry Apker. "In my mind, I always chalked it up to the fact that people's attention must have really been much more focused on the Gulf War." Yet perhaps more important than events half a world away was the tone set by those nearby, the people who knew Scott Lancaster best. Among Scott's friends and family a consensus emerged that his death, sad and untimely though it was, had somehow been acceptable. "It was kind of fitting for him," said James Valdez. "He was a real outdoorsy guy." Scott's girlfriend, Heather Tilley, consoled herself and others: "He would have been happy to have gone this way. I mean, if he has to go, this would have been a better way." "It felt natural," said classmate Abby Heller. "It felt like it was part of nature, and it was part of the earth, and it was part of the way that things work and the way that the cycle happens. It seemed kind of pure." English teacher Mike Dallas went so far as to say, in the pages of the *Denver Post*: "[Scott] would have been angry that the lion was shot. He would have been angry that his body was not left there for the lion to finish."

On a scale of purity of death, being eaten by a cougar may, indeed, rank higher than dying in a car crash, an end that claimed far too many Clear Creek High School students, but to label Scott Lancaster's death "natural" is an oversimplification. His demise was as natural as Boulder's wolfless foothills, its gold-mine lairs, its irrigated lawns and urban deer.

"Next speaker is from University of Colorado. Someone whose name I'm sure we're all familiar with, Jim Halfpenny." The crowd applauded as Jim ascended the dais, placed his notes on the podium, and glanced out at the audience. He had dressed up for the occasion—broad-lapelled jacket of brown polyester, vintage western shirt with faux mother-of-pearl buttons, and a bolo tie made from a slice of elk antler carved scrimshaw-style with the image of a bobcat—yet Jim's long, black hair and thick beard gave the ever-present appearance of a man who'd just wandered in from the wilds.

A deep breath, a pause, and Jim began. "Today, I'd like to report to you on what has become known as the Boulder human-lion interaction database," he said. "This is a database that we started putting together many years back, and it's now grown to what you see over here on the wall." Jim gestured with his left hand toward the side of the Holiday Inn ballroom, where a speckled map of Boulder County hung. "There are 398 entries." The abundant dots on the map were nondescript, but each told a story: the cougar that swatted a plastic owl on Pat and Eugene Kayser's roof, the Knollwood lion, the attack on Fifi, the death of Mark Malan's red deer, the cougar among University Hill frat houses on an August night. "Myself and a speaker coming down the line, Michael Sanders, have been making extensive use of this database to look at the interactions here in the Front

Range," Jim continued, acknowledging his research partner, who sat in the front row.

Behind Michael Sanders, in metal chairs that lined long tables, sat several hundred lion biologists, wildlife managers, National Park Service employees, local officials, and interested citizens from across the United States and Canada who had assembled in this suburban Denver hotel, in view of the distant Flatirons, for three days of discussion on the West's growing cougar problems. The occasion was the Colorado Division of Wildlife's Mountain Lion–Human Interaction Symposium and Workshop, a meeting planned in the aftermath of Lynda Walters's ordeal but which had taken on added urgency after Scott Lancaster's death.

Many in the audience had attended the 1988 mountain lion meeting in Arizona, where the suggestion was made—and largely dismissed—that recent attacks in Orange County and Big Bend National Park portended a worrisome trend. Three years and two fatal maulings later, skeptics were few. The new questions to be addressed were: What had caused the growing threat from cougars? And what could be done to stop it?

"Can we have the slides?" Jim Halfpenny said from the podium. Lights dimmed, and a projector illuminated. "The 1980s were marked by an apparent increase in human-lion interactions here in the Front Range of Colorado, particularly in Boulder County," Jim said. "What I'd like to do today is look at the pattern of interactions that we've found within the database, how these have changed over time, and explore the question of: Are lions habituating to people here on the Front Range?"

Jim and Michael had taken their 398 data points—each alone a mere anecdote—and aggregated them, seeking trends that told a larger story. They had compared sightings from the first half of the study, through 1987, to those that occurred since 1988. The two time periods revealed significant differences, which Jim displayed in diagrammatic form. "You'll notice, prior to 1987, lion reports peaked in February and they hit a bottom in August," he said, using a laser pointer to highlight a graph of lion sightings by month. "Since 1987, the last three years, there's been a dramatic change. Reports are leveling out. We're getting many more reports in the summer, which is particularly important, because that's the time at which lions are often with cubs, and the cubs are now learning from their mother that it's all right to be around people."

With more graphs, Jim demonstrated other recent trends. Lion sight-

FROM DARKNESS TO LIGHT
LION SIGHTINGS BY TIME OF DAY

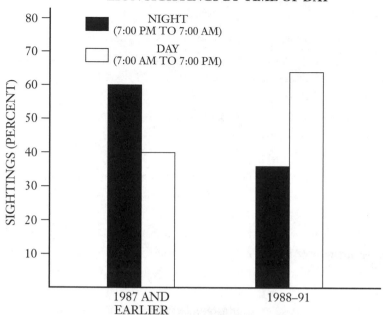

TIME PERIOD
[ADAPTED FROM HALFPENNY, SANDERS,
AND McGRATH (1993).]

ings had moved nearer to town. "The original mode of reports was [at an elevation of] 7000 feet," he explained. "This is shifted now in the last three years down to 6000 feet, a drop of a thousand feet. When you drop a thousand feet in Boulder County, that puts you right in the city limits of Boulder." What's more, the cats were no longer running away from people as readily as they used to. "We are getting a large number of reports now where people are up closer to the lions," he said. And, as he and Michael had instinctively sensed, a growing percentage of cougar sightings were made during the day. "In the baseline period, most of the reports occurred here in the night time," he showed on a chart. "Now we are getting many more reports during daytime hours. Not only are we getting more reports during daylight hours, [the lions are] also coming into the city limits more during daylight hours."

The conditions that had led to these shifts in behavior seemed clear to Jim. "We have more people and pets in Boulder County, and it's growing rapidly," he explained. "We have more deer than we've ever had before. We have more *lion* probably than we have ever had since European man—the settlers—arrived in Boulder County," he added. This New Western landscape, where suburban homes and suburban attitudes had replaced the ranches and mining towns of old, where wildlife had been invited to live among people, had become an incubator for potentially dangerous lions. Like storms that develop where weather systems meet, Boulder's cougar problems, and Scott Lancaster's death, had resulted from the collision of two worlds—rebounding nature and civilization's sprawl—each moving in toward the other, neither showing signs of slowing its advance.

Jim was careful not to exaggerate the risk. He estimated that for an individual Boulder resident, the odds of being attacked by a lion on any given day were about one in thirty-five million. "You're much more likely to win the lottery," he pointed out. But from a societal standpoint, the problem was big enough to be of concern, and it was likely to grow. "Will another mountain lion attack occur possibly along the Front Range?" Jim asked rhetorically in concluding his talk. "The answer seems to be yes. And it's not an *if* question, it's a *when* question. It'll probably be pretty soon."

Some time later, after the applause had faded and the symposium had ended, Michael Sanders found himself back in Boulder with an evening free, now that the Lion Search was over and his spare time was no longer filled with sightings to document and data to analyze. Alone at home, he packed a sandwich and some pickles and headed out for a solo hike up Flagstaff Mountain, on the edge of town. After traversing a few city blocks, he embarked on a steep trail, scrambling over rocks and pine needles, ascending through the butterscotch scent of warm ponderosa. Ever since moving to Boulder from Yellowstone four years earlier, this had been a favorite pastime of Michael's: a late-day climb to a sunset picnic. Raptors circled in the evening sky—among them, a pair of endangered peregrine falcons that had recently nested on city parkland, the first of their kind to do so in more than three decades, evidence of the species' remarkable comeback from years of devastation by DDT.

Michael halted his climb and turned back toward the city for a view over Boulder and the boundless plains. The setting sun projected a jagged shadow, the saw-toothed outline of the Rockies, across the land. Michael sat and watched as darkness reached slowly toward the distant Atlantic—

across Boulder's rooftops and urban forest, its highways and man-made lakes, its plowed-under prairie. In the town below, streetlights and head-lights and porch lights popped on. And where, just a few years earlier, Michael had seen expanses of black—voids among the houses—he now saw a twinkling sea, an ever-spreading mass of humanity.

THE MYTH OF WILDERNESS

April 30, 1998, presented a fine specimen of Front Range spring weather: warm and bright, wildflowers blooming beside melting snow, the Rockies rising into cerulean splendor. A Thursday, it was also Andy Peterson's day off, time for his usual hike up Carpenter Peak. The small mountain rose a thousand feet above the plains in a state park called Roxborough, and the summit afforded a panoramic view west to the Continental Divide, north to the foothills of Boulder, northeast to the skyscrapers of Denver, and immediately below to an upscale community of custom homes. The deer-filled neighborhood, complete with golf course, was populated by nature lovers who lived on sinuous roads with bucolic names. Condor Run. Sleepy Bear Trail. West Yucca.

Andy arrived at the trailhead around noon dressed in green shorts, a white T-shirt and fanny pack. The twenty-four-year-old was small and trim, his face narrow and delicate, his build similar to Scott Lancaster's. Andy worked as a ranger at a nearby suburban park. He felt comfortable out-of-doors. He often took this hike alone.

The 3.2-mile climb commenced among rust-red sandstone outcroppings—mini-Flatirons—that thrust skyward like abstract sculpture. The path wound its way through groves of Douglas fir and broad hillsides of scrub oak to a north-trending ridge that rose to the granite peak. Walking at a leisurely pace, Andy made the ascent in under two hours. Alone on the summit, he took a swig from his water bottle and sunned himself, bare-chested, for a brief spell before turning toward home, his shirt tied around his waist.

A hundred yards down the trail, as Andy stopped to examine a pair of purple flowers that had somehow avoided being trampled, a sudden breeze induced him to turn his gaze leftward, where, fifty feet away, a mountain lion lay beneath a ponderosa pine. The cat, oblivious to the shirtless hiker, appeared to be chewing on a stick.

Admiring the cougar from a distance, Andy quietly backed up along the narrow trail, which was bordered by dense brush. Unsure how he was going to sidestep the cat, Andy decided to arm himself, just in case. He gently unzipped his fanny pack, removed his Swiss Army knife, and—in the process of folding and unfolding blades—accidentally allowed the tool to close with a *snap*. Andy cringed. When he looked up, he found the lion peering at him from a turn in the trail.

As a park ranger, Andy knew the recommended procedures for scaring off a cougar. He made himself look big and menacing. He shouted obscenities. He waved his arms. The lion merely stared. After approximately seven minutes of futile standoff, Andy concluded, *Okay, this is not going anywhere,* and began to inch backward. The maneuver proved counterproductive. As soon as the cat was out of view, obscured by the tangle of scrub oak, it took the opportunity to rush forward until it stood little more than an arm's length away. Andy screamed, "Get out of here!" The cat answered with a combination hiss and growl. It bared its teeth, squinted, flattened its ears, and pounced.

Andy survived the first skirmish relatively unscathed. The cat slashed his chest and knocked him to the ground, but he quickly righted himself and began trotting in reverse down the trail, the lion in pursuit. "It's either going to be you or me!" Andy shouted, swatting the cat with his fanny pack and brandishing his T-shirt. "You wanna go? Let's go!" The cat leapt again. Its momentum carried Andy ten feet into the trees and shrubs.

Andy found himself on his knees, genuflecting into the lion's mouth. The bottom row of the cat's teeth clenched the top of his forehead, its upper teeth the back of his scalp, its claws his neck. His mind entered a curious realm. Time slowed, and he grew conscious of sounds: ripping flesh, chafing bone. His arms flailed. Andy had been a wrestler in high school, but this opponent was immovable. Still clutching the Swiss Army knife in his left hand, he attempted to stab the beast in the throat and head, but the lion's fur and skin were so thick that the blade couldn't penetrate. The cat continued to chew on Andy's skull. Blood spilled. The world turned monochromatic; Andy saw only red.

With time and options diminishing rapidly, and without really thinking, Andy reached up with his right hand and felt the cat's face. He found two lumps: eyes. Andy placed his thumb over the lion's right eye and plunged it in, causing the monster to emit a tiny chirp, retract its claws, open its jaws, and back up. Rising, Andy heaved a rock the size of a volleyball into the lion's side, and he ran.

America is engaged in a grand and largely unintentional experiment. As wildlife invades suburbs, and as suburbs invade wildlife habitat, we are changing animal behavior in unexpected and sometimes troubling ways. It is a widespread phenomenon—applicable to deer, geese, coyotes, raccoons, bears, and many other creatures—but seldom have the consequences been so dire, and rarely has the behavioral shift been so well documented, as in the case of Boulder's lions. Jim Halfpenny and Michael Sanders, in the data they collected, captured a species in transition. They identified the moment of change, the beginning of a trend.

Indeed, Jim Halfpenny's prophecy at the Division of Wildlife's 1991 symposium has, regrettably, proved true. Lion attacks and close encounters have become a recurrent fact of life on Colorado's Front Range, as evidenced by periodic headlines: "Boulder man stabs mountain lion with sword to free Saint Bernard," "Runner survives standoff with lion," "Man escapes cougar attack outside his rural home," "Bicyclist gets best of cougar: Savvy rider puts bike between himself and cat." And in 1997, Colorado suffered its second fatal lion attack, thirty miles from Boulder, just across the Divide in Rocky Mountain National Park. Ten-year-old Mark Miedema was mauled while hiking down the North Inlet Trail a short distance ahead of his family. By the time Mark's parents arrived on scene, the cat—a pregnant lioness—was dragging their son into the bushes.

It would be a gross exaggeration to say that cougar attacks have become commonplace; they have not. Dogs, bees, and snakes kill many more humans each year than mountain lions do. So do mosquitoes and deer, given those creatures' roles, respectively, in disease transmission and automobile crashes. Even in Colorado, residents are far likelier to die from a lightning strike, avalanche, or skiing mishap than from a puma attack. In fact, if one considers the actions of serial cannibal Daniel Blue during the Pikes Peak Gold Rush of 1859, the state can boast more documented cases of people being eaten by other *people* than by mountain lions.

Yet, for all their rarity, mountain lion attacks are far more common than they once were. Throughout the western United States and Canada, the cats have killed more humans since 1991 than in the preceding half century. In 1994, California recorded two fatal maulings, both victims—adults—hunted in parks near sprawling urban communities. Nonfatal attacks and other brazen encounters have grown exponentially and have spread geographically. At a day camp in Missoula, Montana, a six-year-old bringing up the rear on a hike was picked off by a cougar—and rescued by the brave actions of a teenage counselor. Along the Nevada shore of Lake Tahoe, a 120-pound lion smashed through a bedroom window, startling a house-guest who hid beneath the covers until the cat departed. In suburban Los Angeles, a lion crept into the loading dock of a J. C. Penney at Montclair Plaza, a shopping mall just off the San Bernardino Freeway. In Olympia, Washington, wildlife officers killed a cougar in a vacant lot down the street from St. Michael Catholic Church, about eight blocks from city hall.

Boulder is no longer alone. Nor will the West be for much longer.

Some time ago on Fire Island, New York, one of many eastern communities vexed by an overpopulation of deer, a sign appeared by the beach on a summer day. "DEER PROBLEM NOTICE," it read at the top. The broadside outlined the troubles caused by the abundant ungulates—the spread of Lyme disease, the destruction of vegetation—then continued,

What is the Intelligent Solution?

Introduction into Fire Island of a natural enemy of the deer—this is the only safe, sensible, humane, and ecologically-sound approach.

Scientists, environmental specialists, and public-health experts are in unanimous agreement that the ideal method of deer control is the puma or "mountain lion." The puma is quick, silent, effective, and neat (the deer is entirely consumed except for the antlers).

Contrary to erroneous opinion, pumas present ABSOLUTELY NO DANGER to humans or pets:

Pumas are afraid of humans, and will always flee from them. Moreover, pumas are nocturnal animals, so it is unlikely that children or adults will ever even see one.

Pumas do not represent any danger to dogs (in fact, it is the other way around, since dogs are used to hunt pumas), or to cats (since pumas ARE cats).

When Will Action Commence?

In Fall 1991, 30 "breeding pairs" (a total of 60 pumas) will be released in the occupied areas of Fire Island. Results will be apparent immediately.

The poster, produced by the "Fire Island Puma Committee," was intended as a joke. Yet environmentalists and conservation biologists contend that many eastern forests, denuded by a population of white-tailed deer that has ballooned fortyfold in a hundred years, could use nothing better than a natural, carnivorous culling. They may soon get their wish.

Having repopulated the West in large numbers, mountain lions are spreading inexorably toward the rising sun. The cats have solidly recolonized South Dakota's Black Hills and have been seen in growing numbers on the plains of Nebraska. In August 2001, a motorist in western Iowa struck a 130-pound tom, the state's first documented lion since 1867, prompting the *Des Moines Register* to proclaim, "They're baaaacccckkkk." A year later, a Pontiac Bonneville collided with a cougar on Interstate 35 in Kansas City, the first known lion in that part of Missouri in a hundred years. In July 2000, Illinois confirmed its first cougar since the nineteenth century—struck by a train southeast of St. Louis. In May 2002, a couple on an evening stroll in a suburban Minneapolis park spied a cougar in the underbrush; police killed the cat when efforts to scare it away proved ineffective. Farther east— in Michigan, Maine, Vermont, Virginia—where people have long reported glimpses of leopard-sized cats running through the woods, and where such claims have generally been considered as plausible as alien abductions, evidence is building that a few cougars may be living and reproducing in remote areas. The resilient cats are reclaiming old territory, and as they do, the nation should heed Boulder's lessons. Pumas may never reach Fire Island, but they could come close. They will probably retake Connecticut.

Seven months after his narrow escape from a cougar, having been stitched and stapled back together, Andy Peterson sat in the living room of his third-floor apartment in the Denver suburbs, by a Home Depot and Toys "R" Us. Dressed casually, in black sweatpants and a gray sweatshirt turned inside out, Andy looked healthy, uninjured, until he pulled back his bangs to expose a large suture where the cat's lower teeth had met his forehead. He raised a pant leg to display a grid of scratches. He gestured at rows of red dots that arced down either side of his neck. "Claw mark. Claw, claw, claw," he explained while pointing at the scars.

Andy commented that the lion encounter had cleaved his life into distinct eras: pre- and post-attack. He rarely hiked anymore, and never alone. When performing everyday tasks—walking to his car, for instance, or going to the mall—he instinctively and repeatedly checked over his shoulder. He suffered nightmares. In one, he is driving when he notices a pair of Bengal tigers walking into a 7-Eleven gas station. He wheels his car around to warn the unsuspecting customers, only to watch helplessly as one of the cats shreds a man.

Yet the bigger change in Andy's life was due not to the cougar attack itself but to what occurred immediately afterward. As Andy ran from the lion, blood pouring from his head, he glanced back to see if the cat was chasing him. First, he saw what he thought was the lion's face staring from the trees. When he looked again, he saw something else. "It was the face of Jesus," Andy said. Two and a half months later, he was baptized—born again.

Andy perceived a divine purpose behind his mauling. The near-death experience prompted him to reconcile with his father and led him to change careers. He had been studying for a degree in park management; now he aimed to be an inspirational speaker, bringing the tale of his violent struggle and heavenly vision to churches and youth groups. (The following year, he told his story to a national television audience on *Oprah*.) Of the lion attack, Andy said, "I look at it as an absolute gift." Yet a tinge of vengeance remained.

Immediately after the attack, the Colorado Division of Wildlife tried to hunt down Andy Peterson's assailant, but the effort proved unsuccessful. "I tell people, 'If you find [a lion] with one eye, let me know,'" said Andy. "'I want the tooth, and I want the fur.'"

Whether guided by a divine hand or biological imperative, the mountain lions *are* sending a message; they are signaling a change of era, not just to those few who have had direct encounters with them but to America as a whole. The cats, emboldened and proliferating, are heralds of a new stage in the nation's evolution, a changed relationship between man and nature that will require an attendant adjustment in cultural attitudes.

Several years back, William Cronon, a prominent environmental historian at the University of Wisconsin, wrote a controversial essay called "The Trouble with Wilderness; or, Getting Back to the Wrong Nature." The piece provoked ire and debate because it challenged a widespread, romantic notion. Cronon argued that the very concept of wilderness promotes a fallacy—"the illusion that we can somehow wipe clean the slate of our past and return to the tabula rasa that supposedly existed before we began to leave our marks on the world"—and that this fiction, so glorified by the modern environmental movement, paradoxically harms attempts at protecting nature. Cronon contended that by focusing so much effort on saving "virgin" landscapes, which don't really exist, activists have diverted attention from where people live, from getting the public to make environmentally sound choices in their daily lives, from determining the proper place for humankind *in* nature. "The myth of wilderness," he wrote, "is that we can somehow leave nature untouched by our passage."

In the twenty-first century, human fingerprints cover the natural world. We have altered the terrain by plow and bulldozer. We have removed native species and introduced a legion of exotics. We have changed the way water flows, fire burns, nutrients cycle—even how the wind blows and rain falls, given industrial society's effect on the climate. Humankind's influence is inescapable. Yet to proclaim the death of wilderness is not to denigrate attempts at protecting wildlife habitat and undeveloped land. On the contrary, the accelerating spread of civilization obliges us to preserve what's left of the natural world before it's gone. The question is how to achieve that goal.

For a century, environmentalism has divided itself into warring camps:

conservationists versus preservationists, or—in author Evan Eisenberg's more colorful language—Planet Managers versus Planet Fetishers. The struggle pits those who would meddle with nature against those who would leave it be. Situations like those in Boulder have shown, however, that in modern America, the only sensible way forward lies in a melding of the two philosophies. If nature has grown artificial, then restoring wildness requires human intervention. We must manage nature in order to leave it alone.

Historically, "managing" the natural world has meant manipulating it for economic gain—growing forests as glorified tree farms, treating wildlife as a harvestable crop. In this sense, management implies controlling nature to maximize its output, sometimes at the expense of healthy ecosystems. (Recall that wildlife managers once tried to improve deer harvests by exterminating cougars.) For this reason, the term has gained a sinister reputation among many environmentalists. But new forms of management have arisen under different names—conservation biology, restoration ecology—and with revised goals. Scientists working in these disciplines rebuild wetlands, reestablish populations of endangered species, and work to return modified landscapes to more natural functioning.

Unfortunately, wildlife management remains largely old school. Fish and game agencies, funded by hunting and fishing licenses, are still beholden to the interests of sportsmen. In rural areas with rural values, where land is open to hunting and where the public accepts it, this style of management works adequately, but in an increasingly suburbanized America and when dealing with endangered species, wildlife managers need new tools.

A few organizations, communities, and agencies are innovating. The state of Montana and the National Park Service, faced with a growing clash between people and grizzlies, have instituted remedial training for problem bears; when the hulking creatures approach homes or campgrounds too closely, biologists chase the animals with specially trained dogs and shoot them with beanbags to provide a dose of aversive conditioning. To prevent wolves from raiding sheep and cattle herds, environmental groups—working with the federal government and Idaho ranchers—have deployed volunteers and radio-controlled noisemakers to scare away approaching packs with strobe lights, shouts, and the recorded sounds of highway traffic and gunfire. To address its urban deer problem, Fire Island—which never did import cougars—now injects does with contraceptive vaccines to slow reproduction. Many communities plagued by Canada geese employ dogs to chase the destructive flocks.

Such efforts are to be applauded, but the most critical element of wildlife management in twenty-first-century America will be modifying the behavior of the most pervasive species of all. Reducing conflicts between people and wild animals will require controls on human actions: where we build our homes, how we landscape our yards, the way we dispose of our trash and house our pets. People, especially those who live along the new frontier between civilization and wildland, must accept that they are participants in the natural world, not mere observers.

Edward Abbey, repeating a comment by friend and fellow eco-warrior Doug Peacock, once wrote, "It ain't wilderness . . . unless there's a critter out there that can kill and eat you." That may be true, but the inverse is not; just because there's a critter out there that can kill and eat you doesn't mean it *is* wilderness. Time does not run backward. We can bring the lions and wolves and bears back to America, and there are many good reasons to do so—ecological reasons, spiritual ones—but these great animals will not restore a mythic past, cannot erase the need for human intervention.

Regarding the riddle of Scott Lancaster's death—why the tragedy did not elicit more public furor—there is another answer not previously suggested: the tragedy helped assuage societal guilt. After all, when you look at the ledger—66,665 cougars killed by humans in just half of the last century, only fifteen humans known to have been killed by cougars during the *entire* century—some environmentalists argue that the occasional death by wild predator is the least our species can endure considering past sins. In this way, such tragedies are a form of self-flagellation or sacrifice, a modified version of what some mothers in India once did: tossing their infants to sharks at the mouth of the Ganges "to sacrifice the fruit of their body for the sin of their soul." But feeding our own to the lions will not undo the damage done. It will not restore wilderness.

On a blue-skied Sunday morning in early 1999, nine months after Andy Peterson's attack and fifteen miles north, the telephone rang at the home of Joe and Sue Beckner. The sixty-ish couple inhabited a tidy ranch-style house in Lakewood, Colorado, in an area locals once called Rattlesnake Hill, though the venomous serpents had since been displaced by sod lawns, concrete sidewalks, and asphalt driveways that led to two-car garages. Just eight miles from Denver's skyscrapers, the Beckners' subdivision was densely packed, solidly suburban. Joe, a former high school basketball coach and art teacher, now made a living painting pastoral watercolors: children playing amid hollyhocks, a moose wading in a mountain stream.

Joe answered the phone. It was a neighbor alerting him to look out the back window; a large creature appeared to be loitering in his tree. *We've got raccoons again*, Joe assumed as he ambled over to the breakfast nook, where sliding glass doors led to a patio. Peering out at the ponderosa that rose above his barbecue grill, Joe was astonished to find a tremendous cat with cinnamon fur taking in the scenery from a perch fifteen feet up. The cougar seemed calm and content. It rested on a branch with forepaws elegantly crossed.

Over the following hours, the cat would cause much commotion—Joe would call 911, the police would cordon off the street, and TV reporters and neighbors would congregate in his house while wildlife officers tranquilized the animal, affixed a purple tag to its ear, and hauled it back to the mountains southwest of town—but first, before notifying the authorities, Joe wanted some time alone with the majestic creature.

He studied the cat. He considered the contours of its face and the way it posed in the tree; he wanted to remember this sight so he could capture it in watercolor later. Sunlight glinted off the cougar's left eye, which glowed like a marble. Yet something about the lion didn't look right. Joe puzzled momentarily, then recognized what was odd: the cat was missing its right eye.

POSTSCRIPT

Michael Sanders remained a biologist with Boulder County until 1998. In his later years on the job, in an effort to reduce the prey that attracted lions into town, he fought to open county lands to deer hunting, but the proposal failed repeatedly. Frustrated by the politics of managing wildlife among the growing hordes on the Front Range, Michael resigned his post to launch an ecotourism business. Today, he lives in Livingston, Montana, and operates the Environmental Adventure Company.

Jim Halfpenny departed the University of Colorado and Boulder in 1992. He now lives in Gardiner, Montana, at the northern entrance to Yellowstone National Park, and writes wildlife books, produces nature videos, lectures, and teaches courses on predators and tracking. He continues to warn about the dangers of habituated cougars, and he fears that habituated wolves will be the next challenge facing many western communities.

Jerry Apker, Kathi Green, and **Tom Howard** remain employees of the Colorado Division of Wildlife, where Apker now serves as the agency's carnivore biologist, Green is statewide disease coordinator, and Howard continues as district wildlife manager for the area south of Boulder. **Kristi Coughlon** left the division in 1991 to pursue an advanced degree at Col-

orado State University, focusing on the human aspects of wildlife management. She now works as a technical writer for the U.S. Forest Service in Fort
Collins.

Lynda Walters, who graduated from medical school in 1992, took a job
as an emergency room physician in western Colorado, where she still practices. "I chose that place because I felt safe in the environment," she says of
her new home, a more arid and open landscape than the forested Front
Range. "There's no bushes, there's no shrubs, there's no trees. You can see
from here to infinity."

Rick and Teresa Overmyer, still residents of Coal Creek Canyon, no
longer mind the occasional lion (or bear) on their property. In January
2003, Teresa glimpsed a cougar near the house and, thrilled by the sight,
loaded daughter Jennie in the car and searched the neighborhood for
the majestic animal. The family continues to believe that the dog-eating
cougar of 1989–90 was a rogue and was appropriately killed.

Matt Miller and **Mark Malan**, their red-deer ranch outlawed by new regulations in 1990, received compensation from the state and disbanded their
operation in 1991. The men went their separate ways and eventually left
Colorado. Today, Miller works for the Western Area Power Administration
in Billings, Montana.

Don Kattner, after pursuing lions in Colorado for sixteen years, returned
to Northern California in 1991 to take a job as a government trapper and
hunter. He continues in that position today, tracking down stock-raiding
cougars, bears, and coyotes for the U.S. Department of Agriculture.

Scott Lancaster's schoolmates, in the months after his death, collected
donations and organized volunteer labor to construct a lasting tribute to
their friend—the Scott Lancaster Memorial Bike Path, visible today along
the south side of Interstate 70 in Idaho Springs. Scott's mother, who paints
watercolors, keeps her son's memory alive in another way; when she signs
her artwork, she twists the tail of the R at the end of her name into a bicycle wheel.

NOTES ON SOURCES

This book is nonfiction. All characters, places, and events are real. No names have been changed, except where noted in the text. During some of the time covered by the book, Colorado Division of Wildlife biologist Kathi Green was known by her married name, Demarest; for simplicity's sake, I have used her maiden name throughout.

Writing factually and comprehensively about events I did not observe, more than a decade after they occurred, felt at times like assembling a giant jigsaw puzzle from pieces that had scattered to the wind. Finding the missing parts and figuring out where they fit required the assistance of an enormous number of people (see "witnesses," below) who, in telephone conversations, e-mail exchanges, and more than two hundred hours of tape-recorded interviews, shared memories of what they had done, thought, and seen. Many of these individuals also graciously dug around in attics, basements, and dusty, back-office filing cabinets for old letters, photographs, videotapes, audiotapes, computer discs, diary entries, field notes, scrapbooks, calendars, memos, maps, telephone messages, receipts, rosters, race results, police reports, trial transcripts, meeting minutes, neighborhood newsletters, newspaper clippings, press releases, and anything else that could provide direct documentation of the tale I had set out to chronicle.

A thorough recounting of the help offered by my witnesses is impossible to give, but some important examples may serve to illustrate how this book was assembled. Michael Sanders and Jim Halfpenny provided me with their original Lion Search Observation Report Forms, which listed information on nearly four hundred cougar encounters and the people who phoned in the reports. In almost all such cases that I have described in detail, I followed up with the reporting party to check facts and to gain additional information. Many of these individuals were able to provide further documentation of what had occurred. Ponce Gebhardt shared minute-by-minute notes of the Knollwood lion's wanderings and her phone calls to government agencies. Don Kattner sent me photographs from his cougar hunt. In a large number of cases, witnesses accompanied me to where their lion encounters occurred; for instance, Bernice McCain spoke to me on the porch where she confronted Fifi's assailant, Lynda Walters bravely returned to the ponderosa she climbed, and Bob Bachant met me at the Boulder Community Hospital patio where he had his unexpected, late-night feline visit. Similarly, Michael Sanders took me to the abandoned Monarch Mine ("The Hilton of mountain lion dens"), Dave Wohlers escorted me to Scott Lancaster's attack site, and John Peleaux led me up the hillside from which he guided the pursuit of Scott's killer.

Scott Lancaster's father, Larry, provided me with a copy of his son's ski meet video made the weekend before he died; Eric Simonich then watched the video with me to interpret whom and what I was seeing. Scott Reuman, photographer for the Red Zinger Mini Classic, lent me slides of the 1988 Boulder Mall Criterium; Mike and Brendan Dallas deciphered those images for me. Later, Tom Fairlie—whose son Kevin competed in the Zinger—unearthed a videotape of the criterium; I relied on Colby Pearce, another participant in the race and now a professional cyclist, to interpret the video.

Other tape recordings proved critical. Cary Richardson of Boulder's Open Space and Mountain Parks Department found a video of Jim Halfpenny's lion-tracking seminar of February 17, 1988, which enabled me to write that scene in chapter 3. Teresa Overmyer showed me a home video of her family assembling the artificial Christmas tree in November 1989, an event described in chapter 9. Scott Hoover of the Colorado Division of Wildlife provided me with a law enforcement videotape of Scott Lancaster's body and the surrounding hillside filmed on January 16, 1991. The division's Tom Howard gave me an audiotape of his debriefing with Alpine Rescue Team, made at the Idaho Springs firehouse that same day. Michael Sanders supplied a videotape of Jim Halfpenny's presentation at the Mountain Lion–Human Interaction Symposium and Workshop in April 1991.

When writing about events for which I could find no direct documentation, in which case I had to rely solely on people's memory, I attempted to verify statements by comparing one person's account with another's, and I often checked back with witnesses to resolve any discrepancies. In the few cases where recollections still diverged, invariably on minor points, I selected the account that seemed most credible.

Where, in the text, I quote my witnesses in the present tense (e.g., "Michael Sanders says," "Teresa Overmyer recalls"), the source of the comment is almost always one of my present-day author interviews. Quotations written in the past tense derive from various sources: contemporaneous news reports, tapes (video and audio), and the recollections of those who said or heard the words. All thoughts attributed to characters are as recalled by those individuals.

THE WITNESSES
(Grouped by their affiliation during the time period covered by the book.)

Residents of Boulder and the surrounding area: Joseph and Kirtan Aentara, Fran Aguilar, Miriam and Wally Allen, Rob Altschuler, Andy Amalfitano, Bob Bachant, Barbara and John Bennett, Marge Black, Vicki Cherner, Len Crimmins, Warren DeHaan, Jerry Dickinson, Sondra Donovan, Anne and Steve Dubovsky, Gary Emerson, Cathy Eppinger, Joe Evans, Kent Gapter, Ponce and Rich Gebhardt, Beverly Goldthwaite, Ellie Halliday, Steve Headley, Bill Held, Bob Hodgetts, Sydney Hope, Eugene Kayser, Pat Kayser, Jimmy Keith, Bodil and Ralph Knull, Bill Krantz, Doug and Tami Kremer, Dawn Kummli, Bill LaMorris, George and Judy Lehmkuhl, Melanie and Mike Maish, Mark Malan, Bernice and Merle McCain, Christie Ann Miller, Mary Miller, Matt Miller, Peggy Moore, Peter Moore, Dick Moreland, Rick and Teresa Overmyer, Shari Owen, Richard Partridge, Ryan and Shelley Partridge, Althea and Elihu Pearlman, Leah Persons, Bill Pierce, Don Proebstel, Peter Ramig, Mary Beth Reith, Scott Reuman, Stuart Robertson, Paul Ruth, Vincent Scarelli, Suzy Schemel, Steve Steffek, Doug Straub, Roxy Walker, Bill and Betty Walters, Lynda Walters, Atashnaa Werner, Nan Young, Bud and Joyce Zorichak.

At the Colorado Division of Wildlife: Bill Adrian, Jerry Apker, Gary Berlin, Len Carpenter, Kristi Coughlon, Bruce Gill, Kathi Green, Brownlee Guyer, Jim Hekkers, Scott Hoover, Andy Hough, Tom Howard, Laurie Kuelthau, Jim Lipscomb, Tom Lytle, Todd Malmsbury, Lauren Martin, Bruce McCloskey, Perry Olson, Steve Steinert, Bob Tully, Dave Weber.

At the University of Colorado: Jim Halfpenny.

Boulder city and county employees: Dave Allen, Randy Coombs, Brad Frederking, Pascale Fried, Janet George, Mark Gershman, Dave Hallock, Jim Hughes, Clay Leeper, Glen McCarthy, Brian Peck, Michael Sanders, Jim Smith, Rich Smith, Ann Wichmann.

Attendees of the Third Mountain Lion Workshop in Prescott, Arizona: Lee Fitzhugh, Lisa Haynes, Phil Koepp, Sue Morse, Doug Padley, Harley Shaw, Shawn Smallwood, Nick Smith, Tice Supplee, Ron Thompson.

Scott Lancaster's family, friends, and teachers: Trip Coffin, Aaron Dallas, Brendan Dallas, Mike Dallas, Shelly Donahue, Conradt Fredell, John Gould, John Gumina, Abby Heller, Kirk Hobbs, Heather Tilley Hutto, Einar Jensen, John Klieforth, Brett Lancaster, Gail and Larry Lancaster, Todd Lancaster, Candice Michael, Greg Miller, Janet Romarine, Steve Selle, Eric Simonich, James Valdez.

Individuals involved in Colorado cycling: Kevin Fairlie, Tom Fairlie, Rich Gängl, Fred Owen, Colby Pearce, Andy Rosen, Henny Topp, Yvonne van Gent, Beth Wrenn-Estes.

Idaho Springs Police Department and Clear Creek County Sheriff's Office: Rick Albers, Bob Cahill, Don Krueger, Stu Nay, Darren White, Dave Wohlers, Monica Woznicki.

Alpine Rescue Team: Shane Becker, Bill Butler, Tom Fiore, John Peleaux, Robin Schmutzler, Steve Shelafo, Paul Woodward, Brian Wrenshall.

Journalists: Howard Berkes, Gary Gerhardt, Barbara Lawlor, Judy Miller, Carol Wilcox.

Others: Mike Aderhold, Joe Beckner, Mary Bonnell, Dan Flenniken, Ben Galloway, Bob Glock, Vince Hennigan, Carol Hopkins, Don Kattner, Dennis Madden, Kerry Murphy, Andy Peterson, Wilbur Richie, Ray Skiles, Donald and Susan Small, Laura Small, Chris Tomford.

What follows are references for previously published quotations and facts, as well as notes on important works I consulted.

Abbreviations

BCN	*Boulder County News*
BG	*Boston Globe*
CCC	*Clear Creek Courant* (Idaho Springs)
CD	*Colorado Daily* (Boulder)
DC	*Daily Camera* (Boulder)
DP	*Denver Post*
GT	*Golden Transcript*
HCN	*High Country News*
LAT	*Los Angeles Times*
M-E	*Mountain-Ear* (Nederland)
NYT	*New York Times*
RMN	*Rocky Mountain News*
T-C	*Times-Call* (Longmont)

Prologue: Death in the Ecotone

Davis (1998), McKibben (1995), and Nash (1982) provided influential ideas for this chapter.

7 **on a Colorado hunting trip while vice president–elect:** Roosevelt (1925:1–75).

7 **first adult known to be killed and consumed:** For a list of confirmed fatal attacks by cougars from 1890 to 1990, see Beier (1991).

7 **"Lion suspected . . .":** *DP*, Jan. 17, 1991.

7 **"Human remains . . .":** *DC*, Jan. 19, 1991.

7 **"Fatal attack believed . . .":** *Canyon Courier* (Evergreen, Colorado), Jan. 23, 1991.

7 "Cougar Mystery": *USA Today*, Jan. 18, 1991.

8 "There is no . . .": Roosevelt ([1916]1925:16–17). A similar statement can be found in Roosevelt (1893a:272). He expressed a somewhat contraditory opinion in Roosevelt (1914:26–31).

8 from the Old English *wilddēornes*: Nash (1982:1–2).

8 "In Wildness is . . .": Thoreau ([1862]1982:609).

8 "In Europe people . . .": Tocqueville ([1840]1945:74).

9 it is impossible to place oneself: NPR's *All Things Considered*, Dec. 8, 1998.

9 Phoenix's urban edge: Waits et al. (2000:16).

9 Atlanta's swelling metropolitan region: *Atlanta Journal*, May 8, 2001.

9 When asked in a recent poll: *LAT* poll, study #458, April 2001, question 39. For a summary of the survey results, see *LAT*, April 30, 2001.

9 Between 1998 and 2002: *NYT*, Nov. 16, 2002.

10 giving the range back to the bison: *HCN*, Jan. 15, 2001.

10 ballot measures that restrict the hunting and trapping: Minnis (1998).

10 black bears have encroached: *BG*, July 4, 1998. Also see Cardoza (1976).

10 New Jersey's ursine population: *NYT*, March 21, 2003.

10 "rapidly adapting to human presence": Merrill and Mech (2000:430).

10 Coyotes, previously confined to a swath: *NYT*, July 27, 1999.

11 South End doorstep: *BG*, April 12, 1999.

11 Central Park: *NYT*, April 13, 1999.

11 Henry M. Jackson Federal Building: *Seattle Times*, Dec. 4, 1997; *Seattle Post-Intelligencer*, Dec. 4, 1997.

11 "the meeting point . . .": G. Taylor (1949:2).

Chapter 1: A Land without Carnivory

16 "Send us two missiles . . .": *DC*, May 9, 1987.

16 "the little town nestled . . .": Glenn and Brown (1998:1).

16 "the Peaceable Kingdom . . .": *CD*, Aug. 21, 1990 [the "Welcome Back '90" issue].

16 "laid-back city": *Newsweek*, July 28, 1980.

17 "computer technicians . . .": Snyder ([1974]1993:177).

18 in 1986, a yearling wandered: *DC*, March 4, 1986.

18 "the encroachment of wild creatures . . .": K. Thomas (1996:77–78).

18 "higher than all . . .": John (1958:230).

18 "What fruit does . . .": Louth (2001:42).

18 "Man walk'd with Beast . . .": Pope ([1734]1969:46).

19 "where large bands preyed . . .": Cary (1911:169).

19 on September 23, 1979: Petersen (1995:72–96), Murray (1987:134–37, 139).

19 "Control wildlife aggression . . .": *DC*, Dec. 20, 1987.

22 On October 7, 1986: Details of Bill Tesinsky's fatal mauling come from official

documents received from Yellowstone National Park under a Freedom of Information Act request.

22 **"Animals normally flee . . .":** p. 13 of the board's final report.

Chapter 2: Return of the Native

24 **red-green color-blind:** This is presumed to be true of cougars, as it has been demonstrated in domestic cats. See, e.g., Sechzer and Brown (1964).

24 *Caloplaca*: Mutel and Emerick (1984:64).

25 **"[The cougar] never makes any noise . . .":** Eastman (1904:242).

25 **"as you and I know the floorplan . . .":** Shaw (1989:8).

26 **"THE NEW ELDORADO!!!":** West (1998:107).

26 **Illinoisan Daniel Blue:** Blue ([1860]1968).

26 **"Will quit and try and get back . . .":** Jackson's diary was published in the *Colorado Transcript*, March 26, 1884. A transcription is also given by Hafen (1935), with slightly different punctuation.

28 **dynamited grizzlies:** Cahalane (1939:232).

28 **catnip oil:** Dobie ([1950a]1990:132), Barnes (1960:144–45), Young and Goldman (1946:105–6).

28 **wired their mouths shut:** Lopez (1978:196).

28 **set them on fire:** Lopez (1978:196).

28 **sawed off their lower jaws:** Hornby (1945:71–72).

28 **earliest recorded bounty:** Clavigero (1937:80).

28 **"bring the heads & taile . . .":** Burt (1899:348).

28 **"whosoeuer shall kill . . .":** Hoadly (1868:135).

28 **doubled its bounty:** Hoadly (1870:406).

28 **"Panthers and wolves . . .":** Shoemaker ([1917]1993:29–30).

29 **By the time the United States:** Dates of extirpation of cougars from eastern states derive from Young and Goldman (1946), Seton (1929), Rhoads (1903), True (1891), Nowak (1974), Spargo (1950), and Hoagland (1971).

29 **"a hunted criminal . . .":** *DP*, Oct. 2, 1932.

29 **"Crooked Nose":** Grinnell, Dixon, and Linsdale (1937:582).

29 **"Old Five-toe Tom":** Evans (1951:186).

29 **"hundreds of cattle . . .":** *DP*, Feb. 21, 1905.

29 **at least one woman:** Kennedy (1942).

30 **Lee Brothers:** *DP*, June 20, 1948.

30 **"Uncle Jim destroyed . . .":** Dodge (1927:73).

30 **"dean of lion hunters":** Hibben (1948:3).

30 **"I never saw a lion . . .":** Dobie ([1950a]1990:55).

30 **"He is a religious fanatic . . .":** Roosevelt (1919:210).

30 **"It seemed that Ben Lilly . . .":** Hibben (1948:4).

30 **"menace to other . . .":** Hawes (1935:53).

30 **"no respect for hunting seasons . . .":** H. Johnson (1942:2).

31 "spent practically a lifetime . . .": *NYT*, March 7, 1937.

31 "The only thing . . .": Hornaday (1913:x).

31 "The eradication of the puma . . .": Hornaday (1914:155).

31 "a great deal of mischief": *Report* (1890:6).

31 **between three dollars and fifty dollars:** The history of lion bounties in Colorado is as follows: Feb. 11, 1881—$10 bounty enacted. Feb. 27, 1885—bounty repealed. April 18, 1889—$10 bounty reinstated. April 8, 1893—bounty reduced to $3. May 7, 1929—bounty increased to $50. April 3, 1965—bounty repealed and mountain lion declared "big game," effective July 1, 1965.

31 "Come on-n-n-n-n-n-n . . .": *DP*, Jan. 22, 1920.

32 **In the summer of 1891:** A record of James Walker's bounty can be found in the *Treasurer's Record of Bounties Paid, Boulder County*, at the Boulder Public Library's Carnegie Branch Library for Local History.

32 "Fortunately for us . . .": *DC*, Sept. 19, 1950.

32 **eighty-five-pound lioness glimpsed:** *DC*, July 13, 1944.

32 **66,665:** Anderson (1983:55).

32 **4,000:** Cahalane (1964:3).

32 **124:** K. Dixon (1967). This was a low, and probably unrealistic, estimate.

33 "By 1924, deer . . .": Thompson (1935:48).

33 **revisionist thinkers:** Burk (1973).

33 "going out after . . .": *The Pine Cone* (the official bulletin of the New Mexico Game Protective Association), Jan. 1919; reprinted in Flader (1974:x).

33 "By killing off all . . .": Meine and Knight (1999:62).

34 "The 'control of nature' . . .": Carson ([1962]1964:261).

34 **an opinion survey in Canada:** Hancock (1980:209–11).

34 **rock star–like following in Boulder:** See Abbey (1994:269, 280).

34 "We need mountain lions . . .": Abbey (1970:52B).

34 "There is no authentic record . . .": Abbey apparently recognized later that this statement was false. When the *Life* article was reprinted in his book *The Journey Home*, the text was changed to read, "There are few authentic records of a lion actually attacking a human being."

35 "the careless extermination . . .": *DP*, Feb. 11, 1965.

35 **between 1,100 and 1,500:** Currier, Sheriff, and Russell (1977:11).

36 "natural sneaks": Barnes (1960:150).

36 "Only the very lucky . . .": Abbey (1970:52B).

36 **tracks in the snow:** Boulder naturalist Dave Hallock found fresh tracks of this lion on Dec. 20, 1987. I have reconstructed its wanderings on the basis of his field report.

Chapter 3: Happy Times

40 **one of the cat's bearers:** City of Boulder park ranger Ann Wichmann.

41 "It's a pretty unhappy end . . .": *DC*, Jan. 12, 1988.

41 "the destroyer of the deer . . .": Roosevelt ([1916]1925:22).
41 "Humanity has four billion . . .": Abbey (1994:299).
41 "A world without mountain lions . . .": Abbey and Nichols (1984).
41 "I am appalled . . .": *DC*, Jan. 12, 1988.
41 A month later: Jim Halfpenny's lion tracking seminar was held on Feb. 17,
      1988. A videotape of the presentation, possessed by the City of Boulder Open
      Space and Mountain Parks Department, was used to reconstruct this scene.
43 "the ancient script of the woods": Seton (1958:20).
43 an embarrassing episode: *DC*, March 18, 1977.
44 "shun close association . . .": Coleman (1965:3).
45 "Seen a mountain lion lately?": *DC*, Jan. 7, 1987.

Chapter 4: City of Nature

46 "little spiritual quotes" and "people living happy with nature": *DC*, Oct. 6,
      1974.
48 "Nature should appear . . .": Olmsted ([1910]1967:27).
48 "take away the barren look . . .": *BCN*, Feb. 8, 1871.
48 three hundred thousand trees: *DC*, Oct. 20, 2000.
48 ten- to twentyfold: Personal communication, Merrill Kaufmann. See also Kauf-
      mann et al. (2001) and Veblen and Lorenz (1991).
49 "What's with these Boulder residents . . .": *DC*, Dec. 20, 1987.
49 concerned Boulder's deer: For more on Boulder's deer problem, see Southwick
      et al. (1990), Nelson (1997:171–82).
49 "because of its great ears . . .": Roosevelt et al. ([1902]1924:28).
50 *increased* 57 percent: Memo, "Deer Study Road Kill Update," Sept. 5, 1988,
      found in the files of City of Boulder Open Space and Mountain Parks Department.
50 "The mountain lion is something . . .": Mills (1909:9).
51 scientists dried, washed, and sifted: Ackerman, Lindzey, and Hemker (1984).
51 "34 out of 43 . . .": J. Dixon (1925:40).
51 "bread and butter": A. Starker Leopold (1959:476).
51 "the lion's staff of life": Dobie (1928:9).
51 "How much part . . .": Thompson (1935:51).
51 "the puma 'goes with the deer'": Young and Goldman (1946:145).

Chapter 5: Lion Search

54 "Boulder County and the University . . .": *DC*, Sept. 22, 1988.
57 "Zookeepers generally agree . . .": Hancock (1980:24).
58 seventy times in one day: Eaton (1978:43).
58 infanticide and cannibalism: Adult male cougars frequently kill cubs sired by

others. See Logan and Sweanor (2001:120); Anderson, Bowden, and Kattner (1992:73). Shaw (1989:13) does not rule out the possibility of toms occasionally killing their own offspring.

58 six times the fat of cow's milk: Ben Shaul (1962:337).
59 "The kittens play . . .": Hibben (1937:34).
60 "panthers often leaped on roofs . . .": Shoemaker ([1917]1993:28).

Chapter 6: The Day Shift

63 "Wherein consisteth . . .": Gouge (1684:27–28).
66 "They fed most during sunset . . .": Kufeld, Bowden, and Schrupp (1988:519).
66 "Predators are known to synchronize . . .": Curio (1976:34–36).
71 "Beasts of prey have no history": Buber (1965:73).
72 "So light, silent and cautious . . .": Singer (1914:254).
72 significantly longer than its front legs: Gonyea (1976).
75 "Young lion prowls . . .": *DC*, Nov. 12, 1988.
75 "I thought [Kip] was . . .": *DC*, Nov. 14, 1988.
75 "false alarm": *DC*, Nov. 16, 1988.
75 "I would feel lucky . . .": *CD*, Nov. 18–20, 1988.
75 "We've received reports . . .": *RMN*, Nov. 26, 1988.
76 "wildlife enthusiasts . . .": Kellert (1985:188).
76 "Ain't nature wonderful? . . .": *CD*, Nov. 18–20, 1988.

Chapter 7: Sterkfontein Redux

81 "that seized living quarries . . .": Dart (1953:209).
82 "One may visualize *Dinofelis* . . .": Brain (1981:104).
82 "The tipping of this balance . . .": Brain (1981:273).
82 "the most compelling . . .": Chatwin (1987:241).
83 "Could it be, one is tempted . . .": Chatwin (1987:255–56).
83 a thousand people annually: McDougal (1987:442).
83 "had prevented her from killing . . .": Corbett (1946:29).
83 "conceived a most unfortunate . . .": Patterson (1927:119).
84 exceeded 130: There is considerable debate over the number of people killed by the Tsavo lions. For a discussion of the issue, see Kerbis Peterhans and Gnoske (2001:7).
84 67 people in Zambia: Brelsford (1950).
84 "man-eating leopard of Rudraprayag": Corbett (1948).
84 "once every 10 days . . .": *Asiaweek*, April 24, 1998.
84 "The least dangerous to man . . .": Roosevelt ([1916]1925:16).
84 "a cowardly brute . . .": Hittell (1911:196).
84 "We do not recollect . . .": Audubon and Bachman (1851:311).

84 "under no normal circumstances . . .": Seton (1929:126).

85 "terribly ferocious appetite": Simms (1997:154).

86 "ten feet and nine inches . . .": *RMN,* April 14, 1876.

86 "the almost universal tendency . . ." and following two quotations: McGuire (1914).

87 "Miss Kennedy ran . . .": *Morgan Hill Times,* July 9, 1909, as reprinted by Storer (1923:46). For more on this incident, see Anonymous (1909*a*) and Anonymous (1909*b*).

87 "Let us put a stop . . .": McGuire (1914:536).

87 one mountain lion proved McGuire wrong: The victim was James Fehlhaber, age thirteen, killed Dec. 17, 1924, near Okanogan, Washington. Sources disagree on the identity and physical condition of the boy's killer. See Finley (1925), Hall (1925), Haley (1953).

87 "In one instance, a man . . .": C. Moore (1953:115).

89 "I was just standing next to her . . .": This quotation and details of the attack on Laura Small (as well as lion encounters that preceded it) derive from trial transcripts and related documents in the case of *Small v. County of Orange.*

90 "appeared very emaciated . . .": Incident report by Tony Gimbrone, park district supervisor, dated March 23, 1986.

90 "When I saw the lion . . .": *LAT,* Oct. 20, 1986.

92 "These traits indicate predatory . . ." etc.: Lee Fitzhugh's remarks were published in R. Smith (1989:74–77).

92 "When we offered . . .": Bogue and Ferrari (1976:37).

93 "will devise numerous articulations . . .": Kuhn (1970:78).

94 "The reasons for the attack . . .": Big Bend National Park, Case Incident Record #840559. (Incident occurred Aug. 2, 1984.)

94 "The lion circled around . . .": Big Bend National Park, Case Incident Record #870173. (Incident occurred April 19, 1987.)

96 twenty-five ounces of gold: (Boulder) *Weekly Herald,* May 19, 1886.

Chapter 8: Cats and Dogs

98 "It is one of the strange . . .": Barnes (1960:35–36).

98 "The panther always runs . . .": Stone (1883*b*:1188), also Stone (1883*a*:204).

98 "I could train a poodle . . .": Lesowski (1967:47).

98 "to terrify [the mountain lion] to a degree . . .": Ingersoll (1897:56).

99 "At some time in the lions' history . . .": Seidensticker and Lumpkin (1992:117).

99 "the great cat's worst enemy . . .": Calkins (1902:454).

99 "One black Wolf . . .": Boyd and Neale (1992:524).

100 "fraidy cat": Musgrave (1927).

102 "Stimulus-specific waning . . .": Immelmann and Beer (1989:126).

104 an exhaustive study: Anderson, Bowden, and Kattner (1992).

105 "If we reported that a circus train . . .": *DC*, Dec. 11, 1983.

105 An embarrassing tragedy: McDougal (1999:9).

106 "It might have just thought . . ." and following quotation: *T-C*, Feb. 9, 1989.

107 "*the* sports town": *Outside*, May 1989.

107 "This newspaper stands . . .": *DC*, July 8, 1989.

107 "Little did I know . . .": Kummli (1990:73).

107 "like a blast furnace": Kummli (1990:76).

107 "a train coming . . .": Maclean (1992:35).

108 "The beauty of summertime . . .": Kummli (1990:44).

109 "Honey, you've sure got . . .": Philip Thompson, as stated in a letter to Jim
      Halfpenny, March 31, 1989.

109 "You may be old enough . . .": *DC*, Jan. 7, 1990.

110 "We've had at least three females . . .": *RMN*, Feb. 19, 1989.

112 "Mountain lion apparently kills Montana boy": *DP*, Sept. 12, 1989.

114 "Cats possess an exceptionally . . .": Leyhausen (1979:75).

Chapter 9: Trouble in the Canyon

115 one Montana home, flush toilets: Oard (1993:166).

116 more than one hundred miles per hour: The wind gust was reported in the
      Dec. 1989 issue of the *Leaflet*, a newsletter put out by the Coal Creek Canyon
      Improvement Association.

117 radioactive rabbits: *DC*, Oct. 6, 2002.

117 "BOOM TIME IN THE ROCKIES": *Time*, Sept. 6, 1993.

117 "Crisis looming in western timber supply": Sullivan (1989).

117 "giving up and getting out": *NYT*, May 1, 1985.

122 cougar fur is easily distinguished: Moore, Spence, and Dugnolle
      (1974:142–43).

123 "It frightens me": This extended statement by Teresa Overmyer and others by
      her and Rick were made in a taped interview with NPR reporter Howard Berkes
      in March 1990. Portions of the interview were included in a story broadcast by
      NPR's *Morning Edition* on March 27, 1990.

124 Vilhjalmur Stefansson: Gantt (1944:33). The significance of his observation is
      explored by Wyrwicka (1978:72) and Wyrwicka (1981:ix).

124 "There was no doubt . . .": Bruce (1953:17).

124 "clean precision": Hibben (1948:78).

125 "He looked like a well-worn pincushion . . .": Dr. Cathy Eppinger in an
      author interview.

126 "ooze and goo": Bill LaMorris in an author interview.

127 "Coal Creek area on cougar alert": *RMN*, Jan. 30, 1990.

127 "Why, it's for you!": *M-E*, Feb. 1, 1990.

128 "We're not going to solve . . .": *DP*, Jan. 31, 1990.

128 "For one thing . . ." and following quotations: *RMN*, Jan. 30, 1990.

Chapter 10: The Hunt

129 "The mountain lion . . .": Bruce (1925:1–2).

129 an additional thousand dollars: Bell (1921:291).

130 New Zealand's red deer irrupted: Allen (1954:191–92), Fennessy and Taylor (1989:310–11).

132 "Persistence, patience, and Coors": Parfit (1988:77).

133 "a nose as delicate as . . .": Hibben (1948:26).

133 "unless you [can] strike . . .": Carroll (1983:101).

133 "Catch the dog in the act": Carroll (1983:101).

133 "If, after he had trained a dog . . .": Dobie ([1950*a*]1990:172).

135 Old Cripple-Foot . . . and Old Lady Scar-Heel: Barker (1946).

135 "usually in the form of a loop . . .": Bruce (1925:4–5).

135 figure-eight circuits: Vosburgh (1949:54).

135 "As soon as some part . . .": Bruce (1922:112).

135 "arrived at the designated point . . .": Grinnell, Dixon, and Linsdale (1937:577).

138 "The conservation of our natural resources . . .": Hart and Ferleger (1989:102).

138 "Conservation means development . . .": Hart and Ferleger (1989:102).

139 "Wild beasts and birds . . .": Roosevelt (1915:160).

139 "manly out-of-door sports . . .": Roosevelt (1893*b*).

140 "often traveling 25 or 30 miles . . .": Bruce (1925:5).

141 "with nose close to the ground": Bruce (1922:113).

141 "The trail is lost . . .": Barker (1946:144–45).

142 "Lion hounds, with cougar scent . . .": Hibben (1948:20–21).

144 "The shooting of a cougar . . .": Pack (1930:81).

145 "It would be impossible to wish . . .": Roosevelt (1925:75).

146 "Mountain lion's death upsets . . .": *DC*, Feb. 8, 1990.

146 "Disposal of cougar's body . . .": *RMN*, Feb. 8, 1990.

146 "Man who killed . . .": *T-C*, Feb. 8, 1990.

148 the local paper ran a touching feature: *M-E*, Aug. 31, 1989.

148 "Gestapo-type": *DP*, Sept. 22, 1989.

148 "[Mark Malan] understood very clearly . . .": *DC*, Feb. 8, 1990.

148 "no way of knowing . . .": *RMN*, Feb. 8, 1990.

148 "That led to him hunting...": *DC*, Feb. 8, 1990.

148 "We are discussing . . .": *RMN*, Feb. 8, 1990.

149 "I just did something . . .": *T-C*, Feb. 8, 1990.

149 "It was only a matter of time . . .": *DC*, Feb. 10, 1990.

Chapter 11: *Culture—Human and Animal*

150 "I took my fieldglass . . .": *BCN*, Oct. 17, 1873. This story was later retold, with slightly different wording, in *BCN*, July 14, 1876, and by Bixby (1880:379).

150 intervening hills obscure: Meier (1993).

151 "Go away": *BCN*, Oct. 17, 1873.

151 "He wished his white brethren . . .": *RMN*, May 1, 1861.

151 Left Hand, mortally wounded: There has been considerable confusion over Left Hand's fate. Coel ([1981]1987) argues convincingly that the chief, injured at Sand Creek, died a short time later.

151 "men had cut out . . .": *War of the Rebellion* (1893:970–71).

152 "No other task . . .": Roosevelt (1911:252, 254).

152 "[Profit motive] was the passion . . .": Limerick (1987:77).

152 "nationalistic history . . .": Limerick (1987:219).

152 "You can make a game . . .": M. Johnson (1996:11).

153 "split moon" or "failure-to-make-successful-hunt moon": Hilger (1952:85–86).

153 the Division of Wildlife's mountain lion meeting: The meeting in Coal Creek Canyon on Feb. 9, 1990, received wide coverage by the local media. Many of the quotations I use derive from an edited videotape of the gathering found in the archives of Denver's KCNC-TV, as well as articles in the following publications: *DC*, *DP*, *RMN*, Feb. 10, 1990; *GT*, *M-E*, Feb. 15, 1990; Coal Creek Canyon *Mountain Messenger*, March 1990; *DP*, April 1, 1990.

156 "one of the most extraordinary . . .": Nash (1989:4).

156 "from conqueror of . . .": Aldo Leopold (1949:204).

156 "Quit thinking about . . .": Aldo Leopold (1949:224–25).

157 callous attitude toward nature: See L. White (1967).

157 "Be fruitful and multiply . . .": Genesis 1:28.

157 "non-Indian 'wannabes' . . .": Riebsame et al. (1997:115).

160 "When the white man came . . .": Stone and Cram (1903:289–90).

160 "A young officer of the Eighteenth . . .": *Forest and Stream*, Dec. 3, 1874.

161 popular material for making quivers: For the tribes mentioned, see Dyer (1896:99–100), G. Grinnell ([1923]1972:I 184), Spinden (1908:213), Donaldson (1887:401), C. Taylor (2001:64), Hill (1938:168), Dumarest (1919:211), Gunnerson (1998:240), Hoffman (1877:95).

161 "were believed to possess...": G. Grinnell ([1923]1972:I 184).

161 killed lions for meat: For the tribes mentioned, see Russell (1908:81), Barnett (1955:63), Catesby (1754:xxv).

161 "is very white . . .": Darwin ([1839]1966:135).

161 "Consequently, no opportunity . . .": Opler (1941:327).

161 Cochití men: Lange (1959:134).

161 Blackfeet: Wied (1843:251), Southesk ([1875]1969:208).

161 Lakotas: Bolgiano (1995:18).

161 **Osages:** La Flesche (1925:251, 257).

161 **Senecas:** Shoemaker ([1917]1993:52).

161 **a startling discovery:** Culver et al. (2000).

163 **"There are even several reports . . .":** Fisher and Hinde (1949:354). Also see Fisher and Hinde (1951), Sherry and Galef (1984), and Sherry and Galef (1990).

163 **ghoulishly fascinating experiment:** Wyrwicka (1978).

163 **"no doubt that most of these lions . . .":** Rushby (1965:204).

165 **"Lion attacks on people . . .":** Kathi Green spoke to Howard Berkes for a report broadcast by NPR's *Morning Edition* on March 27, 1990. This comment comes from the original, unedited interview. Portions of the quotation were included in the story that aired.

165 **"The history of mountain lions . . .":** Also from interview with Howard Berkes.

166 **"educate themselves on . . .":** Kerbis Peterhans and Gnoske (2001:13).

166 **"began by killing pigs . . .":** Perry (1965:198).

166 **"We have an urbanized mountain lion . . .":** *DP*, April 1, 1990.

Chapter 12: The Long Summer

169 **"Boulder is a hideous . . .":** Bird ([1879]1960:197).

169 **"the great braggart city":** Bird ([1879]1960:137).

169 **"He has large grey-blue eyes . . .":** Bird ([1879]1960:79).

169 **"hideous nocturnal caterwaulings":** Bird ([1879]1960:104).

169 **"bloodthirsty as well as cowardly":** Bird ([1879]1960:217).

170 **"I . . . found it in flavour . . .":** Bird ([1883]1983:228).

170 **"The Malays have many . . .":** Bird ([1883]1983:353–54).

170 **"a regular form of government":** Marsden (1811:292).

170 **"made out of human bones . . .":** Mayer (1924:172).

170 **"They can be distinguished . . .":** This is a translation by Boomgaard (2001:192) of a quotation from A. L. van Hasselt's *Volksbeschrijving van Midden-Sumatra*, 1882.

171 **"The 'birth' of man-eaters . . .":** Boomgaard (2001:85, 230–31).

174 **harvested wild oregano, parsley, and raspberry leaves:** *DC*, Oct. 6, 1974.

177 **"The balloon tipped over . . .":** *DC*, May 26, 1990.

178 **"[Boulder residents] are up in arms . . .":** June 15, 1990, memo from Dave Weber, acting regional manager, to John Torres et al.

179 **"This I would not consider . . .":** *RMN*, June 4, 1990.

179 **"The bizarre incident . . .":** *DC*, June 7, 1990.

179 **"I think the lions are becoming . . .":** *RMN*, June 5, 1990.

179 **"We need to look at adaptability . . .":** From a tape recording of the July 10, 1990, Boulder County commissioners meeting.

179 **"As you are aware . . .":** July 16, 1990, letter from Ron Stewart, chair, Boulder County commissioners, to Perry Olson, director, Colorado Division of Wildlife.

180 **"The Division shares your concern . . .":** Aug. 1, 1990, letter from Perry Olson to Ron Stewart.

180 "At present there is little . . .": "Dear Resident" letter dated June 11, 1990, and signed by Regional Manager John R. Torres.

183 **have been known to target drunks:** Kerbis Peterhans and Gnoske (2001:20).

186 **"My legs turn to rubber . . .":** *Village Voice*, July 11, 1995.

Chapter 13: Final Run

189 **Mountain goats:** Domenick (1975).

190 **a horse:** *Idaho Springs Mining Gazette*, Jan. 25, 1912.

190 **playground equipment:** Gillette (1978:61).

190 **a sixteen-year-old boy:** *CCC*, Oct. 30, 1996.

191 **released a flood from an untapped mine:** Gillette (1978:140–42), Sowell (1976:63–67).

192 **"When they attempted . . .":** Gillette (1978:177).

198 **"The shock produced a stupor . . .":** Livingstone (1859:12).

200 **"I started seeing good . . .":** Noyes and Kletti (1977:377).

Chapter 14: The Investigation

212 **"Who was involved . . .":** The debriefing at the Idaho Springs firehouse was recorded by Tom Howard. The quotations derive from that tape.

218 **"This is the unembalmed . . .":** Dr. Galloway's dictated notes were transcribed in his official autopsy report.

Chapter 15: Exegesis

222 **"He taught me so much . . .":** Many of the quotations and details from Scott Lancaster's memorial service derive from a story in the *CCC*, Jan. 23, 1991, as well as the original notes by reporter Carol Wilcox.

225 **leaving four young cubs motherless:** *DC*, *RMN*, Feb. 18, 1991. The story of the cubs and their rescue is also recounted in a children's book. See Farentinos (1993).

226 **"[Scott] would have been angry . . .":** *DP*, March 10, 1991.

226 **"Next speaker is from University of Colorado . . .":** The description of Jim Halfpenny's talk comes from a videotape of the meeting in the possession of Michael Sanders. See Halfpenny, Sanders, and McGrath (1993) for a written version of the presentation.

Epilogue: The Myth of Wilderness

233 **"Boulder man stabs . . .":** *DC*, July 30, 1993.

233 **"Runner survives . . .":** *DP*, Oct. 22, 1994.

233 "Man escapes cougar . . .": *T-C*, July 25, 1998.

233 "Bicyclist gets best . . .": *RMN*, Oct. 23, 1997.

233 Mark Miedema: *DP*, *RMN*, July 19, 1997.

234 more humans since 1991: According to records kept by Lee Fitzhugh of UC Davis, there were seven confirmed fatal attacks between 1991 and 2002. Beier (1991) lists six such attacks from 1940 to 1990.

234 Missoula, Montana: *Missoulian*, Aug. 1, 1998.

234 Lake Tahoe: *LAT*, Feb. 9, 2000.

234 J. C. Penney: *LAT*, Aug. 25, 1994.

234 Olympia, Washington: *Seattle Times*, April 26, 1998; *DC*, Aug. 10, 1998.

234 "DEER PROBLEM NOTICE": *Wall Street Journal*, Aug. 21, 1991. Also see Kellert et al. (1996:982).

235 "They're baaaaccccckkkk": *Des Moines Register*, Jan. 7, 2002.

235 Kansas City: *Kansas City Star*, Oct. 15, 2002.

235 southeast of St. Louis: July 17, 2000, news release from the Illinois Department of Natural Resources. Also see Heist, Bowles, and Woolf (2001).

235 suburban Minneapolis park: This mountain lion, like others that turn up far from known cougar country, was first thought to be an escaped or abandoned pet, but scientists who examined the cat's carcass "were not able to find any evidence that it had been a captive animal," according to a June 6, 2002, news release from the Minnesota Department of Natural Resources.

235 Michigan: *Detroit Free Press*, Nov. 1, 2001; K. Johnson (2002).

235 Maine, Vermont, Virginia: Bolgiano et al. (2003).

237 "the illusion that we . . .": Cronon (1995:80).

237 "The myth of wilderness . . .": Cronon (1995:88).

238 Evan Eisenberg: See Eisenberg (1998).

239 "It ain't wilderness . . .": Cahalan (2001:165).

239 only fifteen humans known to have been killed by cougars: Beier (1991) lists nine human fatalities from 1900 to 1990. According to records kept by Lee Fitzhugh of UC Davis, another six people were killed by cougars from 1991 to 1999. Additional deaths may well have occurred, but they are not as solidly documented.

239 "to sacrifice the fruit . . .": G. Smith (1887:248).

SELECT BIBLIOGRAPHY

Abbey, Edward. 1970. "Let Us Now Praise Mountain Lions." *Life* 68 (9):52B–58.

———. 1977. *The Journey Home: Some Words in Defense of the American West*. New York: E. P. Dutton.

———. 1994. *Confessions of a Barbarian: Selections from the Journals of Edward Abbey, 1951–1989*. Edited by David Petersen. Boston: Little, Brown.

Abbey, Edward, and John Nichols. 1984. *In Praise of Mountain Lions*. Albuquerque: Albuquerque Sierra Club.

Ackerman, Bruce B., Frederick G. Lindzey, and Thomas P. Hemker. 1984. "Cougar Food Habits in Southern Utah." *Journal of Wildlife Management* 48 (1):147–55.

Ackland, Len. 1999. *Making a Real Killing: Rocky Flats and the Nuclear West*. Albuquerque: Univ. of New Mexico Press.

Acuff, David Samuel. 1988. "Perceptions of the Mountain Lion, 1825–1986, with Emphasis on *Felis Concolor Californica*." M.A. thesis, Univ. of California at Davis.

Alderton, David. 1993. *Wild Cats of the World*. New York: Facts On File.

Allen, Durward. 1954. *Our Wildlife Legacy*. New York: Funk & Wagnalls.

Anderson, Allen E. 1983. *A Critical Review of Literature on Puma* (Felis Concolor). [Ft. Collins:] Colorado Division of Wildlife.

Anderson, Allen E., David C. Bowden, and Donald M. Kattner. 1992. *The Puma on Uncompahgre Plateau, Colorado*. [Ft. Collins:] Colorado Division of Wildlife.

Anonymous. 1909a. "A Mountain Lion That Did Attack." *Outdoor Life* 24 (5):491–93.

———. 1909b. "Further Details Regarding the California Lion Attack." *Outdoor Life* 24 (6):598–600.

———. 1929. "Will the Cougar Attack Man or Child?" *Murrelet* 10 (2):41–42.

Armstrong, David M. 1972. *Distribution of Mammals in Colorado*. Topeka: Museum of Natural History, Univ. of Kansas.

Audubon, John James, and John Bachman. 1851. *The Quadrupeds of North America*. Vol. 2. New York: V. G. Audubon.

Barker, Elliott S. 1946. *When the Dogs Bark "Treed": A Year on the Trail of the Longtails*. Albuquerque: Univ. of New Mexico Press.

Barnes, Claude T. 1960. *The Cougar or Mountain Lion*. Salt Lake City: Ralton.

Barnett, Homer G. 1955. *The Coast Salish of British Columbia*. Eugene: Univ. of Oregon.

Barr, Pat. 1970. *A Curious Life for a Lady: The Story of Isabella Bird*. Garden City, N.Y.: Doubleday.

Barrows, Pete, and Judith Holmes. 1990. *Colorado's Wildlife Story*. Denver: Colorado Division of Wildlife.

Bass, Althea. 1966. *The Arapaho Way: A Memoir of an Indian Boyhood*. New York: Clarkson N. Potter.

Beier, Paul. 1991. "Cougar Attacks on Humans in the United States and Canada." *Wildlife Society Bulletin* 19 (4):403–12.

———. 1993. "Determining Minimum Habitat Areas and Habitat Corridors for Cougars." *Conservation Biology* 7 (1):94–108

———. 1995. "Dispersal of Juvenile Cougars in Fragmented Habitat." *Journal of Wildlife Management* 59 (2):228–37.

Beier, Paul, David Choate, and Reginald H. Barrett. 1995. "Movement Patterns of Mountain Lions during Different Behaviors." *Journal of Mammalogy* 76 (4):1056–70.

Bekoff, Marc. 2001. "Human-Carnivore Interactions: Adopting Proactive Strategies for Complex Problems." In *Carnivore Conservation*, ed. John L. Gittleman et al., 179–95. Cambridge: Cambridge Univ. Press.

Bell, W. B. 1921. "Hunting Down Stock Killers." In *USDA Yearbook 1920*, 289–300. Washington, D.C.: U.S. Government Printing Office.

Ben Shaul, Devorah Miller. 1962. "The Composition of the Milk of Wild Animals." *International Zoo Yearbook* 4:333–42.

Benson, Maxine. 1986. *Martha Maxwell: Rocky Mountain Naturalist*. Lincoln: Univ. of Nebraska Press.

Bird, Isabella L. [1875]1964. *Six Months in the Sandwich Islands*. Reprint, Honolulu: Univ. of Hawaii Press.

———. [1879]1960. *A Lady's Life in the Rocky Mountains*. Reprint, Norman: Univ. of Oklahoma Press.

———. [1883]1983. *The Golden Chersonese and the Way Thither*. Reprint, London: Century.

Bixby, A. 1880. "History of Boulder County." In *History of Clear Creek and Boulder Valleys, Colorado*, 379–433. Chicago: O. L. Baskin.

Block, Eugene B. 1927. "Lion-Hunting for a Living." *Sunset* 58 (4):15, 65–66.

Blue, Daniel. [1860]1968. *Thrilling Narrative of the Adventures, Sufferings and Starvation of Pike's Peak Gold Seekers on the Plains of the West in the Winter and Spring of 1859*. Reprint, Fairfield, Wash.: Ye Galleon Press.

Bogue, Gary, and Mark Ferrari. 1976. "The Predatory 'Training' of Captive-Reared Pumas." *World's Cats* 3 (1):35–42.

Bolgiano, Chris. 1995. *Mountain Lion: An Unnatural History of Pumas and People.* Mechanicsburg: Stackpole.

Bolgiano, Chris, et al. 2003. "Field Evidence of Cougars in Eastern North America." In *Proceedings of the Sixth Mountain Lion Workshop,* ed. L. A. Harveson, P. M. Harveson, and R. W. Adams, 34–39. Austin: Texas Parks and Wildlife Department.

Boomgaard, Peter. 2001. *Frontiers of Fear: Tigers and People in the Malay World, 1600–1950.* New Haven: Yale Univ. Press.

Bowden, Charles. 1989. "Love among the Lion Killers." *Buzzworm* 1 (5):41–45.

Boyd, Diane K., and Graham K. Neale. 1992. "An Adult Cougar, *Felis Concolor*, Killed by Gray Wolves, *Canis Lupus*, in Glacier National Park, Montana." *Canadian Field-Naturalist* 106 (4):524–25.

Brain, C. K. 1981. *The Hunters or the Hunted?: An Introduction to African Cave Taphonomy.* Chicago: Univ. of Chicago Press.

Brelsford, Vernon. 1950. "Unusual Events in Animal Life—IV." *African Wild Life* 4 (1):67.

Brown, David E., ed. 1983. *The Wolf in the Southwest: The Making of an Endangered Species.* Tucson: Univ. of Arizona Press.

Brown, Robert L. 1985. *The Great Pikes Peak Gold Rush.* Caldwell: Caxton Printers.

Bruce, Jay C. 1918. "Lioness Tracked to Lair." *California Fish and Game* 4 (1):152–53.

———. 1922. "The Why and How of Mountain Lion Hunting in California." *California Fish and Game* 8 (2):108-14.

———. 1925. "The Problem of Mountain Lion Control in California." *California Fish and Game* 11 (1):1–17.

———. 1953. *Cougar Killer.* New York: Comet Press.

Buber, Martin. 1965. *Between Man and Man.* Translated by Ronald Gregor Smith. New York: Macmillan.

Budiansky, Stephen. 1995. *Nature's Keepers: The New Science of Nature Management.* New York: Free Press.

Burk, C. John. 1973. "The Kaibab Deer Incident: A Long-Persisting Myth." *BioScience* 23 (2):113–14.

Burt, Henry M. 1899. *The First Century of the History of Springfield . . . .* Springfield, Mass.: Henry M. Burt.

Cahalan, James M. 2001. *Edward Abbey: A Life.* Tucson: Univ. of Arizona Press.

Cahalane, Victor H. 1939. "The Evolution of Predator Control Policy in the National Parks." *Journal of Wildlife Management* 3 (3):229–37.

———. 1964. *A Preliminary Study of Distribution and Numbers of Cougar, Grizzly and Wolf in North America.* Bronx: New York Zoological Society.

Cain, Stanley A. 1972. *Predator Control—1971: Report to the Council on Environmental Quality and the Department of the Interior by the Advisory Committee on Predator Control.* [Washington, D.C.:] Council on Environmental Quality.

———. 1978. "Predator and Pest Control." In *Wildlife and America: Contributions to an Understanding of American Wildlife and Its Conservation,* ed. Howard P. Brokaw, 379–95. [Washington. D.C.:] Council on Environmental Quality.

Calkins, Franklin Welles. 1902. "About the Cougar." *Outing* 40 (4):448–55.

Cardoza, James E. 1976. *The History and Status of the Black Bear in Massachusetts and Adjacent New England States*. Westboro: Massachusetts Division of Fisheries and Wildlife.

Carroll, Wiley. 1983. *History of American Lion Hunting*. N.p.: Spearman Publishing.

Carson, Rachel. [1962]1964. *Silent Spring*. Reprint, Greenwich: Fawcett Crest.

Cary, Merritt. 1911. *A Biological Survey of Colorado*, North American Fauna, no. 33. Washington, D.C.: U.S. Government Printing Office.

Catesby, Mark. 1754. *The Natural History of Carolina, Florida and the Bahama Islands: Containing the Figures of Birds, Beasts, Fishes, Serpents, Insects, and Plants*. Vol. 2. London: C. Marsh.

Chatwin, Bruce. 1987. *The Songlines*. New York: Penguin.

Clark, Jeanne. 1985. "The DFG and the 'Devil Cat.'" *Outdoor California* 46 (2):1–8.

Clavigero, Don Francisco Javier. 1937. *The History of (Lower) California*. Translated by Sara E. Lake and A. A. Gray. Stanford: Stanford Univ. Press.

Clutton-Brock, T. H., F. E. Guinness, and S. D. Albon. 1982. *Red Deer: Behavior and Ecology of Two Sexes*. Chicago: Univ. of Chicago Press.

Coel, Margaret. [1981]1987. *Chief Left Hand: Southern Arapaho*. Reprint, Norman: Univ. of Oklahoma Press.

Coffin, Morse H. 1965. *The Battle of Sand Creek*. Waco: W. M. Morrison.

Coleman, Dean. 1965. "Let's Abolish the Bounty." *Colorado Outdoors* 14 (1): 1–3.

Collins, Mary. 1909. "Pioneering in the Rockies." Unpublished manuscript, in possession of Carnegie Branch Library, Boulder, Colo.

Conover, Michael R., et al. 1995. "Review of Human Injuries, Illnesses, and Economic Losses Caused by Wildlife in the United States." *Wildlife Society Bulletin* 23 (3):407–14.

Corbett, Jim. 1946. *Man-Eaters of Kumaon*. New York: Oxford Univ. Press.

———. 1948. *The Man-Eating Leopard of Rudraprayag*. New York: Oxford Univ. Press.

Crawley, Michael J., ed. 1992. *Natural Enemies: The Population Biology of Predators, Parasites and Diseases*. Oxford: Blackwell Scientific.

Cronon, William. 1995. "The Trouble with Wilderness; or, Getting Back to the Wrong Nature." In *Uncommon Ground: Toward Reinventing Nature*, ed. William Cronon, 69–90. New York: W. W. Norton.

Culver, M., et al. 2000. "Genomic Ancestry of the American Puma (*Puma Concolor*)." *Journal of Heredity* 91 (3):186–97.

Curio, Eberhard. 1976. *The Ethology of Predation*. New York: Springer-Verlag.

Currier, Mary Jean P., Steven L. Sheriff, and Kenneth R. Russell. 1977. *Mountain Lion Population and Harvest Near Canon City, Colorado, 1974–1977*. [Ft. Collins:] Colorado Division of Wildlife.

Cushman, Ruth Carol, Stephen R. Jones, and Jim Knopf. 1993. *Boulder County Nature Almanac*. Boulder: Pruett Publishing.

Cutright, Paul Russell. 1985. *Theodore Roosevelt: The Making of a Conservationist*. Urbana: Univ. of Illinois Press.

Danz, Harold P. 1999. *Cougar!* Athens: Ohio Univ. Press, Swallow.

Dart, Raymond A. 1953. "The Predatory Transition from Ape to Man." *International Anthropological and Linguistic Review* 1 (4):201–19.

Darwin, Charles. [1839]1966. *Journal and Remarks, 1832–1836.* Vol. 3 of *Narrative of the Surveying Voyages of His Majesty's Ships Adventure and Beagle between the Years 1826 and 1836.* Reprint, New York: AMS Press.

Davis, Mike. 1998. *Ecology of Fear: Los Angeles and the Imagination of Disaster.* New York: Metropolitan.

Delumeau, Jean. 1995. *History of Paradise: The Garden of Eden in Myth and Tradition.* Translated by Matthew O'Connell. New York: Continuum.

Dixon, Joseph. 1925. "Food Predilections of Predatory and Fur-Bearing Mammals." *Journal of Mammalogy* 6 (1):34–46.

Dixon, Kenneth R. 1967. "Evaluation of the Effects of Mountain Lion Predation." Unpublished study prepared by the Colorado Dept. of Game, Fish and Parks.

Dobie, J. Frank. 1928. "Lion Markers." *Country Gentleman* 93 (5):9–10, 111–15.

———. 1949. *The Voice of the Coyote.* Boston: Little, Brown.

———. [1950*a*]1990. *The Ben Lilly Legend.* Reprint, Austin: Univ. of Texas Press.

———. 1950*b*. "The Greatest Tracker of the West." *Saturday Evening Post* 222 (36):25, 87–90.

Dodge, Henry Irving. 1927. "The Hour and the Man." *Forest and Stream* 97 (2 and 3):72–74, 107–8, 156–59, 182–83.

Domenick, Don. 1975. "Climber of the Cliffs: A Bit of Life History about the Rocky Mountain Goat, One of Colorado's Newer Wildlife Residents." *Colorado Outdoors* 24 (4):24–26.

Donaldson, Thomas. 1887. *The George Catlin Indian Gallery in the U.S. National Museum (Smithsonian Institution) with Memoir and Statistics.* Washington, D.C.: U.S. Government Printing Office.

Duffey, David Michael. 1972. *Hunting Hounds: The History, Training and Selection of America's Trail, Tree and Sight Hounds.* New York: Winchester Press.

Dumarest, Father Noël. 1919. "Notes on Cochiti, New Mexico." *Memoirs of the American Anthropological Association* 6 (3):135–236.

Dunlap, Thomas R. 1988. *Saving America's Wildlife: Ecology and the American Mind, 1850–1990.* Princeton: Princeton Univ. Press.

Dyer, Mrs. D. B. 1896. *Fort Reno; or, Picturesque "Cheyenne and Arrapahoe Army Life," before the Opening of "Oklahoma."* New York: G. W. Dillingham.

Eastman, Charles A. 1904. *Red Hunters and the Animal People.* New York: Harper & Brothers.

Eaton, Randall L. 1978. "Why Some Felids Copulate So Much: A Model for the Evolution of Copulation Frequency." *Carnivore* 1 (1):42–51.

Eaton, Randall L., and Kathryn A. Velander. 1977. "Reproduction in the Puma: Biology, Behavior and Ontogeny." *World's Cats* 3 (3):45–70.

Egan, Timothy. 1998. *Lasso the Wind: Away to the New West.* New York: Alfred A. Knopf.

Eisenberg, Evan. 1998. *The Ecology of Eden.* New York: Alfred A. Knopf.

Evans, G. W. 1951. *Slash Ranch Hounds.* Albuquerque: Univ. of New Mexico Press.

Ewer, R. F. [1973]1998. *The Carnivores.* Ithaca: Cornell Univ. Press, Comstock.

Ewing, Susan, and Elizabeth Grossman, eds. 1999. *Shadow Cat: Encountering the American Mountain Lion.* Seattle: Sasquatch.

Farentinos, Robert C. 1993. *Winter's Orphans: The Search for a Family of Mountain Lion Cubs.* Niwot, Colo.: Roberts Rinehart.

Fennessy, P. F., and P. G. Taylor. 1989. "Deer Farming in Oceania." In *Wildlife Production Systems: Economic Utilisation of Wild Ungulates,* ed. Robert J. Hudson, K. R. Drew, and L. M. Baskin, 309–22. Cambridge: Cambridge Univ. Press.

Finley, William L. 1925. "Cougar Kills a Boy." *Journal of Mammalogy* 6 (3):197–99.

Fisher, James, and R. A. Hinde. 1949. "The Opening of Milk Bottles by Birds." *British Birds* 42:347–57.

———. 1951. "Further Observations on the Opening of Milk Bottles by Birds." *British Birds* 44:392–96.

Flader, Susan L. 1974. *Thinking like a Mountain: Aldo Leopold and the Evolution of an Ecological Attitude toward Deer, Wolves, and Forests.* Columbia: Univ. of Missouri Press.

Fritz, Percy Stanley. 1941. *Colorado: The Centennial State.* New York: Prentice Hall.

Fuehr, Irma. 1943. "Hunting Lions for Pay." *American Mercury* 56 (230):218–23.

Galef, Bennett G., Jr. 1996. "Social Influences on Food Preferences and Feeding Behaviors of Vertebrates." In *Why We Eat What We Eat,* ed. Elizabeth D. Capaldi, 207–31. Washington, D.C.: American Psychological Association.

Gantt, W. Horsley. 1944. *Experimental Basis for Neurotic Behavior.* New York: Paul B. Hoeber.

Gillette, Ethel Morrow. 1978. *Idaho Springs: Saratoga of the Rockies.* New York: Vantage.

Gittleman, John L., ed. 1989. *Carnivore Behavior, Ecology, and Evolution.* Ithaca: Cornell Univ. Press, Comstock.

Glenn, Reed, and Roz Brown. 1998. *The Insiders' Guide to Boulder & Rocky Mountain National Park.* 4th ed. Boulder: Boulder Publishing.

Goldman, E. A. 1925. "The Predatory Mammal Problem and the Balance of Nature." *Journal of Mammalogy* 6 (1):28–33.

———. 1932. "The Control of Injurious Animals." *Science* 75 (1942):309–11.

Gonyea, William J. 1976. "Adaptive Differences in the Body Proportions of Large Felids." *Acta Anatomica* 96 (1):81–96.

Gouge, Thomas. 1684. *The Principles of Christian Religion Explained to the Capacity of the Meanest.* London: J. and J. How.

Gressley, Gene M., ed. 1994. *Old West/New West.* Norman: Univ. of Oklahoma Press.

Grey, Zane. 1922. *Roping Lions in the Grand Canyon.* New York: Grosset & Dunlap.

———. 1925. "Don: The Story of a Lion Dog." *Harper's* 151 (903):257–72.

———. 1926. "The Man Who Influenced Me Most." *American Magazine* 102 (2):52–55, 130–36.

Grinnell, George Bird. [1923]1972. *The Cheyenne Indians.* 2 vols. Reprint, Lincoln: Univ. of Nebraska Press.

Grinnell, Joseph, Joseph S. Dixon, and Jean M. Linsdale. 1937. *Fur-Bearing Mammals of California: Their Natural History, Systematic Status, and Relations to Man.* Vol. 2. Berkeley: Univ. of California Press.

Guggisberg, C. A. W. 1975. *Wild Cats of the World*. New York: Taplinger Publishing.

Gunnerson, James H. 1998. "Mountain Lions and the Pueblo Shrines in the American Southwest." In *Icons of Power: Feline Symbolism in the Americas*, ed. Nicholas J. Saunders, 228–57. New York: Routledge.

Hafen, LeRoy R., ed. 1935. "George A. Jackson's Diary, 1858–1859." *Colorado Magazine* 12 (6):201–14.

Haley, Charles. 1953. "Killer Cougar." *Field & Stream* 57 (11):54–55, 125–27.

Halfpenny, James. 1986. *A Field Guide to Mammal Tracking in North America*. Boulder: Johnson Books.

Halfpenny, James C., Michael R. Sanders, and Kristin A. McGrath. 1993. "Human-Lion Interactions in Boulder County, Colorado: Past, Present, and Future." In *Mountain Lion-Human Interaction: Symposium and Workshop, April 24–26, 1991; Denver, Colorado,* ed. Clait E. Braun, 10–16. Denver: Colorado Division of Wildlife.

Hall, F. S. 1925. "Killing of a Boy by Mountain Lion (*Felis Oregonensis Oregonensis*)." *Murrelet* 6 (2):33-37.

Hancock, Lyn. 1978. *Love Affair with a Cougar*. Toronto: Doubleday.

———. 1980. "A History of Changing Attitudes to *Felis Concolor*." M.A. thesis, Simon Fraser Univ.

Hansen, Kevin. 1992. *Cougar: The American Lion*. Flagstaff: Northland Publishing.

Hart, Albert Bushnell, and Herbert Ronald Ferleger. 1989. *Theodore Roosevelt Cyclopedia*. 2nd ed. Oyster Bay: Theodore Roosevelt Association.

Hawes, Harry Bartow. 1935. *Fish and Game, Now or Never: A Challenge to American Sportsmen on Wild-Life Restoration.* New York: D. Appleton-Century.

Heald, Weldon F. 1948. "The Americans Come." In *The Inverted Mountains*, ed. Roderick Peattie, 129–49. New York: Vanguard.

Heist, Edward J., Jennifer R. Bowles, and Alan Woolf. 2001. "Record of a North American Cougar (*Puma Concolor*) from Southern Illinois." *Transactions of the Illinois State Academy of Science* 94 (4):227–29.

Henderson, Charles W. 1926. *Mining in Colorado.* U.S. Geological Survey, Professional Paper, no. 138. Washington, D.C.: U.S. Government Printing Office.

Herbert, Marvin J., and Charles M. Harsh. 1944. "Observational Learning by Cats." *Journal of Comparative Psychology* 37 (2):81–95.

Herrero, Stephen. 1985. *Bear Attacks: Their Causes and Avoidance*. New York: Lyons Press.

Hibben, Frank C. 1937. "A Preliminary Study of the Mountain Lion (*Felis Oregonensis* sp.)." *University of New Mexico Bulletin* 5 (3):1–59.

———. 1939. "The Mountain Lion and Ecology." *Ecology* 20 (4):584–86.

———. 1948. *Hunting American Lions.* New York: Thomas Y. Crowell.

Hilger, M. Inez. 1952. *Arapaho Child Life and Its Cultural Background*. Smithsonian Institution Bureau of American Ethnology Bulletin, no. 148. Washington, D.C.: U.S. Government Printing Office.

Hill, W. W. 1938. *The Agricultural and Hunting Methods of the Navaho Indians*. New Haven: Yale Univ. Press.

Hittell, Theodore H. 1911. *The Adventures of James Capen Adams, Mountaineer and Grizzly Bear Hunter of California*. New York: Charles Scribner's Sons

Hoadly, Charles J., ed. 1868. *The Public Records of the Colony of Connecticut, from August, 1689, to May, 1706*. Hartford: Case, Lockwood and Brainard.

———. 1870. *The Public Records of the Colony of Connecticut, from October, 1706, to October, 1716*. Hartford: Case, Lockwood and Brainard.

Hoagland, Edward. 1971. "Hailing the Elusory Mountain Lion." *New Yorker* 47 (25):26–33.

Hoffman, W. J. 1877. "List of Mammals Found in the Vicinity of Grand River, D.T." *Proceedings of the Boston Society of Natural History* 19:94–102.

Hoig, Stan. 1961. *The Sand Creek Massacre*. Norman: Univ. of Oklahoma Press.

Holland, Marjorie M., Paul G. Risser, and Robert J. Naiman, eds. 1991. *Ecotones*. New York: Chapman and Hall.

Hornaday, William T. 1913. *Our Vanishing Wild Life: Its Extermination and Preservation*. New York: New York Zoological Society.

———. 1914. *Wild Life Conservation in Theory and Practice: Lectures Delivered before the Forest School of Yale University, 1914*. New Haven: Yale Univ. Press.

Hornby, Harry P. 1945. *Going Around*. Uvalde: Hornby Press.

Hornocker, Maurice G. 1969. "Stalking the Mountain Lion—to Save Him." *National Geographic* 136 (5):638–55.

———. 1992. "Learning to Live with Mountain Lions." *National Geographic* 182 (1):52–65.

Howard, Chas. B. 1915. "An Instance of a Mountain Lion's Attack upon a Boy." *Outdoor Life* 36 (2):162–63.

Hudson, Suzanne. 1993. *A History of Boulder's Parks and Recreation (or How We Got to Be So Pretty)*. Boulder: Boulder Parks and Recreation Dept.

Immelmann, Klaus, and Colin Beer. 1989. *A Dictionary of Ethology*. Cambridge: Harvard Univ. Press.

Ingersoll, Ernest. 1897. *Wild Neighbors: Out-Door Studies in the United States*. New York: Macmillan.

Jensen, Einar N. U. 1998. "Landscapes of the Mined: An Environmental History of Mining in the Clear Creek Watershed, Clear Creek County, Colorado, 1859–1997." M.A. thesis, Univ. of Montana at Missoula.

John of Damascus, Saint. 1958. *Writings*. Translated by Frederic H. Chase Jr. New York: Fathers of the Church.

Johnson, Harlen G. 1942. "Mountain Lion Bags New Kaibab Record." *Arizona Wildlife and Sportsman* 4 (5):2, 11.

Johnson, Kirk. 2002. "The Mountain Lions of Michigan." *Endangered Species UPDATE* 19 (2):27–31.

Johnson, Michael L. 1996. *New Westers: The West in Contemporary American Culture*. Lawrence: Univ. Press of Kansas.

Julian, Lesley T., and Paul R. Julian. 1969. "Boulder's Winds." *Weatherwise* 22 (3):108–12, 126.

Kaufmann, Merrill R., et al. 2001. "Cheesman Lake—A Historical Ponderosa Pine Landscape Guiding Restoration in the South Platte Watershed of the Colorado Front Range." In *Ponderosa Pine Ecosystems Restoration and Conservation: Steps toward Stewardship, 2000 April 25–27, Flagstaff, AZ*, coord. Regina K. Vance, W. Wallace Covington, and Carleton B. Edminster, 9–18. Ogden, Ut.: U.S. Dept. of Agriculture, Forest Service, Rocky Mountain Research Station.

Kaye, Evelyn. 1999. *Amazing Traveler Isabella Bird.* 2nd ed. Boulder: Blue Panda Publications.

Kellert, Stephen R. 1985. "Public Perceptions of Predators, Particularly the Wolf and Coyote." *Biological Conservation* 31 (2):167–89.

Kellert, Stephen R., et al. 1996. "Human Culture and Large Carnivore Conservation in North America." *Conservation Biology* 10 (4):977–90.

Kennedy, Bess. 1942. *The Lady and the Lions.* New York: McGraw-Hill.

Kerbis Peterhans, Julian C., and Thomas Patrick Gnoske. 2001. "The Science of 'Man-Eating' among Lions *Panthera Leo* with a Reconstruction of the Natural History of the 'Man-Eaters of Tsavo.'" *Journal of East African Natural History* 90:1–40.

Khan, Mohammad Ali Reze. 1987. "The Problem Tiger of Bangladesh." In *Tigers of the World*, ed. Ronald L. Tilson and Ulysses S. Seal, 92–96. Park Ridge, N.J.: Noyes.

Kitchener, Andrew. 1991. *The Natural History of the Wild Cats.* Ithaca: Cornell Univ. Press, Comstock.

Knight, John, ed. 2000. *Natural Enemies: People-Wildlife Conflicts in Anthropological Perspective.* London: Routledge.

Krech, Shepard, III. 1999. *The Ecological Indian: Myth and History.* New York: W. W. Norton.

Kroeber, Alfred L. [1902, 1904, 1907]1983. *The Arapaho.* Reprint, Lincoln: Univ. of Nebraska Press.

Kruuk, Hans. 1972. "Surplus Killing by Carnivores." *Journal of Zoology* 166 (2):233–44.

———. 2002. *Hunter and Hunted.* Cambridge: Cambridge Univ. Press.

Kufeld, Roland C., David C. Bowden, and Donald L. Schrupp. 1988. "Habitat Selection and Activity Patterns of Female Mule Deer in the Front Range, Colorado." *Journal of Range Management* 41 (6):515–23.

Kuhn, Thomas S. 1970. *The Structure of Scientific Revolutions.* 2nd ed. Chicago: Univ. of Chicago Press.

Kummli, Dawn, ed. 1990. *Sugar Loaf's Black Tiger Fire.* Boulder: Sugar Loaf Community.

La Flesche, Francis. 1925. "The Osage Tribe: The Rite of Vigil." In *Thirty-ninth Annual Report of the Bureau of American Ethnology to the Secretary of the Smithsonian Institution, 1917–1918,* 31–636. Washington, D.C.: U.S. Government Printing Office.

Lange, Charles H. 1959. *Cochití: A New Mexico Pueblo, Past and Present.* Austin: Univ. of Texas Press.

Lawrence, R. D. 1983. *The Ghost Walker*. New York: Holt, Rinehart and Winston.

Lechleitner, R. R. 1969. *Wild Mammals of Colorado*. Boulder: Pruett Publishing.

Leopold, A. Starker. 1959. *Wildlife of Mexico: The Game Birds and Mammals*. Berkeley: Univ. of California Press.

Leopold, Aldo. 1949. *A Sand County Almanac and Sketches Here and There*. New York: Oxford Univ. Press.

Lesowski, John. 1967. "The Silent Hunter." *Outdoor Life* 140 (1):44–47, 104, 106–8.

Leyhausen, Paul. 1979. *Cat Behavior: The Predatory and Social Behavior of Domestic and Wild Cats*. Translated by Barbara A. Tonkin. New York: Garland STPM Press.

Limerick, Patricia Nelson. 1987. *The Legacy of Conquest: The Unbroken Past of the American West*. New York: W. W. Norton.

Linnaeus, Carl. [1771]1961. *Mantissa Plantarum*. Reprint, New York: Hafner.

Livingstone, David. 1859. *Missionary Travels and Researches in South Africa*. New York: Harper & Brothers.

Logan, Kenneth A., and Linda L. Sweanor. 2000. "Puma." In *Ecology and Management of Large Mammals in North America*, ed. Stephen Demarais and Paul R. Krausman, 347–77. Upper Saddle River: Prentice Hall.

———. 2001. *Desert Puma: Evolutionary Ecology and Conservation of an Enduring Carnivore*. Washington, D.C.: Island Press.

Lopez, Barry Holstun. 1978. *Of Wolves and Men*. New York: Charles Scribner's Sons.

Lorbiecki, Marybeth. 1996. *Aldo Leopold: A Fierce Green Fire*. Helena: Falcon.

Louth, Andrew, ed. 2001. *Ancient Christian Commentary on Scripture: Genesis I–II*. Downers Grove: InterVarsity Press.

Maclean, Norman. 1992. *Young Men & Fire*. Chicago: Univ. of Chicago Press.

Manfredo, Michael J., et al. 1998. "Public Acceptance of Mountain Lion Management: A Case Study of Denver, Colorado, and Nearby Foothills Areas." *Wildlife Society Bulletin* 26 (4):964–70.

Manville, Richard H. 1955. "Report of Deer Attacking Cougar." *Journal of Mammalogy* 36 (3):476–78.

Marsden, William. 1811. *The History of Sumatra, Containing an Account of the Government, Laws, Customs, and Manners . . .* London: J. McCreery.

Matthiessen, Peter. 1987. *Wildlife in America*. Rev. ed. New York: Viking.

Mayer, Charles. 1924. *Jungle Beasts I Have Captured*. Garden City, N.Y.: Doubleday, Page.

McDougal, Charles. 1987. "The Man-Eating Tiger in Geographical and Historical Perspective." In *Tigers of the World,* ed. Ronald L. Tilson and Ulysses S. Seal, 435–48. Park Ridge, N.J.: Noyes.

———. 1999. "Tiger Attacks on People in Nepal." *Cat News* 30:9–10.

McGuire, J. A. 1914. "Wild Animal Attacks–in the Newspapers." *Outdoor Life* 34 (6):534–37.

———. 1916. "The Cougar." *Outdoor Life* 37 (6):536–44.

McIntyre, Rick, ed. 1995. *War against the Wolf: America's Campaign to Exterminate the Wolf.* Stillwater: Voyageur Press.

McKee, Thomas Heron. 1924. "'Uncle Jim' Owen and His Dogs Have Killed 1500 Cougars." *American Magazine* 97 (4):50–51, 172–74.

McKibben, Bill. 1995. *Hope, Human and Wild*. Boston: Little, Brown.

Meier, Thomas J. 1993. *The Early Settlement of Boulder: Set in Type—Cast in Bronze—Fused in Porcelain; "It Ain't Necessarily So."* Boulder: Boulder Creek Press.

Meine, Curt. 1988. *Aldo Leopold: His Life and Work*. Madison: Univ. of Wisconsin Press.

Meine, Curt, and Richard L. Knight, eds. 1999. *The Essential Aldo Leopold: Quotations and Commentaries*. Madison: Univ. of Wisconsin Press.

Mello, Nancy K., and Neil J. Peterson. 1964. "Behavioral Evidence for Color Discrimination in Cat." *Journal of Neurophysiology* 27 (3):323–33.

Merrill, Samuel B., and L. David Mech. 2000. "Details of Extensive Movements by Minnesota Wolves (Canis Lupus)." *American Midland Naturalist* 144 (2):428–33.

Mighetto, Lisa. 1991. *Wild Animals and American Environmental Ethics*. Tucson: Univ. of Arizona Press.

Mills, Enos A. 1909. *Wild Life on the Rockies*. Boston: Houghton Mifflin.

———. 1918. "The Mountain Lion." *Saturday Evening Post* 190 (38):125–26.

———. 1932a. *Watched by Wild Animals*. Boston: Houghton Mifflin.

———. 1932b. *Wild Animal Homesteads*. Boston: Houghton Mifflin.

Minnis, Donna L. 1998. "Wildlife Policy-Making by the Electorate: An Overview of Citizen-Sponsored Ballot Measures on Hunting and Trapping." *Wildlife Society Bulletin* 26 (1):75–83.

Montgomery, Sy. 1995. *Spell of the Tiger: The Man-Eaters of Sundarbans*. Boston: Houghton Mifflin.

Moore, Clifford B. 1953. *Ways of Mammals: In Fact and Fancy*. New York: Ronald Press.

Moore, Tommy D., Liter E. Spence, and Charles E. Dugnolle. 1974. *Identification of the Dorsal Guard Hairs of Some Mammals of Wyoming*. Edited by William G. Hepworth. Cheyenne: Wyoming Game and Fish Department.

Murphy, J. G. 1867. *A Critical and Exegetical Commentary on the Book of Genesis*. Boston: Draper and Halliday.

Murray, John A. 1987. *Wildlife in Peril: The Endangered Mammals of Colorado*. Boulder: Roberts Rinehart.

Musgrave, M. E. 1927. "The Mountain Lion Is Just a 'Fraidy Cat.'" *Farm & Fireside* 51 (6):8–9, 61.

———. 1938. "Ben Lilly—Last of the Mountain Men." *American Forests* 44 (8):349–51, 379–80.

Mutel, Cornelia Fleischer, and John C. Emerick. 1984. *From Grassland to Glacier: The Natural History of Colorado*. Boulder: Johnson Books.

Nash, Roderick. 1982. *Wilderness and the American Mind*. 3rd ed. New Haven: Yale Univ. Press.

———. 1989. *The Rights of Nature: A History of Environmental Ethics*. Madison: Univ. of Wisconsin Press.

Nelson, Richard. 1997. *Heart and Blood: Living with Deer in America*. New York: Alfred A. Knopf.

Noel, Thomas J., and Dan W. Corson. 1999. *Boulder County: An Illustrated History*. Carlsbad, Calif.: Heritage Media.

Nowak, Ronald M. 1974. "The Cougar in the United States and Canada." Report to the New York Zoological Society and the U.S. Fish and Wildlife Service.

Noyes, Russell, Jr., and Roy Kletti. 1977. "Depersonalization in Response to Life-Threatening Danger." *Comprehensive Psychiatry* 18 (4):375–84.

Oard, Michael J. 1993. "A Method for Predicting Chinook Winds East of the Montana Rockies." *Weather and Forecasting* 8 (2):166–80.

O'Connor, Jack. 1939. "A Lee for a Lion." *Outdoor Life* 83 (5):48–50, 82.

Olmsted, Frederick Law, Jr. [1910]1967. *The Improvement of Boulder Colorado*. Reprint, Boulder: Thorne Ecological Foundation.

Opler, Morris Edward. 1941. *An Apache Life-Way*. Chicago: Univ. of Chicago Press.

Pack, Arthur Newton. 1930. "Trailing the Mountain Lion." *Nature Magazine* 15 (2):75–81.

Padley, W. Douglas, ed. 1997. *Proceedings of the Fifth Mountain Lion Workshop: 27 February–1 March 1996; San Diego, California*. San Diego: Southern California Chapter of the Wildlife Society.

Parfit, Michael. 1988. *Chasing the Glory: Travels across America*. New York: Macmillan.

Patterson, J. H. 1927. *The Man-Eaters of Tsavo and Other African Adventures*. New York: Macmillan.

Perrigo, Lynn I. 1946. "A Municipal History of Boulder, Colorado, 1871–1946." Unpublished report to the Boulder County Historical Society and the City of Boulder.

Perry, Richard. 1965. *The World of the Tiger*. New York: Atheneum.

Petersen, David. 1995. *Ghost Grizzlies*. New York: Henry Holt.

Peterson, Andy. 1999. "The Devil on Carpenter's Peak." *Outdoor Life* 203 (1):56–61.

Pettem, Silvia. 1980. *Red Rocks to Riches: Gold Mining in Boulder County, Then and Now*. Boulder: Stonehenge.

———. 1989. *Guide to Historic Western Boulder County*. Evergreen: Cordillera Press.

———. 1994. *Boulder: Evolution of a City*. Niwot, Colo.: Univ. Press of Colorado.

———. 2000. *Boulder: A Sense of Time and Place*. Longmont, Colo.: Book Lode.

Pope, Alexander. [1734]1969. *An Essay on Man*. Reprint, Menston, England: Scolar Press.

Power, Thomas Michael. 1996. *Lost Landscapes and Failed Economies: The Search for a Value of Place*. Washington, D.C.: Island Press.

Rasmussen, D. Irvin. 1941. "Biotic Communities of Kaibab Plateau, Arizona." *Ecological Monographs* 11 (3):230–75.

Report of the Superintendent of the Yellowstone National Park to the Secretary of the Interior. 1890. Washington, D.C.: U.S. Government Printing Office.

Rhoads, Samuel N. 1903. *The Mammals of Pennsylvania and New Jersey*. Philadelphia: privately published.

Riebsame, William E., et al., eds. 1997. *Atlas of the New West: Portrait of a Changing Region*. New York: W. W. Norton.

Rivierre, Rene R. 1919. "Kills Lions for a Living." *American Magazine* 87 (3):50–51.

Roosevelt, Theodore. 1893a. *The Wilderness Hunter*. New York: G. P. Putnam's Sons.

———. 1893b. "Value of an Athletic Training." *Harper's Weekly* 37 (1931):1236.

———. 1897. *Hunting Trips of a Ranchman*. New York: G. P. Putnam's Sons.

———. 1900. "What We Can Expect of the American Boy." *St. Nicholas* 27 (7):571–74.

———. 1911. *The Strenuous Life: Essays and Addresses*. New York: Century.

———. [1913]1985. *Theodore Roosevelt: An Autobiography*. Reprint, New York: Da Capo Press.

———. 1914. *Through the Brazilian Wilderness*. New York: Charles Scribner's Sons.

———. 1915. "The Conservation of Wild Life." *Outlook* 109:159–62.

———. [1916]1925. *A Book-Lover's Holidays in the Open*. New York: Charles Scribner's Sons.

———. 1918. "My Life as a Naturalist." *American Museum Journal* 18 (5):321–50.

———. 1919. *Theodore Roosevelt's Letters to His Children*. Edited by Joseph Bucklin Bishop. New York: Charles Scribner's Sons.

———. 1925. *Outdoor Pastimes of an American Hunter*. New York: Charles Scribner's Sons.

Roosevelt, Theodore, et al. [1902]1924. *The Deer Family*. Reprint, New York: Macmillan.

Rushby, G. G. 1965. *No More the Tusker*. London: W. H. Allen.

Russell, Frank. 1908. "The Pima Indians." In *Twenty-sixth Annual Report of the Bureau of American Ethnology to the Secretary of the Smithsonian Institution, 1904–1905*, 3–512. Washington, D.C.: U.S. Government Printing Office.

Russo, John P. 1964. *The Kaibab North Deer Herd—Its History, Problems and Management*. Phoenix: Arizona Game and Fish Dept.

Sandfort, Wayne W., and Robert J. Tully. 1971. "The Status and Management of the Mountain Lion and Bobcat in Colorado." In *Proceedings of a Symposium on the Native Cats of North America, Their Status and Management*, ed. S. E. Jorgensen and L. David Mech, 73–85. Twin Cities, Minn.: U.S. Department of the Interior, Fish and Wildlife Service.

Schmidt, John L., and Douglas L. Gilbert, eds. 1978. *Big Game of North America: Ecology and Management*. Harrisburg: Stackpole Books.

Sechzer, Jeri A., and John Lott Brown. 1964. "Color Discrimination in the Cat." *Science* 144 (3617):427–29.

Seidensticker, John. 1987. "Managing Tigers in the Sundarbans: Experience and Opportunity." In *Tigers of the World*, ed. Ronald L. Tilson and Ulysses S. Seal, 416–26. Park Ridge, N.J.: Noyes.

Seidensticker, John, with Susan Lumpkin. 1992. "Mountain Lions Don't Stalk People. True or False?" *Smithsonian* 22 (11):113–22.

Seidensticker, John, and Susan Lumpkin, eds. 1991. *Great Cats: Majestic Creatures of the Wild*. Emmaus, Pa.: Rodale Press.

Setnicka, Tim J. 1980. *Wilderness Search and Rescue*. Boston: Appalachian Mountain Club.

Seton, Ernest Thompson. 1929. *Lives of Game Animals*. Vol. 2, pt. 1. *Cats, Wolves, and Foxes*. Garden City, N.Y.: Doubleday, Doran.

———. 1958. *Animal Tracks and Hunter Signs*. Garden City, N.Y.: Doubleday.

Shakespeare, Nicholas. 2000. *Bruce Chatwin*. New York: Doubleday.

Shaw, Harley. 1989. *Soul among Lions: The Cougar as Peaceful Adversary*. Boulder: Johnson Books.

Shepard, Paul. 1996. *The Others: How Animals Made Us Human*. Washington, D.C.: Island Press.

Sherry, David F., and Bennett G. Galef Jr. 1984. "Cultural Transmission without Imitation: Milk Bottle Opening by Birds." *Animal Behaviour* 32 (3):937–38.

———. 1990. "Social Learning without Imitation: More about Milk Bottle Opening by Birds." *Animal Behaviour* 40 (5):987–89.

Shoemaker, Henry W. [1917]1993. *Extinct Pennsylvania Animals*. Reprint, Baltimore: Gateway Press.

Simms, William Gilmore. 1997. *The Cub of the Panther: A Hunter Legend of the "Old North State."* Edited by Miriam Jones Shillingsburg. Fayetteville: Univ. of Arkansas Press.

Singer, Daniel J. 1914. *Big Game Fields of America, North and South*. New York: George H. Doran.

Smith, George. 1887. *The Life of William Carey, D. D. Shoemaker and Missionary*. London: John Murray.

Smith, Phyllis. 1981. *A Look at Boulder: From Settlement to City*. Boulder: Pruett Publishing.

Smith, Ronald H., ed. 1989. *Proceedings of the Third Mountain Lion Workshop: December 6–8, 1988, Prescott, Arizona.* Prescott: Arizona Chapter of the Wildlife Society and Arizona Game and Fish Department.

Snyder, Gary. [1974]1993. *Turtle Island*. Reprint, Boston: Shambhala.

Southesk, James Carnegie, earl of. [1875]1969. *Saskatchewan and the Rocky Mountains: A Diary of Travel, Sport and Adventure. . . .* Reprint, Rutland, Vt.: C. E. Tuttle.

Southwick, Charles H., et al. 1990. "Boulder's Deer Population." In *Close to Home: Colorado's Urban Wildlife,* ed. Frederick R. Rinehart and Elizabeth A. Webb, 101–14. Boulder: Roberts Rinehart.

Sowell, Merle L. 1976. *Historical Highlights of Idaho Springs: Mining Camp Days*. Idaho Springs: Idaho Springs Friends of the Library.

Spargo, John. 1950. *The Catamount in Vermont: An Account of the Animal Variously Called "Catamount," "Painter" and "Panther" Which Holds an Important Place in the Legends and Folklore of Vermont — To Which Is Added a Brief Explanation of the Catamount Tavern Marker*. Bennington: n.p.

Spinden, Herbert Joseph. 1908. "The Nez Percé Indians." *Memoirs of the American Anthropological Association* 2 (3):165–274.

Stoehr, C. Eric. 1975. *Bonanza Victorian: Architecture and Society in Colorado Mining Towns*. Albuquerque: Univ. of New Mexico Press.

Stone, Livingston. 1883*a*. "The Panther of the McCloud River." *Forest and Stream* 20 (11):203–4.

———. 1883*b*. "Habits of the Panther in California." *American Naturalist* 17 (11):1188–90.

Stone, Witmer, and William Everett Cram. 1903. *American Animals: A Popular Guide to the Mammals of North America North of Mexico. . . .* New York: Doubleday, Page.

Storer, Tracy I. 1923. "Rabies in a Mountain Lion." *California Fish and Game* 9 (2):45–48.

Sullivan, Michael D. 1989. "Crisis Looming in Western Timber Supply." *Forest Industries* 116 (3):33–34.

Taylor, Colin F. 2001. *Native American Weapons*. Norman: Univ. of Oklahoma Press.

Taylor, George Rogers, ed. 1949. *The Turner Thesis*. Boston: Heath.

Thomas, Elizabeth Marshall. 1994. *The Tribe of Tiger: Cats and Their Culture*. New York: Simon & Schuster.

Thomas, Keith. 1996. *Man and the Natural World: Changing Attitudes in England, 1500–1800*. Oxford: Oxford Univ. Press.

Thompson, Ben H. 1935. "National Parks and Wilderness Use." In *Wildlife Management in the National Parks*, ed. George M. Wright and Ben H. Thompson, 47–55. Washington, D.C.: U.S. Government Printing Office.

Thoreau, Henry David. [1862]1982. "Walking." Reprint in *The Portable Thoreau*, ed. Carl Bode, 592–630. New York: Penguin.

Tinsley, Jim Bob. 1987. *The Puma: Legendary Lion of the Americas*. El Paso: Texas Western Press.

Tocqueville, Alexis de. [1840]1945. *Democracy in America*. Pt. 2, *The Social Influence of Democracy*. Translated by Henry Reeve. Reprint, New York: Alfred A. Knopf.

Trefethen, James B. 1967. "The Terrible Lesson of the Kaibab." *National Wildlife* 5 (4):4–9.

Trenholm, Virginia Cole. 1986. *The Arapahoes, Our People*. Norman: Univ. of Oklahoma Press.

True, Frederick W. 1891. "The Puma, or American lion, *Felis Concolor* of Linnaeus." In *Report of the U.S. National Museum . . . for the Year Ending June 30, 1889,* 591–608. Washington, D.C.: U.S. Government Printing Office.

Turner, Alan. 1997. *The Big Cats and Their Fossil Relatives*. New York: Columbia Univ. Press.

Van der Kolk, Bessel, Alexander C. McFarlane, and Lars Weisaeth, eds. 1996. *Traumatic Stress: The Effects of Overwhelming Experience on Mind, Body, and Society*. New York: Guilford.

Veblen, Thomas T., and Diane C. Lorenz. 1991. *The Colorado Front Range: A Century of Ecological Change*. Salt Lake City: Univ. of Utah Press.

Vosburgh, John R. 1949. *Texas Lion Hunter*. San Antonio: Naylor.

Waits, Mary Jo, et al. 2000. *Hits and Misses: Fast Growth in Metropolitan Phoenix*. Tempe: Morrison Inst. for Public Policy, Arizona State Univ.

Walker, Woods. 1945. *Walker Fox Hounds: Their Origin and Development*. Cynthiana, Ky.: Hobson Book Press.

Wallihan, Allen Grant. 1902. *Hoofs, Claws and Antlers of the Rocky Mountains, by the Camera*. Denver: Frank S. Thayer.

———. 1944. "Photographing Wild Life in Early Colorado." *Colorado Magazine* 21 (5):171–77.

Wallmo, Olof C., ed. 1981. *Mule and Black-Tailed Deer of North America*. Lincoln: Univ. of Nebraska Press.

The War of the Rebellion: A Compilation of the Official Records of the Union and Confederate Armies. 1893. Ser. 1, vol. 41, pt. 1. Washington, D.C.: U.S. Government Printing Office.

Warren, Edward Royal. 1910. *The Mammals of Colorado: An Account of the Several Species Found within the Boundaries of the State. . . .* New York: G. P. Putnam's Sons.

Weddle, Ferris. 1966. "The Cougar in Our National Parks and Monuments." *National Parks Magazine* 40 (224):4–7.

Wessing, Robert. 1986. *The Soul of Ambiguity: The Tiger in Southeast Asia*. DeKalb: Northern Illinois Univ., Center for Southeast Asian Studies.

West, Elliott. 1998. *The Contested Plains: Indians, Goldseekers, and the Rush to Colorado*. Lawrence: Univ. Press of Kansas.

White, Lynn, Jr. 1967. "The Historical Roots of Our Ecologic Crisis." *Science* 155 (3767):1203–7.

White, Paula A., and Diane K. Boyd. 1989. "A Cougar, *Felis Concolor*, Kitten Killed and Eaten by Gray Wolves, *Canis Lupus*, in Glacier National Park, Montana." *Canadian Field-Naturalist* 103 (3):408–9.

Wied, Maximilian, prince of. 1843. *Travels in the Interior of North America*. Translated by H. Evans Lloyd. London: Ackermann.

Winn, Frederic. 1923. "Ben Lily, a Twentieth Century Daniel Boone." *American Forestry* 29 (355):398–99.

———. 1937. "Ben Lily—Trapper, Mountaineer." *American Cattle Producer*, Feb., 13–14.

Wohl, Ellen E. 2001. *Virtual Rivers: Lessons from the Mountain Rivers of the Colorado Front Range*. New Haven: Yale Univ. Press.

Wyckoff, William. 1999. *Creating Colorado: The Making of a Western American Landscape, 1860–1940*. New Haven: Yale Univ. Press.

Wyrwicka, Wanda. 1978. "Imitation of Mother's Inappropriate Food Preference in Weanling Kittens." *Pavlovian Journal of Biological Science* 13 (2):55–72.

———. 1981. *The Development of Food Preferences: Parental Influences and the Primacy Effect*. Springfield, Ill.: Charles C. Thomas.

Yahner, Richard H. 1988. "Changes in Wildlife Communities Near Edges." *Conservation Biology* 2 (4):333–39.

Young, Stanley P., and Edward A. Goldman. 1944. *The Wolves of North America*. Washington, D.C.: American Wildlife Institute.

———. 1946. *The Puma: Mysterious American Cat*. Washington, D.C.: American Wildlife Institute.

ACKNOWLEDGMENTS

In 1996, I traveled to Auburn, California, a small city in the Sierra foothills, where a mountain lion had killed a jogger two years earlier, to produce a story on the politics of cougars for NPR's *All Things Considered*. I planned a straightforward report on a ballot measure that, had it passed, would have legalized lion hunting in the state, but my boss, NPR science editor Anne Gudenkauf, encouraged me to dig deeper, to look at the attitudes of people who live in cougar country, to examine what the resurgence of mountain lions says about America's changing physical and cultural landscape. Anne's prodding pushed me to produce a better story, and it planted an idea in my mind—to write a book about the nation's growing clash between humans and large predators.

As a broadcaster with no book-writing experience, however, I had no idea where to begin. Todd Shuster, a good friend and a great agent, served as my coach; he helped shape my thinking, bolstered my confidence, and guided me down the long road from abstract idea to concrete book. The nascent project received a boost in 1998 when the University of Colorado's Center for Environmental Journalism, headed by the inspiring Len Ackland, granted me a Ted Scripps Fellowship in Environmental Journalism—nine glorious months during which I conducted preliminary research and sought focus for my still amorphous book. The fellowship also brought me to Boulder, where I met Michael Sanders, who introduced me to the amazing tale of the city's lions and, with openness and irrepressible good humor, endured seemingly interminable interviews and endless requests for information. One year later, Bob Weil, my stalwart editor at Norton, took a chance on an untested author, saw how to mold my original concept into something far richer, and gave me the time and support I needed. I am indebted to Anne, Todd, Len, Michael, and Bob. Without them, *The Beast in the Garden* would not exist.

Hundreds of other people graciously assisted my endeavors in large and small ways. First among them are my witnesses (see pages 245–46), many of whom provided far more help than any author could reasonably expect. Scott Lancaster's parents and brothers generously aided my research despite the painful memories it unearthed. Jim Halfpenny, chronically overworked, carved out time for several all-day interviews and constant queries about events from a decade ago. Other witnesses who spent an inordinate amount of time answering my questions, searching for documents, and fact-checking my prose included Jerry Apker, Kristi Coughlon, Mike Dallas, Lee Fitzhugh, Ponce Gebhardt, Kathi Green, Tom Howard, Einar Jensen, Don Kattner, Matt Miller, and Rick and Teresa Overmyer.

Mary Axe, Al Bartlett, Paul Danish, Ricky Weiser, and Gilbert White educated me about the evolution of modern Boulder. Majorie Bell gave me a primer on the history of Idaho Springs. Maurice Hornocker taught me about cougar ecology. Jane Bock helped me identify Front Range plants (including the buckthorn bush at Scott Lancaster's attack site). Elisabeth Vrba spoke to me about her excavations at Sterkfontein. Sandy McFarlane and Atul Gawande provided expertise on the psychological and physiological effects of trauma. Keith Aune of the Montana Department of Fish, Wildlife, and Parks permitted me to witness a cougar necropsy. Rich DeSimone, of the same state agency, and Bob Wiesner, an extraordinary houndsman, allowed me to accompany them for a thrilling day of lion tracking near Missoula, giving me a valuable firsthand experience with wild cougars.

For help with my descriptions of what the world looks like through the eyes of a mountain lion, I am grateful to Alan Bachrach, Christopher Murphy, and Jay Neitz. Thanks to Karen Anderson in the Law Offices of Wylie Aitken for providing me with a trial transcript (all 3,593 pages) from *Small v. County of Orange*. Barbara Powers gave me a tour of the necropsy room at CSU's Veterinary Diagnostic Laboratory. Rosanne Humphrey provided information on mountain lion specimens at the CU Museum. Cheri Jones gave me access to the cougar collection at the Denver Museum of Nature and Science, where Joyce Herold showed me Native American lion-hide quivers and Elaine Anderson taught me about prehistoric fauna of the Front Range. Boulder animal control officer Bill Eeds helpfully demonstrated the equipment used to tranquilize the lion on University Hill in 1990.

Many friends and colleagues influenced the content and style of this book as it evolved over the years. Richard Nelson and his exquisite *Heart and Blood: Living with Deer in America* provided inspiration and ideas. Bill McKibben and Sue Halpern gave advice and encouragement. Steve Woodruff of the *Missoulian* first alerted me to the widespead nature of the West's modern cougar problems. Candace Slater and other participants in the spring 2000 residential seminar on rain forests at the University of California Humanities Research Center pushed me to explore the larger themes in my story. Katy Human served as an enthusiastic sounding board and, sleuth-like, assisted me in finding people who had departed Boulder long ago. Conversations with Jennifer Bowles, Deborah Brosnan, Paula Dobbyn, Steve Downs, Harriet Feinberg, Cate Gilles,

Michael Goldstein, Todd Hartman, Susan Huse, Dick Jones, Rachel Nowak, and Tom Yulsman shaped my thinking in valuable ways. Kathy Sylvester provided superb editing and advice, especially during my earliest drafts. In its later stages, the manuscript benefited greatly from comments by Jason Baskin, Marc Bekoff, Howard Berkes, Andy Bowers, and Harley Shaw, as well as careful copyediting by Otto Sonntag. Brendan Curry deftly guided my book through the final stages of production. Hiking partners Amy Gahran, Cathy Koczela, Jennifer Lindsey, and Andrea and Dana Meyer accompanied me on forays into lion country to visit locales that figure in the book. And I am grateful to Milton Meltzer for his book-writing advice and for serving as a role model.

Others who provided facts, documents, and ideas: Steve Armstead, Dave Armstrong, Doug Bamforth, Diane Benedict, Del Benson, Elizabeth Benson, Peter Boomgard, Jennifer Bray, Mark Brennan, Jim Burrus, Valerius Geist, Tom Gnoske, Dan Grossman, Wyck Hay, Dave Hoerath, Lee Hood, Steve Jones, Tina Jungwirth, Merrill Kaufmann, Wendy Keefover-Ring, Rich Koopman, Cindy Lair, Jim Lawler, Cameron Lewis, Larry Loendorf, Steve Lucero, Bob Pickering, Steve Pozzanghera, Cary Richardson, Michael Robinson, Nick Saunders, Matt Taylor, Pete Taylor, Dock Teegarden, Keith Thomas, Matt Thomas, Wally Toevs, Steve Torres, Bill Travis, Meg Van Ness, Jan and Dave Waddington, Deward Walker, Morgan Wehtje, Adrian Wydeven, and Tom Zuidema.

For assisting my research into local history and the scientific literature, I thank the Boulder Public Library (especially Kathleen Cassaday, who was able to find even the most obscure and ancient books that I requested, and Wendy Hall, at the Carnegie Branch Library for Local History), Denver Public Library (in particular, its Western History Department), Idaho Springs Public Library, Norlin Library at the University of Colorado, the Colorado Historial Society's Stephen H. Hart Library, the National Center for Atmospheric Research Library, *Daily Camera* librarian Carol Taylor, and Jackie Boss, librarian for the Colorado Division of Wildlife.

Thanks to my family—especially Buzzy (a.k.a. "Dad"), Dianne, Sam, Jessica, Ira, Sharon, and Josephine—for their constant encouragement, for reading my early drafts, and for enduring my years-long cougar obsession. Most importantly, I am indebted (for so many reasons) to Paul Myers, who gave honest and insightful feedback on each stage of the manuscript, cheerfully tolerated my workaholic tendencies, and, when I raised the wild idea of moving from Boston to Boulder, unexpectedly said yes.

ABOUT THE AUTHOR

David Baron has reported on science and environmental issues for National Public Radio for more than fifteen years and is a three-time recipient of the American Association for the Advancement of Science's annual journalism award. He lives in Boston and Boulder.